DAVID LEAN

DAVID LEAN

BY STEPHEN M. SILVERMAN

INTRODUCTION BY KATHARINE HEPBURN

Cover: *Lawrence of Arabia*, 1962. © 1962 Horizon Pictures (GB). All rights reserved. Courtesy Columbia Pictures Industries, Inc.

Page 1: David Lean and the "clear screen" developed to capture the great storm for *Ryan's Daughter*, Ireland, 1970.

Pages 2–3: T. E. Lawrence crosses the Sinai with his servants, Faraj and Daud (Peter O'Toole, Michael Ray, and John Dimech); *Lawrence of Arabia*, 1962.

Page 4: David Lean, Jordan, 1961.

Pages 6–7: The desert initiation of T. E. Lawrence (Peter O'Toole), with his guide Tafas (Zia Mohyeddin); in Jebel Tubeiq, southeastern Jordan, for Lean's masterpiece, *Lawrence of Arabia*.

Editor: Beverly Fazio
Designers: Samuel N. Antupit and Ellen Nygaard Ford
Photo Researcher: Charles Brannan

Library of Congress Cataloging-in-Publication Data
Silverman, Stephen M.
David Lean / by Stephen M. Silverman ; introduction by Katharine Hepburn.—Updated pbk. ed.
p. cm.
Includes bibliographical references and index.
ISBN 0–8109–2507–9 (pbk.)
1. Lean, David, 1908– . 2. Motion picture producers and
directors—Great Britain—Biography. I. Title.
PN1998.3.L43S55 1992
791.43'0233'092—dc20
[B]   92–5039
                                                    CIP

CONTENTS

Ronald Neame, who four decades before had served as Lean's cinematographer, told how Lean sets up a scene to the exact specifications that exist in his head, and how nothing, "but nothing," can alter this vision. "Film is his life," said Neame. "If you were to tell him that his very best friend was dying, David would answer, 'I'm so sorry, but I have to get this next shot.'"

There was more. Lean's consternation with Sam Spiegel, his formidable producer on *The Bridge on the River Kwai* and *Lawrence of Arabia*. Lean's consternation with actors. With writers. With cameramen. With the weather.

And Lean's reaction to all this? Who knew?

David Lean was nowhere to be seen.

He was on holiday in Africa, recuperating from the rigors of finishing *A Passage to India*.

That seemed only to add to his legend.

David Lean has alternately charmed and confounded interviewers for nearly half a century. "He has the kind of face that years ago was stamped on coins," reported *Time* correspondent Denise Worrell in 1984, on the occasion of that magazine's cover story on Lean. A few weeks earlier, Aljean Harmetz in *The New York Times* painted the same subject as follows: "He has a large, imperial face that would be the envy of a caricaturist," she wrote. "His handshake is hearty, his voice loud, and he tosses his head like a lion tossing his mane."

The look of Lean has long impressed. "David Lean, with his coal-black hair, lean face, straight, neat nose, and piercing eyes, is a strikingly good-looking fellow, something between a popular juvenile lead and Jane Eyre's portrait of Mr. Rochester," suggested the noted critic for *The Observer*, C. A. [Caroline] Lejeune. The year was 1947. "Seen in a crowd or at the studio by a stranger, he is immediately taken for an actor. Five minutes' fruitless attempt to make

him talk about himself convinces you, without a shadow of a doubt, that he is not."

"Drawing Lean out was like pulling water from a very deep well," reported *Time*'s Worrell. "Mr. Lean is willing to give no more than unsatisfactory half-answers," complained Harmetz. "Getting a personality piece about David Lean," said Lejeune, "is like drawing teeth, and the knowing investigator doesn't attempt it. He goes to Mr. Lean's partner, Ronald Neame. 'Ronnie' has no inhibitions about talking about his collaborator and their partnership."

"I used to have the most terrible time with Ronnie," Lean confides in 1988. "He was absolutely mad for publicity, and I wasn't the least bit interested. Used to get me into the worst trouble. I finally had to say to him, 'Look, Ronnie, do what you like, but leave me alone.'"

In 1947, Neame informed Lejeune what he repeated nearly verbatim about Lean at the 1985 Sardi's dinner: "His only passionate interest in life is films, because it's the one thing he knows backward."

I first met David Lean on December 10, 1984, in preparation for a series of newspaper articles about *A Passage to India*. The setting was his suite at the Bel-Air Hotel in southern California, a spacious, well-lived-in bungalow in which every square inch of free tabletop was covered with books. The seventy-six-year-old Lean, impeccably dressed in gray trousers, a white shirt buttoned to the top (no necktie), and a navy blue pullover, entered the room. There was no doubt as to who would be in charge of the interview.

Lean's first—his only—words of greeting were, "You'll not get much out of me, I'm afraid."

Lean and I met again on February 18, 1987, thanks to the New York film publicist Renée Furst. She had arranged that I accompany Lean and his friend Sandra Cooke to the Mamaroneck editing studio of Bob Harris, at the time Lean was inspecting Harris's work restoring *Lawrence of Arabia* to its full, original length. Comfortable in his surroundings, Lean told colorful stories about his favorite subject—making movies. This book grew out of that occasion and a subsequent visit, eighteen days later, to Lean's home in London's Docklands.

Since July 5, 1987, when he granted permission for this book, Lean and I have held ongoing, face-to-face conversations in London, Los Angeles, and the south of France. We have also shared lengthy discussions over the telephone, New York–London, and, when he was on holiday, New York–Kenya. One early, concentrated session occurred on the site of our initial meeting, the Bel-Air Hotel, the weekend of May 6, 1988. The day before, Lean and Columbia Pictures representatives had viewed the fully restored *Lawrence of Arabia* in the Samuel Goldwyn Theatre at the Academy of Motion Picture Arts and Sciences. Lean, exhausted from the week spent overseeing the final edit but thrilled at the prospect of the film's being rereleased internationally, spoke all afternoon and evening into my tape-recorder, recalling the past and the people with whom he had worked. At one point, when told there was no need to clutch the instrument's tiny microphone so tightly, he replied, "Well, you see, it's sort of like an old friend."

David Lean has a most distinctive way of speaking. Robust. Dramatic. Unmistakably English. As his words are few, every one carries weight. So do his silences.

Perhaps the greatest insight into Lean comes from two suggestions he made for this book. The first, delivered gravely one night on the way to dinner, was, "You know, you really should speak to people who don't like me." The other, spoken after he had been told that the manuscript appeared to be taking shape, was, "Well, good. But it's not sweet, is it?"

If there is one thing David Lean abhors, it is sentiment. The most damning label he can apply is to call something "sentimental."

"To David," says Maggie Unsworth, Lean's script supervisor since her school days in 1942, "sentiment makes it all sort of slushy."

"David absolutely detests sentiment," concurs his friend, Katharine Hepburn. "There's not a sentimental bone in David's body."

"If there is one reason the films have lasted," Lean says of his own work when the question is thrust upon him, "I think it is because they are not sentimental."

Yet this is the same man who cried when he heard the news that Fred Astaire had died.

At the 1988 Cannes Film Festival, the British Film Industry and the British Academy held a banquet in honor of David Lean. This one he showed up for.

On May 20, the afternoon of the event, a press conference with a reluctant Lean was held aboard a yacht. Afterward he reported that, surprisingly, he had enjoyed it.

"They were very kind," he said of the journalists, adding, "They asked intelligent questions."

One of the inquiries during the session was about this book and its author. Having been told this by Rita Kempley of *The Washington Post,* I, in turn, queried Lean.

"*They* brought it up," said Lean. "They wanted to know how the book came about. I told them. 'Very simple. He asked me and I said, "Yes."'"

Lean cracked a half-smile. "People are always looking for some kind of secret," he said, "some dark, tangled web. They should realize, there's no magic to it."

That's what he thinks.

Stephen M. Silverman

INTRODUCTION

David Lean is a name in motion pictures that stands for perfection. Every department—the sound, the photography, the casting—is delegated to persons at the very top of their profession. The locations are chosen with the utmost care.

There is a great story about the making of *Doctor Zhivago.* A friend of mine was playing a villain. He had been sent back to London from Madrid where they were working and had been told that they would need him again when the corn had ripened. Time passed. Finally, he got a wire: "THE CORN IS RIPE."

Back he went to Madrid and was picked up by the studio car and taken to the cornfield location, along with about fifty other men who were his soldiers. They were costumed. They were allotted horses and they waited by the side of the field to be told what to do. The idea of the scene was that these soldiers would attack a small army that was hidden in the cornfield. David was sitting in his chair looking at the cornfield. David was obviously studying the situation.

Suddenly he got up and said, "No, this really won't do at all. This battle took place in 1917, and at that time, this cornfield would have been full of red poppies."

Immediately he sent out a crew to dig up red poppies from another field and plant them in the cornfield. It took all day. David looked delighted. "Yes, that's nice," he said. "Authentic. Really authentic. And so much more colorful."

Here's another story. Zhivago is kidnapped and taken to a glade of trees which had a stream running through it. David decided to send the soldiers through the stream on horseback, which he thought would make a very pretty shot with the splashing water. They finished the shot and David said, "I can't see the water splashing."

John Box, who was the set designer, said, "David, if you want to see the water splashing, the stream will have to be deeper."

"Yes, I agree with you," said David.

"Let's dam it up." They did.

And yet another story was told me by his property man, Eddie Fowlie. They were working at a castle in Spain—the Arab headquarters of *Lawrence of Arabia*—and a car was driving up to the front door dispelling passengers. David called Eddie.

"Listen, Eddie, when that gray Rolls gets to the door, I want you to be sure that the double Rs on the axle stand absolutely upright. You understand—I don't want them lying down."

"Of course," Eddie answered.

There was only one thing that interested David—perfection.

I knew this. I'd made a picture with him in 1954—*Summertime,* in Venice. We share

Above: With Lean and shutterbug Noël Coward.

Opposite: Katharine Hepburn, in Venice for *Summertime,* 1954.

13

Above and opposite: Venice,
1954.

over a narrow alleyway lighting the scene as he wished—in a certain way. I was always terrified that I might not be able to deliver exactly what he wanted on the dot. But the fascinating thing to me was that he picked the particular location with such imagination and such sensitivity that you couldn't miss doing the scene properly. His sense of the mood was always exactly right.

Summertime was my only experience of working on a film with David Lean. He took a play—*The Time of the Cuckoo*—and removed about all of the rather complicated and extraneous happenings and turned it into a very simple story of a woman approaching forty who took a trip to Venice one summer and had a love affair with a fascinating Italian.

I can remember being so wildly impressed with what he chose to include—all the things which a woman of this sort would know about and would seek. Nothing too highfaluting or arty, just the simple sights and atmospheres which really make Venice what it is—the canals, the Piazza San Marco, the gondolas, the neighboring islands, the pensione on the Grand Canal, the little shops . . .

He was a famous cutter as a young man, and of course this gives one a real knowledge of film as a medium. I think he really understands film as a painter understands his paint—his brushes—canvas. It was really thrilling working with him and at the end of the picture just watching him in the cutting room for a few brief visits.

To work with someone who really knows what he is doing—who has an enthusiasm for working in film beyond one's imagination—whose capacity for work has no end—whose determination is to produce the best possible result—to whom nothing matters—discomfort, exhaustion—so long as it contributes to a perfect result.

My admiration for David is infinite.

that quality. We don't give up. If we say we'll be there, we'll be there—we'll do it. You say you'll get to the top of the hill—you do!

David is sweet—simple and straight—and strong and savage; and he is the best movie director in the world. And nothing—did you hear me?—I said nothing gets in his way. He'll stand and look and stare. He won't be hurried. He won't budge until he can smell perfection. That's his aim, work or play: do it as well as it can possibly be done. Or don't do it.

For an actress, this has its advantages. You get a pure point of view. I'm not prejudiced about his direction. I see what I see, and I don't just see it through rose-colored glasses. But he's far, far superior to most people.

Some scenes in *Summertime* could only be shot at a certain hour of the day, actually a certain minute, when the sun would be

Katharine Hepburn

14

BEGINNINGS

David Lean, circa 1909: "I had a childhood you could call happy."

"I remember working with somebody once," recalls David Lean, "a wonderful art director named John Bryan, who was going to do *Lawrence of Arabia,* only he had to have a terrible kidney operation. A year or two afterward he died, poor chap. But I remember, we were setting up something on *Lawrence,* and John said to me, 'I suddenly realize what you are.' 'What's that?' I said. He said, 'You're a bloody Boy Scout.'

"And there's great truth in that, you know."

David Lean was born on March 25, 1908, at 38 Blenheim Crescent, in the gray, Edwardian suburb of Croydon, located in South London. "Croydon was so respectable in its dreary way," says Lean, "all the houses one the same after the other. Every-

one was so careful of what they were wearing and doing. I hated it."

Lean's parents had been married in a Quaker ceremony at Birmingham's Bull Street Friends' Meeting House on July 26, 1904. His mother was the former Helena Annie Tangye; his father, Francis William le Blount Lean, a chartered accountant in London since 1900. "He was someone," says his son, "who gave advice to big companies that went into bankruptcy." Three years after the arrival of David, another son was born, Edward Tangye Lean.

Handsome, strong looks distinguished both sides of the family. Helena Tangye's father, Edward Tangye, grew up on his father's fruit farm in Cornwall, and took his first job as a locomotive driver on the West Cornwall Railway. In 1855, he decided to emigrate to America, a journey overruled by fate when his New York–bound ship sank because captain and crew were drunk. While most on board perished, Tangye lived to tell the story.

Some months later, successfully landing in America, he settled in a remote outpost of Wisconsin, and, living alone in a wooden shanty, survived as a lead miner. Simultaneous to Tangye's time abroad, his elder brothers in Birmingham formed their own machinist business and christened it James Tangye and Brothers. After three years in America, Edward Tangye returned to join them, and the company prospered. The brothers invented several mining devices and helped inaugurate the Great Eastern Railway and erect Cleopatra's Needle on the Thames Embankment in London. It was also shortly after joining his brothers that Edward Tangye married his cousin, Ann Cowlin, and began to raise a family.

David Lean recalls his mother's family as "rather artistic, an interesting lot. My grandfather invented gas engines, which, as a boy, I would see at various train stations." The machinery was plainly marked "Tangye Gas Engines."

"He also," Lean remembers, "invented a famous hydraulic jack." One such model, it so happened, was responsible for one of the great face-saving rescues in British naval history. "Just up the Thames not far from here," says Lean as he points over his shoulder while sitting on one of the terraces of his London home, "there was a great launching ceremony for a ship called *The Great Eastern*."

Came time for the 18,914-ton vessel—the largest of her day—to ease her way into the river, says Lean, "She just got stuck."

Edward Tangye and one of his brothers rushed to the scene intending to place some of their jacks under the ship as a means to force *The Great Eastern* into the water. "Everybody said, 'Look here, it's ridiculous,'" says Lean. "Here they had invented these small jacks, three or four feet high. I don't know how they did it, but they placed a series of these tiny jacks underneath the boat."

The ship finally set sail in late January 1858—thanks to the Tangye jacks.

"That," says Lean, "made their name. They used to say, 'We launched *The Great Eastern,* and she launched us.'"

Edward Tangye died in 1909, when David Lean was a year old.

David Lean's paternal grandfather was a lifelong educator, William Scarnell Lean, born June 3, 1833, at Camp Hill, Birmingham, the eldest of eight children. In 1850, he started teaching at a Quaker school in York and followed with posts at the Flounders Institute and in Darlington. In 1864, two momentous events occurred: he became classics master at University College in London, and he married Marianna Bevan, a Greek scholar, a rare calling for a woman of her time. She and Lean were to have ten children.

In 1870, William Lean founded a Quaker University, the Flounders Institute at Ackworth, where he was reputed to be one of the most eloquent preachers of his era. He

died in 1908, the same year David Lean was born.

"My mother was a sweet woman, rather pretty," Lean told *Time* magazine in 1984, after being pressed for family information. "My father was tall, and I think he was handsome. He wasn't a stern character. He left my mother. I must have been in my early teens. It was sort of a bad part of my life, really. My father, poor man, plagued by guilt. It was a difficult thing in the best of times, but in those days, and being a Quaker, you can imagine. He didn't get married again. He went off with somebody else. She was a nice woman. I got to know her later. I think he was a sad man. I don't really want to talk about these personal things."

Of Cornwall, Lean says, "That's from the toe of England to the extreme west, an area that's wild like Ireland. What you'll find there are a lot of tin mines." The terrain and its resources would prompt Lean's brother to quip, "David, we've certainly come up from the mines."

"Funny," Lean says these many years later, "he was probably right." After a thoughtful pause, Lean adds, "We were never really close, my brother and I, not until the last three years of his life."

Edward Tangye Lean died of a heart attack in his London home on October 28, 1974. "I admired him enormously," says David Lean. "He became head of the BBC Overseas Service. Very clever. He had two books published before he left Oxford. It was always my envy that he was considered worth sending up to university and I wasn't."

Shortly after David was born, the family moved to the country, to Merstham. "We had a nice house there," he recalls, "and I had a happy time." His education, however, presented a problem. "We were Quakers, and the local school, Church of England, wouldn't have me." The family moved back to Croydon.

"In those days," says Lean, "we used to have a Quaker school. It still goes quite strong today, a lovely place, actually, a very small school, only one hundred people. It's called Leighton Park and it's just outside Reading, which is—I don't know how you describe it—where the biscuits come from, Huntley and Palmer. Wonderful grounds. Beautiful trees. Gardens. That sort of thing. Fives court. Lovely swimming pool. And there were many Quakers."

Lean considers the place, especially for its era, "very modern in certain ways. I remember there was a Chinese boy. Highly unusual. Wonderful, really. There was a black boy, which was to be considered most extraordinary. And I remember having been fascinated by the Scriptures class, because I remember spending the whole term with the master, exploring the miracles in the Bible: manna from heaven, that sort of thing. The crossing of the Red Sea, how that probably wasn't a miracle at all, because the Red Sea can go very low at certain times. I remember thinking, in those days, 'This is sacrilege.' But it was also wonderful, of course."

One of Lean's most vivid childhood memories involved aviation. "Croydon was where the Croydon Aerodrome was," says Lean. "Not 'Croydon Airport.' Croydon Aerodrome. I used to go out there on a bicycle when I was a boy, and watch these planes on a grass runway taking off for Paris. It seemed extraordinary."

In 1927, he says, he experienced "the biggest excitement I ever had at Croydon. I saw Lindbergh arrive." Lean describes the event as he usually tells a story, by blocking it out as if fashioning a movie scene. "Now, Lindbergh had flown across the Atlantic," he says, "and arrived at Paris. He had a night's sleep, or two nights' sleep, and then came to Croydon. And the place was packed, waiting for him."

Lean breaks the tempo of the conversation, then stops entirely. "Now look," he says, "I can't talk, because I find these things very emotional." He stares into the distance, focusing momentarily on some imaginary object on the far horizon, his means to collect himself, then continues.

"I remember this plane coming into view, this tiny plane, the *Spirit of St. Louis.* And it landed, everybody cheering. I can see it now. I could stage it. Billy Wilder has done that, of course."

Wilder reenacted Lindbergh's flight in his 1957 film *The Spirit of St. Louis,* with James Stewart.

"But I remember," says Lean, "this slim figure in overalls, standing up out of the cockpit. Everyone going wild. He looked, he *was* so young. I remember his hair. It was sort of blondish."

Lean rests silently and reflects upon the memory. "That sort of thing has always fascinated me, I suppose."

At Leighton Park, Lean's teachers found him to be an indifferent scholar, "either not very bright or incorrigibly lazy," according to one report.

"I never thought I would be able to do anything," Lean says in retrospect. "I was a complete dud in school. Hopeless at mathematics. Still am. I have to count on my fingers if I wish to add. Latin? Hopeless. They asked me to give it up."

His timidity regarding such matters extends also to mastery over simple mechanical devices such as typewriters, despite Lean's decades of experience with highly complex film equipment. Sitting at a keyboard to compose even a letter, let alone a film script, is, he insists, a matter of two-fingered hunt and peck.

Aside from periodic school outings, especially when they meant "expeditions to various places," the class Lean "liked better than anything else was what we called 'musical appreciation,' once a week." The course exerted such a happy influence that, Lean says, "I can still remember the name of the

man who gave it, Scott Goddard. He taught me a tremendous lot, and he used to have an HMV Gramophone, with a wonderful mahogany horn. I still remember him winding it up and how it looked, like a wonderful precision machine. It used a kind of bamboo triangle for the needles. They didn't damage the records as steel needles did and they gave very good reproduction for then."

In all, Goddard's class afforded Lean exposure to an entire new world. "I learned about people like Richard Strauss, the young Strauss, *Don Juan,* that sort of stuff, all of which was madly exciting to me. In those days it was considered rather outrageous modern music, and I suppose I imagined myself as becoming, perhaps if the river had taken a different turn, a sort of wonderful jazz pianist."

Lean now laughs at such a notion. "I would have loved it, actually," he says. Asked what musical instruments he plays today, he answers, "Well, that's the funny

Above: Ann Cowlin Tangye, maternal grandmother. "My mother's family was *enormous,*" says Lean. "Twelve children or something."

Opposite, above: Edward Tangye, maternal grandfather, who died when grandson David was one.

Opposite, below: Marianna Bevan Lean, paternal grandmother, whom young David found imposing.

19

Lean's parents, Helena Annie Tangye Lean and Francis William le Blount Lean, both of whom lived well into their nineties.

thing, you see. I'm afraid I don't play a note."

When he was about twelve years old, Lean was presented with a gift by his Uncle Clement, on the maternal side of the family. It was a Kodak Box Brownie, the simple camera of its day.

"Everybody remarked and said, 'He'll never be able to use it,'" Lean recalls, "but I actually became very good, and mad, keen for taking pictures. In fact, in school I used to spend most of my spare time in the darkroom, enlarging, learning composition."

His camera accompanied him on foreign trips with his father and brother to such places as Switzerland, France, and, a place of true fascination, the Mediterranean. It was also on these holidays that the young, impressionable Lean began photographing magnificent scenery. "That camera," he says, "became my great friend."

At home, Lean devoted a voracious reading appetite to stories that provided strong narrative structures and larger-than-life heroes. "I was brought up on Jules Verne and R. M. Ballantyne," he says. "I remember a man called Captain Charles Gilson, who wrote in an English magazine called *The*

Boy's Own Paper, which I think has completely vanished."

In his 1939 essay "Boys's Weeklies," George Orwell happily recalled "*Chums* and the old *B.O.P.* [as] the leading papers for boys, and they remained dominant till quite recently. Each of them carries every week a fifteen- or twenty-thousand-word school story, complete in itself, but usually more or less connected with the story of the week before."

"I used to wait for the news agent to bring the copy on Wednesdays, whenever it came out," says Lean, "so I could continue reading Gilson's serials. I don't know what they would be like to read today, but, at the time, they had an enormous narrative power, obviously, being serials."

Lean's father regularly used to take the boy to religious meetings. Ironically, the one place Lean was strictly forbidden was the cinema, even though, by Lean's adolescence, the moving-picture had gained wide popular acceptance. The first public performance of a film program in England had taken place February 20, 1896, at the Marlborough Hall on Regent Street. By the end of the same year, films were required bill of fare at every music hall.

20

"Because I was Quaker," says Lean, "I wasn't allowed to go to the cinema. Now, my father and mother were pretty advanced, as a lot of Quakers in those days were, but they thought the stage was pretty wicked, and the cinema was much worse. Absolute dens of vice. I think it had to do with what they portrayed, these wildly emotional people, people like Pola Negri, Theda Bara, Nazimova, and Sarah Bernhardt. These were outlandish human beings, and I think Quakers, being very keenly aware of the passions and trying to keep them under control, wanted to put a cap on these actresses and the wickedness that went on backstage."

Despite years of curiosity, "Not until I was about seventeen," says Lean, "did I ever go to the cinema." He sneaked in with friends one day after school.

Prior to that furtive initiation, the young Lean had only heard stories about movies from the family housekeeper. "During the first World War," he says, "we lived in a big house in Croydon and a woman used to come—they used to be called 'charwomen,' they're 'charladies' now—and she was Irish and called Mrs. Egerton, and she was mad about the movies. I remember once asking her, 'When they talk, how do you know what they're saying?' She said, 'Well, they talk, and then writing comes up on the screen,' and I said, 'But that can't look right.' She said, 'Oh, it looks perfectly natural.'"

Mrs. Egerton was married to a man who drove a horse cab, although, remembers Lean, "Her great love was Charlie Chaplin. She used to show me how Chaplin walked down the street and around corners, by her walking around the kitchen table. I'd sit there in stitches, eyes glued to Mrs. Egerton, until finally I went to the movies myself."

In contrast to the drab uniformity of Croydon, he says of those early attractions, especially the sweeping adventures from America, "I looked upon them as a kind of wonderful escape. At the movies I saw

things I thought I would never see in my entire life. *Nothing* ever daunted Douglas Fairbanks."

The first film Lean ever saw was the 1922 *The Hound of the Baskervilles*. "One of Conan Doyle's [Sherlock Holmes] stories," he says, "directed by a man called Maurice Elvey, whom I later worked with as a camera assistant. People laugh at him now, but in his day he was very professional."

Considered Britain's all-time most prolific director, with more than three hundred features to his credit, Elvey (1887–1967) worked as a stage actor, then director, before turning to film in 1913. His *Hound of the Baskervilles* did not rely on traditional

Helena Lean and her two sons, Edward (who was called by his middle name, Tangye) and David.

David Lean, not quite a teenager. Still awaiting him was his first glimpse of cinema—as of yet forbidden by his Quaker parents.

afford to go to the first-run theatres." Particularly appealing was Robert Flaherty's 1922 documentary *Nanook of the North,* as well as British accounts of the explorers Scott's and Shackleton's sweep of the Antarctic. As to features, Lean was impressed by Chaplin's comedic struggle against the elements in *The Gold Rush,* director King Vidor's "sense of terrific movement" in *The Big Parade* (which later Lean emulated for a key sequence in *Doctor Zhivago,* when lovers Zhivago and Lara meet during a caravan scene), and the ground-breaking cinematic techniques of D. W. Griffith, who harnessed an untamed nature as a setting for his human drama.

"One of the best first-run picture houses was the M-G-M theatre in London, in the Strand, called the Tivoli," says Lean. "Today it's part of a department store, sadly. I saw quite a few pictures there."

Of those, Lean's undisputed favorites came from the director Rex Ingram (1892–1950). Born the son of a minister in Dublin, Ingram studied sculpture at Yale and worked as a railway clerk on the New Haven line before, in 1913, he happened to meet Charles Edison, the son of American motion-picture inventor Thomas.

By 1920, Ingram was a leading Hollywood director at Metro-Goldwyn-Mayer, due in large part to screenwriter June Mathis's insistence that he take charge of her script for the 1921 adventure *The Four Horsemen of the Apocalypse,* starring Rudolph Valentino. "My aim," Ingram wrote in a 1928 essay deploring the "artificiality" of Hollywood, "has always been to tell a story as directly, as simply, and as naturally as I could."

Says Lean, "When I first saw Rex Ingram's *The Four Horsemen of the Apocalypse,* and, particularly, his *Mare Nostrum* [1925–26], which he made in the south of France and was the story of a German submarine, I realized that there was somebody behind the camera. Somebody was actually *guiding*

silent-movie title cards. Instead, Elvey employed pictorial devices to spell out the plot: a closeup of a newspaper death notice, a marriage license, letters from Watson to Holmes.

"I was fascinated by these pictures on a screen and by the orchestra playing," says Lean. "People today don't know what silent movies were like. They were a very powerful medium. The silent pictures combined with an orchestra. Its impact was something quite different from a talkie. Just marvelous, really."

Lean's parents conceded their son's infatuation, and he soon became an habitué at the Philharmonic Hall in Croydon. "When I got older," he says, "I began to be able to

it. In some idiotic way, I had never realized this before."

The revelation struck, Lean says, because "Ingram's images had such power. I knew that they were thought-out images. It wasn't that the camera just happened to be there when this was taking place. It was a view of what was taking place. And he had staged it.

"This I found tremendously exciting."

"So there I was," continues Lean, "a complete dud, and I had this very bright younger brother. My father sent him to Oxford. I didn't go to university because my father did not think that would be worthwhile."

Lean distinctly recalls his parent saying at this time, "Look, I think the only thing you can do—and you'll consider yourself very lucky—and this is, I think you'd better come into the office."

Lean's father was the senior partner of the accounting firm of Viney, Price, and Goodyear, whose offices were in the City of London. "And so," says Lean, "I went there. You should have seen me." Lean, who is lounging poolside at the Bel-Air Hotel on an unseasonably cool May afternoon, laughs as he provides a description of his uniform of some sixty years before: "a rolled umbrella, bowler hat, black coat, black striped trousers."

Asked whether a photograph might exist from that period, he answers a stern, "No."

"I absolutely hated it," he says. "I remember, one day, my father going for me and there I was, wearing a pullover sweater. He said, 'You must never wear that. That is not professional.'" His father likewise discouraged the then nineteen-year-old from spending three pennies a day on newspapers, to no avail.

"It's a funny thing, memory, isn't it?" says Lean. "I suddenly get a picture of myself sitting in the corner of a third-class carriage, going back home from that damned office that I hated so much, reading *The Evening Standard,* and reading the once-a-week crit-

Croydon: Lean, his mother, and brother Tangye, at the time the younger sibling entered Oxford.

icisms by this man, Walter Mycroft. He must be dead now. He was never malicious and he obviously loved movies, nowadays another rare commodity. He later became head of one of the big studios, Elstree, obviously because the people, the bosses, the money people, thought, 'Here's a man who knows about movies and has some taste.' And they put him in charge. I think he must have been very successful there. I never met him, but I learned a lot from him, in a way. I mean, he just really said what he thought, said it without malice, and he became, I suppose, like a teacher to me."

By the time he started his first job, Lean says, "My mother and father were parted and my mother and I lived in a wretched little house in Croydon. My brother had just finished school, or was just going up to Oxford. This was really a rather bad part of my life."

Circumstances were about to change. "I came back from the office one evening and my mother said, 'Aunt Edith came for tea today, and she asked how things were going at the office.'"

"I don't think he's very keen on it," Lean's mother replied.

"You know, it's a funny thing," said the aunt. "I look around David's room and I don't see any accountancy books. All I see are film magazines. Why doesn't he go in for films?"

When Lean came home, his mother told him what his aunt had suggested. "Today it seems absurd," says Lean, "especially to young people, who must think it absolutely mad, but in those days it didn't seem so absurd. Somehow, the cinema was such magic to me. I didn't really believe they were made in a studio, or that one could go into the so-called 'business.' Of course, I knew the studios. I used to read film criticisms like crazy, but I never thought *I* personally could go into that box of magic.

"And then, when my Aunt Edith said what she did, I thought, 'Oh, my God, I suppose I could.'"

Lean approached his father. "I said, 'Look, Dad. How much will I earn if I stay here at the office? In ten months' time, how much will I be earning?' And, he said, 'Well, I'm sorry to tell you that if in ten years you earned X thousand a year—I know it's very low—but you would be extremely lucky.'

"Dad, look," countered Lean. "I'm no good at it. I know that."

Thirty years later, Lean took the story and paraphrased it to describe the prewar vocation of the Geoffrey Horne character in *The Bridge on the River Kwai.* Says Lean, "I told my father, 'I go to various places, I check the balance sheets, I add up columns and columns of figures that have been checked by two other people before me, and will be checked by two other people after me, and it's terribly unexciting.' Then I told him the story about Aunt Edith."

Learning that his son wished to enter the movies, the senior Lean was "absolutely shocked," Lean remembers. "Movies in Quaker families were considered to be absolutely beyond the pale. It was like my saying I'd like to join the circus.

"In the end, my father was very good about it," recollects Lean. "He sort of simmered down and said, 'Look, I'll tell you what. If you are really serious about this, then So-and-so'—he mentioned a firm of city accountants—'do the Gaumont-British account, and I'll give What-not'—one of the partners—'a ring to see if there's any possibility of arranging an interview for you.'

"You know," says Lean in a rare, wistful voice, "it's one of my great regrets now that my father never really realized that I've made a success of it. He lived well into his nineties. I don't know precisely how old he was when he died, but I know he was past ninety-five. He got, we became, very distant, and, I remember, I was terribly hurt. I sent him an invitation to the premiere of *Lawrence of Arabia,* and he said it was too far to come.

"And I've often thought of this."

On a Saturday morning when he was nineteen years old, David Lean took the train from Croydon to Victoria Station, and changed there for a bus to Lime Grove, Shepherd's Bush. "I went down to the Gaumont Studio, my father having succeeded in getting this introduction for me," says Lean, "and I interviewed with the studio production manager. He was a very short little man, and he said, 'I'll tell you what we'll do. We need a runner here, and you can come work for a month carrying the camera, making tea, anything we want to put you onto. At the end of the month, we'll give you a pound a week if we consider you suitable. If we do not consider you suitable, then you will go.'"

Lean was extremely grateful. "I said to the man, 'Thank you very much, sir,' and I started to work there."

Lean pauses a moment, then says with a deep sigh, "*I just loved it.*"

One afternoon, during lunch, the recent hireling ventured into the camera storage room. "I'll never forget, there was a Bell and Howell camera on the bench. I'd never touched nor seen a movie camera before, and I went over and put my hand on it. At that precise instant somebody there, not realizing what a magic moment that was for me, said, 'That photographed *Roses of Picardy.*'

"Now, *Roses of Picardy* was directed by the same man who had done *The Hound of the Baskervilles,* Maurice Elvey, and it was a bloody good picture. It uses flashbacks, very modern in those days, to tell the story of how a soldier fell in love with a French girl.

"Anyhow, there I am with this camera, and I thought it was just wonderful to see this thing. It's, again, another sensual pleasure and I sort of repeated it in *The Bridge on the River Kwai,* where I got Alec Guinness, on the day before the train comes over the completed bridge, to stroke the wood of the bridge." Lean laughs. "I think Alec was rather angry about doing it, but he did it and that was that. It's in the film, of course."

At the end of the four-week trial period at the studio, Lean received his hoped-for verdict. "I was in a sort of heaven," says Lean. "I mean, I couldn't wait to get to the studio every day."

"The greatest advantage to those times, which was also the greatest disadvantage," says Lean, "was, of course, there were no unions." This circumstance allowed him to learn different aspects of moviemaking by plying several trades at the studio, among them holding up the slate in front of the camera that recorded the number of takes

Lean's entry into the British film industry was also a matter of propitious timing. The year 1927 marked the passage of the British government's Cinematographic Act, a sweeping protectionist measure conceived wholly as a means to boost employment in the long-sagging British movie industry and to keep at bay the already-realized American monopoly of the world film market. In 1926, thirty-seven British films vied for screen time in England with more than five hundred American imports. The new legislation called for English exhibitors to devote five percent of their screen time to home-produced product in 1928, graduating to seven-and-a-half percent in 1929, and, ultimately, by 1935, when the Act was to expire, to twenty percent.

Chief among the film companies to seize advantage of this law was Lean's employer, Gaumont-British, founded in 1895 by the photographic-equipment merchant Leon Gaumont (1864–1946) in his native Paris. In 1898, the Gaumont company established a London office to distribute its French films in Britain, but slowly the London branch crept into original production, creating both newsreels and features, including a 1908 *Romeo and Juliet* as well as comedies with titles such as *A Stitch in Time* and *Put Papa Amongst the Girls.*

In 1915, Gaumont launched into full-scale, English production. For thirty thousand pounds, considered expensive by British standards but cheap by Hollywood's, the company built a studio at Shepherd's Bush, where, among the earliest output was a serial featuring the continuing adventures of an avenger named *Ultus.*

In 1922, Leon Gaumont totally relinquished control of the company to Colonel A. C. Bromhead and his brother R. C. Bromhead. Gaumont-British expanded production, and created two separate units at Shepherd's Bush. One, British Screencraft, would produce melodramas, and the other, called Westminster, comedies.

Although nothing of real distinction was produced by either branch, the steady stream of pictures they made allowed the company to gain a stronghold in the otherwise shaky British film industry; in fact, in 1926, the worst business year since the World War I, Gaumont-British optimistically built an entirely new studio to replace the original facility.

for a scene. The first feature to which Lean was assigned was the 1927 *Quinneys,* directed by Maurice Elvey.

"I went around to every department," says Lean, "and people laugh when I say I was a one-time wardrobe mistress. Maurice Elvey was the star director at that studio. He did a film called *Balaclava,* which was actually *The Charge of the Light Brigade.*"

The 1928 *Balaclava* (U.S. title: *Jaws of Death*) was a spectacular historical drama, set against the Crimean War and shot in color, but to save money it was released in monochrome. It starred Benita Hume (later to marry Ronald Colman), Miles Mander, Alf Godard, and Cyril McLaglen, brother of Victor. McLaglen played an army officer instrumental in the capturing of a notorious spy, and the film's grand finale reenacted the charge of the Light Brigade.

"On *Balaclava,*" says Lean, "I was in charge of the uniforms, and I had to take them down to Salisbury Plain to the extras and recover them from the extras after the day's shooting. On that I got to learn the crank of the camera. I can still do it. You look at my wrist, now. . . ."

Something remarkable starts to happen. To illustrate the workings of a silent camera, Lean forms a fist with his left hand and starts to wind his right fist around it in a clockwise motion. And, as he does, this eighty-year-old man, who most of the time looks to be in his early sixties anyway, undergoes a metamorphosis. In his facial expressions and movements, Lean becomes a youth in his twenties. He does not sense this, or, if he does, makes no sign of it.

"You turn from the wrist, and at the speed I'm going now," says Lean, his concentration unbroken, "I can assure you, it's sixteen pictures a second." He speeds the rotation of his right fist. "Now it's twenty-four."

Lean apprenticed in every department until landing in the cutting rooms, where he assisted the director. "Directors then had to cut all their own films," he says. "There were no such things as Moviolas. You looked at the films all night with the magnifying glass in the hand, and then you'd have a pair of scissors and the director would measure out three feet."

Lean stretches out his left arm in front of his face. "Now, you take the film, put it to his nose, stretch out his arm, and from the nose to the end of the fingers is about three feet. You then come back again and there's six feet, and the director would cut it. It's a comparatively crude process. We used to go into the theatre and see the film we'd just cut and then come back and alter it."

Lean's obsession with the medium and its techniques propelled him to try latching on to one of the directors on the lot. "I used to say, 'Look, would you mind if I came into the cutting rooms?' In those days, the directors never let us juniors into the theatre to see the rushes, but, I remember, I'd previously made friends with a man called Matthews, the studio projectionist, and he said that if I kept out of the way as he was loading up the reels, I could look through the porthole in the projection room and from back there see the screen."

The right opportunity soon availed itself. "Once I went in there, this Matthews said, 'You don't talk. Don't tell anybody, but I'm running a reel of cut stuff.' I'd been present when we cut it, you see, and I looked through the porthole and there I saw what I'd seen done, now cut together. Close-up of you, as it were, cutting to a close-up of me, and it looked as if we were talking to each other. And then, as somebody talks, up came a title, and it looked quite natural. Next day, all right, a cut to a long shot, or whatever it was, you see. That's how it was in silent days. You know, I've often wondered about directors who have never been editors."

"When sound came in, the studio was turned over to the talkies," says Lean. "I

Gardening in Croydon, 1927, at the time he started in films; both tasks remained favorite pastimes.

remember there was an American director, called Sewell Collins, who did a music-hall skit, and it was only a four-reeler."

The comedy, *The Night Porter,* was based on a play by Harry Wall and ran only forty-five minutes. It centered on an empty-headed hotel worker who mistakes one of his guests for a thief. "Sewell Collins didn't have the remotest idea about cutting sound," says Lean, "and I remember that the editor of the Gaumont Sound News, which was going very well by then, offered to sit there for an hour to teach Collins how to synchronize sound and picture and keep it in sync, you see. So, down he came for an hour, and I was there."

As the news editor provided the explanation, Lean caught on immediately. Sewell Collins did not. Lean ended up making the actual cuts on the picture, with Collins spelling out to him what he wanted.

"Collins would say to me, 'Look, that's playing in the long shot. Now we go to a close-up of her listening. Could we continue? I'd like to hear the sound of the man over her face for the first two sentences, and then cut in speaking. Do you think that's possible?'"

Lean said, "I'm sure, sir. I can do that." He did that. Then he went and did it for seven more directors.

"One day, the man who edited the sound news, the man who had taught us how to synchronize sound, left. Now, cutting the sound news is no bloody joke, I can tell you. With silents, if you made a mistake, all you had to do was stick in another title. But with the sound news, you cut the negative. You didn't have prints made. They might shoot a football match on a Saturday afternoon, and you'd have to cut and splice it and make perhaps five minutes to show that very same night.

"By that time, you see, it was two issues a week, Wednesday night and Saturday night, and they were sent to the cinemas all over. By the time you cut the negative with the

Lean continues to be fascinated by film cutting. "It still is to me a kind of conjuring trick. I know, even now, when I make a good cut, I get a real sense of pleasure out of it. I love flow, you see, and cutting, in a sense, is creating flow like real music. It's playing music in pictures. And often, when I'm constructing a scene, not so much dialogue, but in silent action, I think of it in terms of music." (Lean goes so far as to venture further, "I think perhaps that's why I use too much music in my films.")

To illustrate, Lean cites a scene from *Lawrence of Arabia:* "When Lawrence is leaving [Auda's] camp, and they all go off into the desert. I mean, by any sensible terms the scene is too long. Nowadays you don't hold a shot like that. But if you think of it— and I don't mean to be conceited here—but if you think of it in terms of the second movement of a symphony, it's got to have that kind of weight.

"I don't say that I'm writing music. Of course I'm not. But flow, music, creating images—it's in the same line of country, you know what I mean?"

sound, and by the time you saw your first print with sound, on the screen, something like four hundred copies of the newsreel were out. So if you made one mistake, you made four hundred."

Just such an accident was caused by an assistant working on footage of the Graf Zeppelin. "There it was," says Lean, "going backwards and upside down." This left the heads of the studio to "cast about what the hell to do. They fired the assistant and they came to me and said, 'Will you be the cutter? We'll pay you five pounds a week. Plus overtime.'" Lean gladly took the job.

"I edited the sound news for five pounds a week. I cut it, I wrote the commentaries, and I spoke them. I was in that for two, three years."

In early 1931, at the invitation of producer Keith Ayling, Lean signed on to a job at Movietone News. For a while, he also worked in Paris, editing for Paramount. "I cut a film called *Insult,* directed by Harry Lachman, who had worked with Rex Ingram in the old days. Roger Livesey's father was in it, and I'm not sure John Gielgud wasn't in it as well. It was actually made at British-Dominion, which was the best studio in England, but it was cut in Joinville, which was where I lived on the river. I had a smashing time.

"Then, someone, I've forgotten who it was, said, 'Come into the studios,' and, to make a long story short, I ended up at the British-Dominion Studios at Elstree."

Elstree, built in 1926 by American financier J. D. Williams and English producer Herbert Wilcox, was known for production standards that could rival those of Hollywood. Hitchcock's 1929 *Blackmail,* considered to be the first English talkie, was born at the studio. As sound techniques were perfected, Elstree gained in stature, and it was into this hub of activity that Lean returned to feature-film editing late in 1932.

"I became quite a successful editor," Lean says, "and I used to edit a film, and

then I'd go to Capri, which I just loved in those days. I would stay there until my money ran out, then I'd go back to England and edit another film. There'd be about six weeks like that. I'd go back and edit another film. They used to send for me if a film was in trouble, if it was too long and needed cutting, or if it was loose and they didn't know what to do with it."

The transition from newsreels back to features was not entirely smooth. "I used to overcut horribly," Lean remembers. "When you're dealing with newsreels, you're damned lucky if the cameraman managed to get the goal in the football match and fit it into the frame. You rely on what you are given. But, when suddenly you come to cut a film, everything is placed before you: long shots, medium shots, close-ups. I'm afraid I was so pleased to have all these shots that I overcut terribly.

"Alex Korda, whom I liked very much, produced a film that he said I overcut. I probably did. He fired me. I learned from that."

Another instructor Lean has long credited was an editor he had met in France, Merrill White, "a big curly-haired American who was [Ernst] Lubitsch's chief cutter." During the early days of talkies, Herbert Wilcox had brought White to England from Hollywood, where White had earned a reputation as a film doctor. White used to cut the films that had turned out poorly and attempt to improve them by including close-ups, inserts, or whatever else he thought was required.

Lean was an attentive pupil of White's, which is how, as he says, he "came to be sort of a film doctor."

Lean's career was truly launched—a fact, however, that had yet to be reflected in his earnings. Partly to blame was his own modesty, a trait instilled during his upbringing and held over until today. (One close friend often teases him by saying, "David, your Quaker oats are showing.") Back in his editing days, Lean was severely lacking in confidence, particularly when it came to negotiating with his studio employers.

"The person who really gave me a helping hand with money," Lean says, "was Bobby Wyler, the brother of Willy. It was when I cut a film directed by Dr. Paul Czinner, a famous German director married to Elisabeth Bergner."

Budapest-born Czinner (1890–1972) was a doctor of philosophy, journalist, playwright, and stage producer before he directed his first film in Vienna in 1919. In 1924, he won acclaim for his German film *Nju,* starring his wife, the Polish-born Bergner (1900–1986). She created a faithful European following in subsequent German films the couple made together. In 1933, Czinner and Bergner fled Hitler and settled in England, where, the following year, they made the biographical drama *Catherine the Great.*

In 1935, their melodramatic love story cut by Lean, *Escape Me Never,* starred Bergner as Gemma, an unwed mother, and Hugh Sinclair as the struggling musician she meets and then finally marries. Though the musician cares more for his unfinished symphony than for the welfare of Gemma's child, Gemma and he realize that they cannot possibly live without the other. The film proved a critical and commercial hit and Elisabeth Bergner was nominated for an Academy Award.

"Part of it was done in Venice and part of it in the Dolomites and part of it in the studio," says Lean. "Elisabeth Bergner was a wonderful actress and it was a highly successful film, very prestigious, and I got a great salary of thirty pounds a week for cutting it.

"Now, a very important part of this story is that I knew Bobby Wyler. We lived in the same block of flats, a place called Mount Royal, which still exists today."

One day Bobby Wyler informed Lean that Czinner was working on another film,

As You Like It with Bergner and Laurence Olivier, and that Czinner wanted Lean to cut it. Wyler urged his neighbor to demand a higher salary this time.

"Bobby said, 'Look here, David. They want you for this film, but if this film fails, you can always get another job, can't you? It isn't the end of your career.' I said, 'No, that's right.' 'Well,' said Bobby, 'you put it in my hands, because I think you ought to be earning more. You should be more like the Americans, you see.'"

Lean "sort of hemmed and hawed." Bobby Wyler prodded him.

"Come on," insisted Wyler, "take a chance."

"All right." Lean surrendered. "Over to you."

"Right," said Wyler. "Now you're going to see Dr. Czinner and the production people next week. You're going to recoil, but I tell you, you're going to go in there and you're going to ask for double the salary. Ask for sixty pounds a week."

"Sixty pounds a week!" exclaimed Lean, who fifty-two years after the fact explains, "This was enormous. No editor was ever paid it, in England particularly. I suppose there were a couple of American editors, I don't know. But Bobby said, 'You promise?' I said, 'All right.'"

The conspirators staged a run through. "The first thing Bobby said was, 'You don't wear hats, do you? Let's go out and buy you a hat.' And so I went out with Bobby and bought what was called in those days a Trilby hat. Bobby said, 'It's only a prop. You go into the office, carrying the hat, and there they will be sitting behind their desks, and you put the hat on the desk.'

"And we rehearsed this, Bobby and I, and he played Dr. Czinner and the production people, saying, 'Look here now, I'm sure you'll be very —,' and I said, 'I'd like some more money,' or something like that. And he said, 'Yes, we'll pay you thirty-five,' and I'm to say, 'Well, I'm sorry. That's not what I'm aiming at.' And then Bobby said that they would finally say, 'Well, what do you want?,' and I was to look them straight in the eye, and, Bobby told me, 'You say, "I want sixty." '

" 'They'll recoil,' said Bobby. 'Let them recoil. Then reach forward and pick the hat off the desk. Stand up. And you say, words to the effect, "I'm sorry, gentlemen, to have caused you this irrelevance, but good afternoon. It was nice to see you again." '

"And he said, 'I should think it's a big office, and, I can promise you, I don't think you will ever get to the door, but the worst that can happen is, you'll just open it and they'll say, "Wait a minute." ' And exactly this happened.

"I walked to the door, just as Bobby and I had rehearsed, and put my hand on the handle, and Czinner said, 'Wait a minute,' and I turned back. He said, 'Look, we want you very badly, make no secret of that. But it is an enormous salary. Nobody's been paid this before.' And I said, 'Well, I think I'm worth it.' And Czinner said, 'Let us think this over. We've got to talk this over with the board.' Everybody wants to talk with some mysterious board.

"I came back in two days and they said, 'We've decided to give it to you.' And so I became sort of a star cutter from then on."

Lean cut *As You Like It,* and "quite a lot of films. I ended up by cutting *Pygmalion* with Leslie Howard playing Higgins. That was a damn good film, with Wendy Hiller in her first big part."

Produced at Pinewood Studios in 1938 by Hungarian emigré Gabriel Pascal (1894–1954), who had made it his personal mandate to bring the plays of Bernard Shaw to the screen, *Pygmalion* successfully adapted the dramatist's 1913 comedy of class distinction about a phonetics teacher who introduces a cockney flower girl into society after improving her manner and speech. On the recommendation of Shaw, who had seen her in the role at a Shaw Festival in Malvern, Wendy Hiller was cast as the pupil, Eliza Doolittle. For the ever-intractable Professor Henry Higgins, Shaw wanted Charles Laughton, but acceded to the box-office name of Leslie Howard, who, in tandem with Anthony Asquith (1902–1968), received codirector credit for the briskly paced piece.

"One time David Lean and I were at the cutting stage of *Pygmalion,*" said Asquith, "and we showed a reel of it to Gaby, who asked for some impossible cut, but by this time we knew him. We'd say, 'Right you are. In half an hour we'll show it to you.' Then we'd go and have a leisurely cup of coffee and show him the same reel again." In fact, Asquith and Lean had not altered a single frame. Pascal was none the wiser. In his thick accent, he pronounced their improvement "*parfait.*"

"Leslie got codirector credit," says Lean, "but he didn't direct it." Asquith, to Lean's assessment, was "a very good director, but not a great one. He was too gentle with actors." As for Leslie Howard, says Lean, "He had the charm of the devil, more charm than anyone I've ever met, before or after. But he could never be on time. I used to wait two hours for him at Pinewood and I thought I would kill him."

Still, Lean found Leslie Howard to possess so much charm that it was impossible to stay angry. The actor was also one of those rare few who Lean felt could fit the definition of a movie star. "What is a star?" says Lean. "From an editor's point of view, you can get a wonderful actor, he says the line, you go, 'Bang, cut.' Now, if it's a star, you can hold it for another four frames, because something interesting will always happen. I think it has to do with a star's having a concentration and an energy. Kate Hepburn calls it having 'horsepower.' "

With the outbreak of war in 1939, Lean was issued an artist's deferment from military service, a protectionist measure by the

British government, which had sent off so many film workers into World War I that it effectively wiped out the nation's entire movie industry.

"I edited so many films during the war," says Lean. "I particularly remember Michael Powell's films. I loved very much doing them." Powell's *49th Parallel* concerned six German sailors who, after their U-boat is sunk in the Gulf of St. Lawrence,

venture toward the then-neutral United States. Raymond Massey played a Canadian soldier; Eric Portman, the Nazi captain.

"When I came back from shooting exteriors of *49th Parallel* in Canada," recalls Michael Powell, "that was late in 1940, mid-winter, I don't remember the actual date, but the Blitz was on and there was snow on the ground. I had an enormous amount of material shot in Canada. My editor, John

Lean with Wendy Hiller, when he cut Shaw's *Pygmalion*, 1938. He also directed her screentest for *Major Barbara* (1941)—as well as most of the finished film.

31

Lean, actress Ellen Drew, and director of photography Bernard Knowles, on the set of *French Without Tears* (1939). Lean cut the picture, which was written by Terence Rattigan and directed by Anthony Asquith, "whom we used to call 'Puffin,'" recalls Lean. Knowles also photographed *The 39 Steps* for Alfred Hitchcock.

[including, later, five for director David Lean]. One of the legendary tales of Lean I'd heard was how David would write dialogue on film. While cutting a scene, he'd write a key word on the film, and his assistant would have to create dialogue to fit that scene. What a remarkable change he brought to sound dialogue."

Boxhall set up the meeting between Powell and Lean. "As far as I remember," says Powell, "we ran everything I'd shot in Canada. At the end, David said, 'Well, you need an editor.'"

"And he did," remembers Lean. "What he showed me ran for five and a half hours. I cut it down to two."

49th Parallel marked Lean and Powell's first collaboration. "From then on," says Powell, "I had to mind my P's and Q's. It wasn't just that he was a meticulous cutter—which means a miraculous storyteller, you sometimes forget that—but David supplied more than that. He would disappear one day and appear the next, and say, 'I've discovered some wonderful German film of U-boats.' Or else, 'You know when that ship is sinking, I think we need a [shot of a] wireless op[erator] to give a sense of urgency.' Or else it would be the scene in Hudson's Bay, with the Eskimos, when the survivors from the U-boat start shooting and murdering everybody, David would appear at my elbow and say, 'Michael, you mind if I take a camera and shoot some close shots of hands snatching guns, buckling on knives, that kind of thing?'

"I'd just say, 'Good idea, go ahead.'"

Powell admits dryly that the professional marriage succeeded. "I did what I was told," says Powell, a hint of sarcasm in his voice. "David tolerated me, so when we made our next picture, *One of Our Aircraft Is Missing,* David went along in playing and brought in Ronald Neame as a cameraman. That started them off on what proved to be a long partnership."

The actual camera operator on *One of*

Seabourne, who in the past had cut a lot of my films, was also in charge of the second unit on *49th*. When he came back to England, he got sick, and there were thousands and thousands of feet of material. I said, 'What on earth are we going to do without John the editor?'"

The answer came from one of the executives at Denham, Harold Boxhall, who said to Powell, "I suggest that I get hold of David Lean for you."

"Of course, I knew all about David," remembers Powell. "I'd first heard of him from a brilliant editor, Jack Harris, a man who never did anything but cut pictures

Our Aircraft Is Missing was Guy Green, who on that occasion was introduced both to Lean and to Lean's working technique. Asked the degree to which a camera operator and an editor usually had contact during production, Green answers, "Not much, but an editor of David's tremendous stature was very concerned about all aspects of the film, and he used to come and let me know what he wanted."

Lean's requests, Green recalls, were invariably followed to the letter.

Concurrent with *49th Parallel,* Gabriel Pascal was preparing his second Shaw vehicle, *Major Barbara,* a 1905 stage parable about social reform. Cinematographer Freddie Young, who would later shoot *Lawrence of Arabia, Doctor Zhivago,* and *Ryan's Daughter* for Lean, was to be Pascal's cameraman on *Major Barbara,* until he went to Michael Powell.

"Freddie was tied down to a contract with Pascal," Powell recalls. "He wanted to get out of it to do a war picture, so I said, 'Talk yourself out of it,' and he did."

"Gaby was a difficult chap," allows Freddie Young. Ronald Neame photographed *Major Barbara* (starting with Wendy Hiller's screen test, which Lean directed), and it was at this time that he and Lean met.

As for Shaw, "I met him on both *Pygmalion* and *Major Barbara,*" says Lean. "He used to come down and inspect what was happening. Gaby Pascal used to sit him in a huge chair that the property department would send over, sort of a throne, really, and then Gaby would kiss him on top of the head. I'd stand there and think, 'Oh, no, don't do it. It's a huge mistake,' but obviously I was quite wrong. Shaw loved it."

Expected to duplicate the success of *Pygmalion, Major Barbara* did anything but, with the production riddled with problems from day one. Pascal set about directing himself, which meant that the first choice for leading man, Leslie Howard, backed

out, as *he* had wanted to direct. The part went to a virtual unknown, Andrew Osborn. Because of his inexperience, coupled with Pascal's own, footage shot with Osborn had to be scrapped. A month later, Rex Harrison was signed, although the chaos continued. The budget doubled and the ten-week shooting schedule swelled to six months. Blame could not be laid on Pascal alone; air raids regularly shut down the work at Denham.

In the finished film, Harrison stars as the young professor Adolphus Cusins, who for romance's sake pursues Major Barbara Undershaft (Wendy Hiller) into her post at the Salvation Army. Devoted to saving souls, she is also the daughter of a munitions manufacturer (Robert Morley), whose own religion is money.

"David Lean," Harrison wrote in his 1974 autobiography, *Rex,* "was known to us then as 'the whispering cutter.' It was part of his job to give Pascal guidance even on the set, but so that it should not be too obvious he insisted on whispering his advice into Gabriel's ear—which of course made it far more obvious than if he had come on and shouted his head off."

"Gaby Pascal didn't really know the right end of the viewfinder," says Lean, "and so he employed Harold French and me as what is known as 'Assistants in Direction,' *not* 'Assistant Directors.'"

French was formerly a stage actor and director. He directed his first film, *The Cavalier of the Streets,* about a blackmailer who poses as a prince, for the producer Anthony Havelock-Allan in 1937.

"Harold was there for the dialogue," says Lean, "because he was a stage director, and I was there for the camera setups. And," Lean adds, "I did a fair amount of the direction."

Lean never received credit for it.

"I can imagine that David directed all of *Major Barbara,*" ventures Michael Powell. "Somebody had to."

His reputation for technical expertise well established, Lean was offered a promotion, to direct his own films.

"What was happening then," Lean says, "was that people started with 'Quota Quickies,' we used to call them. There was a British quota. The American companies had to show so many British films for every American film they sold. I've forgotten how many it was—it might have been one for one. The Americans used to pay the English a pound a foot for the finished film, and most of the films were terrible. I had a good go at cutting these 'Quota Quickies' and putting those together."

The "Quickies" were usually made in twelve days each at the studios in Twickenham and Shepperton or at the American-owned facilities in Teddington and Wembley. In 1935, the manager of one Manchester cinema was so embarrassed by the poor quality of these B-pictures that he flashed a message on the screen explaining it was only because of order by law that he was showing it.

"'Round about the time of *Pygmalion* and then old things like *49th Parallel,* I used to get offers for directing these 'Quota Quickies,' and I began to think I might be able to direct," says Lean. "I knew how film went together, at least. I had no experience directing actors, but when these offers came for the 'Quota Quickies,' I always said, 'No,' because I thought that if people go to the theatres and it's pretty lousy, which it was bound to be, because the scripts were terrible, people were not going to say, even if I did a halfway good film, 'Well, he had no money, he had lousy actors, whatever it is.' They were not going to make any excuses, they would just say, 'He's no good.' So I just said, 'No,' and I said, 'No,' 'No,' 'No,' until Noël offered me *In Which We Serve.*"

Noël was Coward.

"That's when I became a director," says Lean, "and, from then on, I learned with each film I made."

Barely twenty years old, Lean lurks in the shadow of the camera on the set of the 1928 *Sailors Don't Care,* "a comedy starring John Stewart and Estelle Brody," says Lean. "I was in a sort of heaven," he says of his start at Gaumont-British. "I couldn't wait to get to the studio every day."

By the time David Lean met Noël Coward (1899–1973), the latter's fame was well established. His mark had been made on his twenty-fifth birthday in 1924, when he wrote, directed, and acted in the controversial West End hit *The Vortex,* a biting depiction of contemporary society hooked on appearance, fashion, and youth, a syndrome Coward called "a vortex of beastliness." Since then, Coward had gone on to write (and oftentimes star in) critically and commercially successful stage pieces reflective of his day, among them *Hay Fever, Easy Virtue, On with the Dance, The Marquise, Semi-Monde, Bitter Sweet,* and *Private Lives.*

On a July afternoon in 1941, some months prior to meeting Lean, Coward had met with the Columbia Pictures representative Charles Thorpe and producers Filippo del Giudice and Anthony Havelock-Allan. Charles Thorpe came to offer £60,000 of his studio's money, for the purpose of the playwright's making a movie. His companions came to offer their support as producers.

Anthony Havelock-Allan was born into the peerage, worked in the film industry since 1933, and had met Lean when he was cutting the Paramount British News. In 1938, Havelock-Allan produced his first film, *This Man Is News,* a takeoff on M-G-M's successful sleuth series *The Thin Man;* it starred his own wife, Valerie Hobson. The following year, Havelock-Allan produced *The Lambeth Walk,* the film adaptation of the West End Cinderella musical *Me and My Girl,* and *The Silent Battle,* a spy drama again starring Hobson as well as John Loder and Rex Harrison.

Filippo del Giudice, who lacked a firm grasp of the English language, was an Italian emigré whose career was often compared to Gabriel Pascal's: both had landed destitute in England in the 1930s; both rose to prominence producing film adaptations of West End plays that were directed by Anthony Asquith and edited by David Lean—in del Giudice's case, Terence Rattigan's battle of

NOËL COWARD
In Which We Serve
(1942)

the sexes, *French Without Tears* (1939); and both ended their careers in the mid-1940s by going lavishly over budget producing films for the mogul J. Arthur Rank. At the time of his meeting with Coward, del Giudice was production manager of his own company, Two Cities Films.

"I received them warily," Coward remembered, "because I knew that the object of their visit was to persuade me to make a film." Coward held moviemakers in low esteem. To him, they were part of a "soul-destroying industry in which actors of mediocre talent were publicized and idolized beyond their deserts, and authors, talented or otherwise, were automatically massacred."

Above: Tea time in the pivotal Carley float; Noël Coward is at center.

Opposite: On Denham's Stage Five, the largest stage at the studio, Coward stands in foreground, flanked by Lean, designer Gladys Calthrop, and, behind Lean, cinematographer Ronald Neame.

As evidence, Coward pointed to the film adaptation of his 1933 stage delight about a workable *ménage-à-trois, Design for Living,* bowdlerized beyond recognition by Paramount Pictures in 1934 as a vehicle for Fredric March, Miriam Hopkins, and Gary Cooper. "I'm told," Coward commented at the time, "that there are three of my original lines left in the film—such original ones as 'Pass the mustard.'"

To assuage his fears, Thorpe, Havelock-Allan, and del Giudice assured Coward that he would retain complete control over subject matter, creativity, and selection of talent and technical crew. "It would have been churlish not to appreciate that this was a very flattering offer, indeed," said Coward.

Lacking only a suitable idea, he was to find it the next evening, when, after attending the cinema, he had dinner with Lord Louis and Lady Edwina Mountbatten. Mountbatten related the story of the recent sinking, off the Greek island of Crete, of the British destroyer he had commanded, the H.M.S. *Kelly.*

Coward's creative fires were lit. "In my bed at the Savoy," he recalled, "I knew that this was a story to tell if only I could tell it without sentimentality but with simplicity and truth." He wrote a first-draft screenplay, which he entitled *White Ensign.*

Enter David Lean.

"I found out," says Lean, "that Noël had apparently been around the industry in a quiet sort of way, asking who was the best technician in the business. And, apparently, various people had recommended me, so I was asked along. Noël had never directed a film before, and I don't think the mechanics were a plus for him. He was very fiddly about that sort of thing. I wouldn't have liked to be with Noël in a car that broke down."

Lean went to Gerald Road with Havelock-Allan. "Noël lived there and had a wonderful great big studio—big grand piano, tall windows," Lean recalls. "I was

pretty scared, because Noël was *the* British sophisticate. I was always frightened that he would make some quip which would make everybody roar with laughter and that I would be the butt of it. As it was, I don't think he admired movies very much to begin with."

Lean's speech becomes severely clipped as he perfectly mimics Coward's words of nearly five decades ago. "'Look, my dear,'" Coward said to Lean. "'I am making a film and I would like you to come on it. It's about the Navy. In fact, it's about Mountbatten and the *Kelly,* although I'm obviously not advertising that.'"

During the session together, Lean was spared any sarcasm by Coward, whom he in fact found "really very sweet."

"Now, my dear," Coward instructed Lean, "come along next Wednesday afternoon and I shall read you what I have written."

"And so I went along the following week," says Lean, "and Gladys Calthrop, who used to design all Noël's stage shows and was also his great friend, was there, and so was Joyce Carey—not the writer but the actress—who was Lillian Braithwaite's daughter. Joyce later played the barmaid in *Brief Encounter.*"

Coward and Calthrop, who was an artist, had met in 1921 when they were both vacationing in Alaisso. He insisted she design the sets and costumes for *The Vortex,* in which Joyce Carey was to play the man-hunting society mother.

"We sat down and Noël read everything he'd written," says Lean. "It lasted for, I don't know, two-and-a-half hours. It was very rambling, contained a lot of dialogue, and, at the end of reading it, he said to me, 'Well, what do you think of that, my dear? What sort of film will that make?'

"I said, 'Well, I think it's simply wonderful, but the trouble is that what you've read me will run for five hours on the screen.'"

"Oh, my God," declared Coward, shattered. "I never thought of that. I thought you could do anything in the movies. I fear this has as many restrictions around it as the stage."

"He was right, of course," affirms Lean. "Noël was terribly, terribly quick. The fact is that the first script, entertaining as it was, with wonderful dialogue, wonderful scenes in it, was what I call a kind of diary: 'Today we did this, next week this happened, and I had bacon and eggs for breakfast, then that afternoon Aunt Sally came and saw me.'

"I said to Noël, 'A remarkable film has come out and I think it might be of some help. You should go see that.'"

"What is it?" asked Coward.

"*Citizen Kane,*" said Lean.

Coward went to see the Orson Welles picture that very day and thought it "absolutely wonderful."

At their next meeting Coward presented instructions for Lean. "Look here," he said, "I'm not going to see you now for a week, ten days, perhaps two weeks. I'm going to rewrite. I've got an idea."

"He went back," says Lean, "and he thought of the idea of the Carley float, all the men around the float, and using that as a device to flashback to some of the best things that he had written in this very, very long version. That's roughly how the script came about."

Two stumbling blocks arose for Coward during the period of the second draft; the first was delivered from Mountbatten himself, who feared Coward might be too faithful to the incidents on board the *Kelly* (called *Torrin* in the script), "lest the film," said Coward, "in any sense become a boost for himself."

That in the first draft the film's hero, like Mountbatten, had a chauffeur-driven Rolls-Royce and a titled wife only heightened Mountbatten's concern. Coward calmed him, insisting that the leading character, referred to in the film as Captain D, would be "an average naval officer." The Rolls was

replaced by a Ford, the driver completely excised, and the wife's title dropped. The final film did, however, rely heavily on the Mountbatten portfolio for many of its speeches and incidents.

Coward's second hurdle came from a merciless press, who deemed it lunatic that the internationally known theatrical personality who was practically synonymous with smoking jackets, dry martinis, and biting repartee should undertake to portray a stalwart naval hero and family man. Particularly rancorous and perceived as a vendetta against Coward and Mountbatten were the attacks by the publisher Lord Beaverbrook.

Beaverbrook's broadside was launched August 29, 1941, on the front page of his

Coward in his Gerald Road studio, where Lean first met him in 1941. "Funnily enough," says Lean in 1989, "just the other day I saw it advertised for sale in one of the glossy magazines."

Daily Express, exposing the plan that Columbia Pictures intended to finance (what indeed had escalated into) a £150,000 film glamorizing the wartime career of Mountbatten, to be directed by and to star an obviously miscast Coward. The Ministry of Information, which could facilitate use of necessary military equipment and issue an export license once the film was finished, read the story and was not amused. Also at issue was the making of a film which featured the sinking of a British ship, particularly during wartime. This was considered bad taste.

"Can you imagine it?" sniped Coward. "When else do ships sink so frequently?"

The journalists belabored their own disapproval. The *Daily Express* film correspondent Jonah Barrington editorialized on September 17 that if such a film were to be produced, it should be played in documentary style, "with real naval men in the leading parts," and should not star an international playboy.

Thirteen days later, Barrington reported that he had personally visited the Admiralty to argue against Coward's "dressing in the clothes of a naval officer." For its part, the Admiralty said that, with the country at war and all, it could not spare a genuine officer to appear in a movie.

Subsequent to that, another ugly incident flared up, and Coward was forced to answer Finance Defense Department charges of currency-export offenses while traveling. That settled, he was allowed on board the H.M.S. *Nigeria* for a quick sail of the North Sea to soak up atmosphere, and the rewrite was completed.

Lean paid another call.

"Now, my dear," said Coward, "I don't know a damn thing about how to shoot things." With that he gave Lean the script, now called *In Which We Serve.* Its title was taken from a daily morning prayer said aboard every British ship.

Coward's story begins during the summer of 1939 and establishes the friendly relationship between the captain and crew of the newly launched H.M.S. *Torrin,* a destroyer in the Royal Navy. With the arrival of the war, the *Torrin* undertakes convoy patrol in the North Atlantic, ferrying soldiers from the shores at Dunkirk. Finally, she is sunk off Crete on May 21, 1941, with half her crew lost. While awaiting rescue as they cling to a Carley float, three of the survivors reflect on their pasts, which unspool for the moviegoer.

Seaman Shorty Blake meets and marries the former Freda Lewis, who gives birth to a son; Petty Officer Walter Hardy loses his wife and mother-in-law when the Germans bomb their home in Plymouth; and Alix, the wife of Captain Edward Kinross (Captain D) and mother of their two children, stoically carries on with her marriage despite her acknowledged rival, the *Torrin.*

"Mountbatten was good enough to give me pretty well a whole evening," recalls Lean. "It was late, and we were in a deserted Denham Studios, in one of the chief offices up in the front. We had sandwiches and coffee, and he told me all about the dive-bombing of the *Kelly* so I would know how to do it for the film. And I remember at one point in that wonderful evening, he was describing the dive-bombing."

Mountbatten told Lean: "The ship was starting to turn over. I realized she was going, and I gave the order to abandon ship. I stood on the deck, trying to balance myself. I grabbed the binnacle, and then the old-fashioned idea popped into my head, that the captain should be the last to leave the ship, so I grabbed the binnacle and down we went. I was actually submerging in water, and I realized I was being dragged under the ship."

"And," recounts Lean, "he said, 'I hung on and hung on, my lungs were pretty well bursting, and then it got lighter and I realized that we were returning right around and coming back to the surface—until I let

go and pushed off. And that saved my life.' I loved his old-fashioned idea, that the captain should be the last to leave his ship."

Mountbatten provided the film crew with a technical advisor, "a man called Terry Lawlor," says Lean, "an ordinary seaman, the naval equivalent of an army batman. Lawlor had been badly burned when the *Kelly* was dive-bombed and turned over, and he came and pretty well lived with me. I lived in Denham in those days."

Lawlor and Lean worked in tandem preparing the shooting script. This included a documentary-style opening, narrated by Leslie Howard, who begins the postcredits sequence with the dramatic declaration: "This is the story of a ship!"

"I would work out and write the big action sequences," says Lean. "Lawlor would tell me, for example, what happened when the raiders appeared, and give me all the technical information. I would write this into a shooting script: long shot of this, close-up of that, guns firing, rubber raft, and so forth. I used this method, which I later did with other writers, and put it into

Coward and the crew on Denham's backlot. "Noël very soon got terribly bored photographing the picture," says Lean, who was soon informed by his co-director, "My dear, I'll leave it to you."

Coward and Leslie Howard, who narrated the opening newsreel segment of the picture. Howard fit Lean's definition of a star.

what I call sort of a blueprint for a film. As you shoot, you may alter it slightly, but it serves as a blueprint at your back all the time."

The *In Which We Serve* shooting script prepared, Lean returned to Gerald Road for another meeting. "Now, my dear," Coward offered, "I think it would be fair, don't you think, if you were called 'Assistant to the Director'?"

"No. I don't think it would," replied Lean.

"What are you proposing?" asked Coward.

"I think," said Lean, "it should say it was directed by you and me."

"You and Noël?" piped up Gladys Calthrop, who was also on hand. "But who's ever heard of you?"

"I hope one day they will," Lean remembers himself saying. Years later, he is amazed at such audacity. "Anyway," he insisted in 1941, "that's what I want."

"You mean," said an incredulous Cal-

42

throp, " 'Directed by Noël Coward and David Lean'?"

"I screwed up all my courage, because it really did require a great deal of moral courage—Noël was such a tremendous figure, you see—and I said, 'If you don't give it to me, I'm not going to do the job for you and you must find somebody else.' "

Lean did indeed have another offer, albeit confined to the cutting room. "Mickey Powell and Emeric Pressburger had an idea that they wanted me to do, a film about the London Symphony Orchestra, set in the Blitz. It could have been good, but I loved the naval thing and once Noël started reading that I was hooked."

Confronted in his own sitting room with Lean's proposal that they share director's credit, Coward turned to his friend Calthrop and said sedately, "Gladys, I think that's fair, you know."

"Then," Lean recalls, "he said, 'Do you mind having Ronnie Neame's name'—Ronnie was the cameraman on it—'on the same card?' And I hadn't the nerve to say, 'Yes,' so if you see the credits today, they read 'Directed by Noël Coward and David Lean, Photographed by Ronald Neame,' and, I think, another one on the front somewhere. Anyhow, I got my credit for being codirector, and we had a wonderful time."

When Lean went to inform Powell and Pressburger that he would not be at liberty to cut their film on the orchestra because he was off to work with Noël Coward, Powell teased him. "Mickey said, 'You're like a Bond Street tart. You see a bright bauble in the window of a jewel shop and you can't resist it.' "

Hearing his own remark of forty-seven years earlier recalled to him in 1988, Powell breaks into a hearty laugh and responds, "Really? That's awfully funny."

Work on the picture proceeded arduously. Columbia had backed out of the project once costs grew to £100,000 and its

Neame, Coward, and Lean at Dunstable Downs, Hertfordshire, for a picnic scene. "Noël had a wonderful natural instinct for the movement of actors," says Lean, "but I don't think he was really a straight actor."

studio chief, Harry Cohn, had determined that Noël Coward did not guarantee sufficient box-office draw to risk such an investment. C. M. Woolf of General Film Distributors was then brought in by del Giudice, but he too withdrew once the production budget rose to £180,000. Photography commenced without a backer until, six weeks in, del Giudice convinced Sam Smith of British Lion to finance and distribute the film. Final cost came to £200,000.

Mountbatten, while wishing to distance himself from the character on screen, exerted a strong hand behind the scenes, especially when it came to casting. When the original group of seamen extras was not up to Mountbatten's requirements, he personally recruited two hundred convalescent patients from the naval hospital at Haslar.

When the actor Bernard Miles was contacted about a possible role, he was informed only that he was to go to a studio in London, where some unspecified dignitaries would be viewing a film he had recently completed about the Home Guard. The viewers were Coward, Mountbatten, and novelist Clemence Dane (who had written the Home Guard script). Following the screening, Mountbatten passed Miles and shot him a glance. "You'll do," he told Miles.

"High praise, dear boy," snapped Coward, trailing Mountbatten.

Miles was hired to play Walter Hardy.

Coward also had a say in such matters. "During the first week of 1942 I received a fantastic New Year's present, the script of the film *In Which We Serve*," said John Mills, who, as time went on, would come to star in five films for Lean (a record topped only by Alec Guinness, with six). Coward had sent Mills the script personally, with the Shorty Blake role underlined. The two had worked together on Coward's stage production of *Cavalcade* (1931), in which the then-twenty-three-year-old Mills played Joe Maryot.

"Noël knew Johnny from Australia," says Lean, "where Johnny was working in the chorus. I think I'm right in saying that Johnny was a chorus boy. I remember having seen him long before this in various musicals, and he could put over a number very well. He was a jolly good idea for *In Which We Serve,* and I think it really did start him off.

"Another person who started off in that was Richard Attenborough. I cast him, actually." The teenaged Attenborough, making his screen debut (he had made his stage debut only the year before), was to play the role of the cowardly stoker, a part that would do much to typecast him for years to come.

"There was an agent in London called Al Parker," says Lean. "He was an American, and before he'd become an agent, he had directed Douglas Fairbanks, Sr., in *The Black Pirate* [1926], and very well. He was the only agent I knew in London who could give you absolutely straight answers, and he wouldn't push his clients on you. If ever you were in trouble, he was the one to call."

Lean rang him up and said, "Look here, Al, we've got a part of a young boy who deserts his post in the middle of a naval engagement. I don't want you to think, and I don't want the audience to think, that he's a wretched rat, but that he's just a frightened rabbit. He's so young, one's heart should go out to him. It's a small part, but it's a very good part. I think people will remember it afterward."

Parker told him, "Look here, David, I don't know. I haven't got anybody on my books, but I'll give you a ring in a couple of days after having looked around." The agent called Lean back a couple of days later and said, "I think I've got him for you. He's only eighteen years old, seventeen or eighteen, his name is Richard Attenborough."

"And I cast him," says Lean, "and Noël was very pleased with his performance, and, you know, he's never stopped."

Lean's praise for Celia Johnson, who played the captain's wife in the film and was later to deliver equally refined, restrained performances for Lean in *This Happy Breed* and, most notably, in *Brief Encounter,* is boundless. After training at the Royal Academy of Dramatic Art, Johnson (1908–1982) appeared on screen for the first time in *In Which We Serve.*

"I was living down in the country most of the time," said Johnson, "but my husband came home on leave and we were asked to a cocktail party." Who should be there but Noël Coward. "I hadn't seen him for a long time," the actress recalled, "and we did the usual sort of 'darling-darling' thing." She asked Coward what he was working on, he told her "the most wonderful film," and she asked brazenly, "Why don't you give me a part in it?"

Coward shot her a look of mock disdain, before recovering and saying, "Right."

"But the film people didn't want me at all," said Johnson. They found her a good actress but not photogenic. "You're supposed to be the cameraman," Coward ordered Neame, "photograph her!" Coward did the screen test with her, and together they recited *The Walrus and the Carpenter.*

Said Noël Coward some years later, "The only thing that prevents Celia Johnson from becoming the greatest actress of her time is her monotonous habit of having babies."

"Noël brought her in for the part of his wife," says Lean. "She was just wonderful, even now I mean, and I saw the film not long ago. She gives a party on board the ship before she actually goes into service, and Celia makes a speech, ending with 'God bless this ship and all who sail on her.' And I cannot see it, even after all these years. . . ." Lean stumbles in his recollection. "I'm doing it now," he says, slightly embarrassed, "I've got a lump in my throat, remembering her. She had a most wonderful quality and was able to transmit emotion some curious way. So highly intelligent."

Lean breaks off speaking.

Shooting lasted from February 5 until June 27, 1942.

"The thing that surprised me about Noël," says Lean, "was that I thought, 'Oh, my God,' this is going to be difficult working with him because he'll be a kind of playboy, as it were. I couldn't have been more wrong. Noël used to come to work at Denham at nine in the morning. He'd work until one, have a sandwich, or some very simple meal up in the office, in what was then called the Old House, where [Alexander] Korda had his office. Noël had a bed in another room, and he'd go there and sleep, until three. Then he'd get up and wherever he was in the script, he would leave at sort of half past five, and then be bang-on early in the morning. Tremendous

discipline, all self-discipline. It was quite an education."

"There were good days and bad days, cheerful days and bad-tempered days," said Coward, who particularly detested "nine very uncomfortable days" when he, Mills, Miles, and twenty others spent a daily ten hours submerged up to their shoulders "in a tank of warm but increasingly filthy water." Their makeup consisted of artificial fuel grease "smeared head to foot . . . only a little of which we were able to scrape off for the lunch break."

John Mills recalls shooting in that muck. "Swimming to one of the Carley floats," he said, "I, as Shorty Blake, was supposed to be

Seventeen-year-old Richard Attenborough, in his film debut as the stoker who deserts his post; "A small part, but a very good part," Lean said at the time. "People will remember it."

The *Torrin* is hit. "I loved his old-fashioned idea," Lean says of Lord Mountbatten, "that the captain should be the last to leave his ship."

shot in the arm by a machine-gun bullet from a German aircraft that was strafing the survivors. The special effects man was suddenly at a loss. How could this be done?" The answer was, with rubber condoms—fastened every twelve inches to a long hollow tube that had been drilled with the necessary holes and wired electrically. "At the planned moment," continues Mills, "I heard the sound of sharp, staccato explosions in the water coming rapidly one after another. Special effects had blown compressed air into the tube and detonated the contraceptives." Mills is certain in his claim to be "the only actor in history who has been shot in the arm by a French letter."

Despite Coward's self-discipline when it

came to writing and performing, the mechanics of the film did prove too much for him. "I was just so lucky," says Lean, "because Noël very soon got terribly bored with the work photographing the picture. He'd say, 'Now, my little darlings, how long are you going to be?' And we'd say, 'This will take about an hour,' because it was terribly complicated, and very often it would be an hour between setups.

"It still sticks in my mind," says Lean. "Noël used to go back to his dressing room with Gladys Calthrop to play this card game of four-pack Bezique, and then we'd call him when we were ready. Finally Noël said, 'Look, my dear, you know what you are doing. I'll just leave it to you, and I'll come down whenever I'm to be photographed.'"

"Noël just let David have his hand," says John Mills. "I mean, he flattered David to a certain extent. Noël didn't want to know about where to put the camera. The two of them would discuss it together, but it was always left up to David to shoot it."

"So I had this huge studio to myself," says Lean. "I used to come into it in the morning. I used to think that the man at the door—Stage Five at Denham, the biggest stage in Denham Studios in those days, it was big all right—would stop me from coming in. I thought I looked rather young to be the director, but he always let me in, so I virtually directed the film myself."

Lean admits to a fear on that first picture of being in above his head. "I was a technician, all right. That was my great trouble. Everybody knew I could cut films. I really didn't know anything about directing actors, and I found it very difficult. I think now I could probably have done it myself, but at the time, I was terribly lucky to have Noël, because he was such an expert. I learned a tremendous lot from him. I mean, he was sort of an outstanding person in my career, of course, because he had unfailingly good taste."

While acknowledging that Coward's

stage training provided much of his gift, Lean says that was only part of the explanation. "He had a wonderful natural instinct for the movement of actors, a wonderful sense of—I hate the term, really—but 'sense of rhythm.' I hate it because I think it's used in so many wrong ways. I remember on one film, *This Happy Breed,* he came back from the Far East and, with fear and trepidation, I showed him the finished film in the theatre at Denham. I remember coming to a scene that I was very unhappy about, and I said as it was coming on, 'Look, Noël, tell me what's wrong with this.' And he said, 'My dear, I think if you had her standing and him sitting, it might have helped.'

"*Bang on,* you see?" says Lean. "He was always dead right at that sort of thing, at being able to put his finger on something that was wrong in the choreography, or in that sort of staging.

"Tremendous amount of things I learned from Noël. One thing he always used to say to me, and I've quoted it to many people, was 'My dear, ideas do not come to you through wandering around in the woods, hoping for inspiration. It just isn't there. It's in your head.' He's dead right again, you know: Face that terrifying blank sheet of paper, at least put 'Fade In' at the top of it, and get on with your work. Don't wait around for some bit of magic."

One incident that illustrates how "Noël was very tough with actors" arose the morning they were to shoot the Christmas party scene for *In Which We Serve.* John Mills recalls it as having taken place on the first day of shooting.

"I remember one actor," says Lean. "We arrived, just about to have a rehearsal, and Noël came in and sat down at the table. The poor wretch didn't know his lines properly, and Noël said, 'You have not studied the part. You can go.' And he went, so there we were. I said, 'Well, whom are we going to use?' Noël turned to the assistant director. He was Mickey Anderson, who later di-

rected *Around the World in Eighty Days,* and Noël said, 'Look, Mickey, I think you can act, can't you?' Mickey said, 'Well, I never tried it.' His father [Lawrence Anderson] was an actor. Noël said, 'We'll put you in the uniform and you try it. And when you get in uniform, all fixed and makeup put on, learn the lines.' And Mickey came in and he played the part in the film, and believe me, every actor from then to the end of the film knew his lines to perfection."

"Noël went on further," recalls Michael Anderson. "He said, 'Take him away, put a mustache on him, give him a haircut, and when you bring him back, make certain he knows his lines.'"

Earlier in his own career, Anderson had

John Mills and Kay Walsh (Mrs. David Lean) as Shorty Blake and Freda Lewis. "Kay Walsh," says Michael Anderson, "encouraged David to direct. 'Of course you can,' she said. 'You'll do wonderfully.'"

Captain Kinross (Coward) bids farewell to his crew. For *Doctor Zhivago*, Lean staged a similar scene at the Holy Cross Hospital, when Yuri says good-bye to his patients and his beloved Lara.

film. David was terribly nervous, terribly worried. He said, 'Noël Coward wants me to do this and I can't, I just can't.'

Lean and Kay Walsh, his second wife, had wed in 1941. His first marriage, to a woman whose married name was Isabelle Lean, produced Lean's only child, a son, Peter. The Lean-Walsh union ended in 1949, when he married his leading lady Ann Todd. They divorced in 1957. In all, Lean has had six wives. The others were Leila Devi (1960–78), Sandra Hotz (1981–85), and Sandra Cooke, whom he wed in 1990.

"It was Kay Walsh," says Anderson, "who encouraged David to direct. 'Of course you can,' she said. 'You'll do it and you'll do it wonderfully.'"

Anderson concurred, and says this indeed was the fact once shooting began. "Any nervousness David felt about working with Noël wore off quickly," he says. "I never felt David was intimidated by anybody but himself. It came from his own humility. He didn't realize how good he was." Summing up Lean as a director on his first film, Anderson remembers him as "a low-profile person, a perfectionist. He had a great technical sense, and a sense for underplaying, which for those days was unusual. It was the tradition then to overplay. In staging, David was very decisive, as opposed to Carol Reed, whom I worked with later. There was a vast difference in the styles of the two directors. Carol didn't know what he wanted. He was indecisive."

On Friday, September 25, 1942, Noël Coward noted in his diary, "Read the London notices of the film, which are absolute superlatives. Nothing but 'great picture' and 'finest film of the war,' etc. The most gratifying thing of all is that even the commonest journalistic mind has observed that it really is a dignified tribute to the Navy."

Not all the notices were positive. Some criticism also grew out of what was deemed

served as assistant to the director Anthony Asquith and had worked with Lean on *Pygmalion*. "David was very genial, and very quiet," says Anderson. "He's a very shy man."

Lean and Anderson were longtime neighbors. At one time they lived on the same block in London, and later (during the making of *In Which We Serve*), their houses were located next door to one another's in Denham Village. Anderson was on hand "the day David came home and told his wife, Kay Walsh, that Noël had asked him to direct a

the film's socially retrogressive attitude toward the lower-deck crew, which seemed patronizing and therefore peculiar for a propaganda film from a democratic country.

"I remember sitting in the theatre, at the premiere," says Lean. "It was a very smart premiere, and the row in front of me was filled with naval commanders, heads of the Admiralty and their wives, and I remember when Noël gave some order on the screen— 'Bup, bup, bup'—in the dialogue, the man in front of me, who was the leader of the Atlantic squadron, Admiral Somebody, started laughing, giving a little chuckle. He couldn't resist. And so, I think Noël—I mean, he's all right in the film, but you wouldn't have cast Noël Coward if he hadn't written it and weren't the producer.

"I am swearing in church," allows Lean, "but I don't think Noël was a good straight actor. It's awfully hard. Noël really isn't a commander as it were, in the sense that Mountbatten was. And, certainly, not as the family man. In fact, very soon after the premiere I remember going to see *Present Laughter* on the stage, and Noël of course acted in it. He was simply wonderful. You know, all the time with a cigarette holder, smoking cigarettes, and in those silk dressing gowns, with that tremendously quick-fire dialogue. He could do it wonderfully. No one could touch him on that. But I don't think he was really a straight actor."

Michael Anderson recalls the day on the set when Coward stood on the bridge and delivered a stirring speech to the crew on the lower deck, of how he expected the *Torrin* to be "a happy ship and an efficient ship," and how the phrase "happy ship and efficient ship" was repeated several times in that precise, clipped, swift manner of speaking that was Coward's— "A happy ship is an efficient ship"—and how a very befuddled sound man came down afterward and asked that someone speak to Coward about his enunciation during "that fish and chips speech."

Michael Anderson's comment on Carol Reed raises the frequently asked question: Who is the better director, Reed or Lean? A rivalry between Reed (two years Lean's senior) and Lean has long been discussed by critics, film historians, and industry workers.

By the late 1940s, the so-called contest for the title of Britain's most acclaimed director had blossomed full-flower, what with the debate fueled by each of the filmmakers' successive string of successes. Reed had created his timely masterpiece, the fatalistic tragedy of Northern Irish politics, *Odd Man Out* (1947), as well as two taut exercises in disenchantment (with witty scripts by Graham Greene), *The Fallen Idol* (1948) and *The Third Man* (1949). From Lean came *Brief Encounter* and his two Dickens adaptations, *Great Expectations* and *Oliver Twist*.

"I'm sure a rivalry *did* exist," Anderson notes. "Carol would spend hours to search for a way to do a scene. David would spend hours to search for a manner to do a scene the way he already visualized it."

"It was good-natured between us," says Lean when asked about his relationship with Reed, whom he considered "a smashing director." Looking back, Lean remembers, "We'd sort of see one another in those days, Carol and I, and say to the other, 'What, you still here? Hasn't a bus hit you yet?'"

"The funniest little story about this rivalry," adds John Mills, "was that right after *In Which We Serve* was out and it was an enormous success and everybody said, obviously, that David was going to be a very fine director, I had dinner with Carol Reed. And Carol said to me, 'You know, when Noël Coward went around asking for suggestions as to who should help him with this film, I suggested David Lean. It's the most insidious goddam thing I ever did.'"

As time passed, the rivalry was defused, given that any competition, real or imagined, had completely ceased to exist as Reed's career was laid to waste by weak Hollywood scripts, while at the same time Lean went on to make his name with international epics. As pinpointed by critic-director Lindsay Anderson in his *Times Literary Supplement* review of a 1988 book on Reed, "Perhaps [Reed] would have survived longer as an artist if, like his colleague David Lean, he had been able to escape from Britain altogether—without falling into the American trap. But Lean made his choices wisely, and Reed was not good at choices."

This Happy Breed (1944)

"Noël was very nice indeed," says Lean. "Toward the end of *In Which We Serve,* he said, 'Look, my dear, you can have anything I've written to do with as a film, anything you like.' Terribly generous, you know."

The choice, which was to mark Lean's officially credited debut as a solo director, was the Coward stage play *This Happy Breed,* a hit that opened in the West End on April 30, 1943. "At the time," says Lean, "it was very successful in England, because it's a portrait of a middle-class family in London, sort of near-cockneys."

In several respects, *This Happy Breed*—its title comes from John of Gaunt's speech in Act II, Scene One of Shakespeare's *Richard II* ("This royal throne of kings, this scepter'd isle . . . This happy breed of men, this little world")—served as a working-class sequel to Coward's earlier *Cavalcade,* which had opened at the Drury Lane on October 13, 1931. When filmed the next year by Hollywood's William Fox, with Clive Brook and Diana Wynward as its stars, it won the Academy Award as Best Picture.

Cavalcade spanned the years from the death of Queen Victoria, through the Boer War, the *Titanic* disaster, to the First World War, following the personal travails of the upper-middle-class Marryot family and their lower-class servants, the Bridgeses.

This Happy Breed, picking up in 1918 and advancing toward 1939, was far less fancy. Coward turned his attention to the Gibbons family, a lower-middle-class clan inhabiting 17 Sycamore Road in London's distinctly unfashionable Clapham Common.

"It was not terribly good," Lean says defensively of his film. "It's a small domestic story, but it was highly successful in England. People liked it. And we did it in color, which was very daring at the time. Color was considered vulgar."

Ronald Neame's cinematography, using one of only four color cameras available in England during the war, kept the hues subdued but still took its toll on Lean's cast,

who lamented the hours it literally took between setups. "One used to wait, and wait, and wait. The lighting took so long," said Celia Johnson, who played Ethel, the mother of the Gibbons household, "that I used to get rather depressed because I was playing the part of a woman of seventy, and in those days I wasn't all *that* old. I'd sit in my dressing room looking at myself in the mirror, thinking, 'That's what you're going to be like any minute now.' It was rather gloomy-making, really."

"When it came to casting," says Lean, "I did a rather daring stroke. On the stage, Noël played the part of the leading man—husband, again, to Celia Johnson—and when it came to doing the film, I was given a pretty broad hint that Noël would like to play the man. Now, Noël Coward playing a

Above: Lean with Robert Newton and Celia Johnson, as Frank and Ethel Gibbons, on set of the Wembley Exhibition.

Opposite: In the catbird's seat (from left), Noël Coward, camera operator Guy Green, and director of photography, Ronald Neame.

51

lower-middle-class man? I mean, I saw it on the stage with Noël, and he j-u-s-t about got away with it, but, really, not good, you know." (That fact is all the more ironic because Coward sprang from precisely such a background, having been born in Teddington the son of a traveling salesman, Arthur Coward.)

When the time came to select the husband of Celia Johnson for the screen role, Lean decided to try Robert Newton. Best known in later films for his rolly-eyed villains, including what was actually a controlled performance as Bill Sikes in Lean's *Oliver Twist,* Newton (1905–1956) had been acting in movies for a dozen years before doing *This Happy Breed.* His initial impact had been made in the role of the slum ne'er-do-well in *Major Barbara.*

"My old friend Robert Newton," said John Mills, "although he had the reputation for being an exciting actor, was known for his devotion to any form of liquid refreshment." This, Mills knew, made filmmakers wary. "Noël and David both wanted him for the part," Mills remembered, "but David, who frowns at anyone even having a light ale at lunchtime during shooting, was uneasy."

Newton's contract stated that if he tippled, he would be out of the picture, and Mills recalled the day he and his wife Mary eyed Newton staggering down the street in front of the Mills cottage in Denham Village—about fifty yards from the home of David Lean. "I grabbed Robert and hustled him as quickly as possible into the cottage," said Mills, describing his and his wife's maneuver as "not an easy procedure, as he had both arms round our necks, hugging and kissing us and informing the village in a loud, clear voice what darling people we were." Coffee and a good sleep set Newton straight for the next day's shoot, for which he rewarded his rescuers with a case of champagne and a note. The message read, "Darling chums, A friend in need etc. Love, Robert."

"Robert was quite good, and, oh, I suppose," says Lean, adjusting his previously voiced opinion, "the film was quite good, this little picture, you know."

Coward did pop in from time to time, merely to check the dailies and the rough cut, and to discuss the next project with Lean. "David directed us all on his own," says John Mills, who played Billy Mitchell, the loyal boy next door. "He and Noël worked on the script together, but David was in charge of all the scenes."

"It was pleasant to be concerned with the picture but not trapped by it," said Coward, who, recalling "so many leaden and difficult days" on *In Which We Serve,* admitted, "I could never quite prevent a sinking of the heart every time I drove through the gates of Denham Studios."

When it came to directing actors, Lean relied on the advice of Coward: "My dear, you must know precisely what every character eats for breakfast, even though you must never show them eating breakfast."

Despite his reputation for disliking actors, who he knows "would say I'm tough"—Trevor Howard once said that David Lean cannot wait to finish shooting a picture just so he can begin cutting the actors out of it—Lean says that only rarely has he had trouble with performers. "Actors," he says, "only get difficult when they get frightened, which is understandable. It's their face, their voice, on the screen. Oh, there are some moments of temperament, of course. Actors are always uncertain, tense, you know. Only the jerks are certain."

Lean's first crack at directing actors, he claims, made him the timid one. "I was frightened of criticizing their performances, but then I realized that's what the director's job is, after all. If you're not malicious, actors take the criticisms in good part."

On *This Happy Breed,* "I remember we had a scene with Celia and Johnny Mills.

They were in the sitting room and they get the news from somebody coming in through a door that one of Celia's children has been killed, and it really knocks her. I was doing the camera setup and all that sort of business, and there was an awful lot of giggling going on."

Lean looked up and discovered the culprits: Celia and Johnny Mills. "I was really furious, actually, because I thought, 'They're going into a scene, they really ought to behave more responsibly.'"

Finally the two pulled themselves together, and Lean went straight into a take. The scene unfolded. "The person came through the door," says Lean, "delivered the news about the death, and Celia reacted to it. And there, standing beside the camera, I found myself choking back the tears. Of course, I printed it. That was the take. One take. She was magical."

C. A. Lejeune concurred in her notice in *The Observer,* May 28, 1944. "Celia Johnson plays the wife, the drably named Ethel Gibbons. She plays her in drab silk blouses, drab skirts, drab hair, and sometimes a positively fierce Technicolor makeup. Often she looks awful, but by thunder! as an actress she's superb." Continuing the praise, Lejeune said, "This is beautiful acting; the sort of acting that the French have been taught to understand; confessional acting from the inside outwards."

So is it also left to Celia Johnson to undercut in the film what might have been a sloppily sentimental ending. After twenty years, the Gibbonses move out of 17 Sycamore Road. It was from this home that they participated in the Wembley Exhibition, the General Strike, the General Election, the funeral of King George V, the Charleston and talkie crazes, and followed the events of Prime Minister Chamberlain's visit to Munich. Here, too, Mrs. Gibbons's mother, Grandmother Flint (Amy Veness), died; Aunt Sylvia (Alison Leggatt) recovered from a severe bout of hypochondria and

embarked upon a life devoted to spiritual healing; daughter Vi (Eileen Erskine) married a "Bolshie" and eased him into being merely a liberal; son Reg (John Blythe) was killed in a car crash; daughter Queenie (Kay Walsh) ran off to South Africa with a married man but eventually came home to marry the sailor next door (John Mills); and a grandchild was born.

Just as he is about to close and lock the front door on the house for the last time, Frank Gibbons (Robert Newton) turns to his wife and says warmly that he's glad he's got her.

"Don't talk silly," she responds.

Top: Lean with Robert Newton and Stanley Holloway, who played Bob Mitchell, neighbor and drinking partner of Frank Gibbons.

Above: Arrival at 17 Sycamore Road; Newton, Amy Veness (grandmother Flint), and Celia Johnson.

Blithe Spirit (1945)

"They were a formidable trio together," Noël Coward wrote in his second autobiography, *Future Indefinite,* discussing the production team of Lean, Neame, and Havelock-Allan, who together called their company Cineguild, "and I owe them much of the success of *In Which We Serve, This Happy Breed,* and, above all, *Brief Encounter.* I will draw a light, spangled veil over *Blithe Spirit,* which they made while I was away in South Africa. It wasn't entirely bad, but it was a great deal less good than it should have been."

Coward's brittle farce of a smart British novelist whose country home is beset by the ghost of his playful first wife, whom only he could see, had premiered at London's Piccadilly Theatre July 2, 1941, and continued to run strong when Coward made Lean the offer to direct the movie version. Onstage Cecil Parker played Charles Condomine, the novelist-husband; Fay Compton, his sensible *living* wife Ruth; Kay Hammond, the ghostly Elvira; and Margaret Rutherford, the eccentric medium Madame Arcati. (A Broadway production opened at the Morosco November 5, 1941, with, in the same roles, Clifton Webb, Peggy Wood, Leonora Corbett, and Mildred Natwick.)

"Noël could be very persuasive," says Lean. "After *This Happy Breed,* the next thing he said was, 'Look, my dear, I want you to do *Blithe Spirit.* I think you could do that rather well.' I said, 'Look, Noël, I know nothing about high comedy. That would be terribly, terribly difficult for me.' It's awfully hard, high comedy, because in ordinary comedy and drama, you've got a sort of real life to go by, but in high comedy, it's completely unreal. You've got no yardstick. I don't know, I suppose I could do it better now. But Noël insisted. He said, 'You certainly could do it, my dear, I'm sure you can.' And I did it, with Kay Hammond and Rex Harrison, who gave me a fine old time."

Obviously this is a matter that, like the spirit of Elvira, has yet to be exorcised. "Rex

got on television the other day, apparently," says Lean. "I didn't see it, but I'm told he started off by saying it was very difficult doing *Blithe Spirit* because the director had no sense of humor."

On December 2, 1987, Harrison was interviewed by Patrick Garland on Thames Television. When Garland asked whether Lean was helpful on *Blithe Spirit,* Harrison said, "He wasn't altogether. He doesn't understand comedy [and] did something that wasn't helpful. I must say, *Blithe Spirit* isn't Noël Coward's best play. I was doing my best. David turned to his cameraman [and said], 'I don't think that's funny, do you, Ronnie?' What do you do then? Go home?"

When the quote that Harrison attributed

Above: Margaret Rutherford as the scene-stealing spiritualist Madame Arcati.

Opposite: Charles Condomine (Rex Harrison) and his late first wife, Elvira (Kay Hammond).

Arcati goes into her trance. Eyeing her skeptically are Rex Harrison (Charles), Constance Cummings (his second wife, Ruth), Joyce Carey and Hugh Wakefield (Mrs. and Dr. Bradman).

to him is recited back to Lean, he says, "I said that?"

Yes, according to Harrison.

"I don't believe it, you see," says Lean. "How funny. I'm sorry about that, because we had a terrible quarrel on the film because he wouldn't do anything I suggested. And, well, I don't want to go into criticizing Rex, but it was a shame. Anyhow, I saw the film the other day and it's not bad at all."

One member of the *Blithe Spirit* crew explains that Harrison refused to take direction if it meant that he would have to be photographed from his "wrong side," which naturally caused flare-ups between him and Lean. Another alleged dispute was over Harrison's refusal to shout his lines to his dead wife as Lean directed, for fear of losing audience sympathy.

Visiting the set in February of 1944, C. A. Lejeune witnessed only happy harmony. Coward had been through the script with his editing pencil, she said. "There was little that could valuably be done to the script,

Mr. Lean tells us," Lejeune wrote, "except break up the dialogue here and there, and add a fresh line or two to get the actors from spot to spot. These addenda Mr. Coward jotted down on the back of an envelope as they went along." (In fact, there were minor changes, including altering the ending so that Charles could join both his by-then-deceased wives.)

Coward did insist that the Condomine house in Kent—this film too was to be shot in Technicolor—look perfectly livable, and Lejeune reported that the residence designed by Gladys Calthrop was "a lulu. We were given a preview of the setup before the first day's shooting. Mrs. Calthrop had just finished 'doing' the flowers, red and yellow artificial roses artlessly arranged in low bowls. Outside the French windows, an amber spot was picking up the lush green of an English studio lawn. A dwarf conifer or two, studio trained, added a cozy note."

When the film was completed and ready to preview, "a terrible thing happened," says Lean. "Noël came back from wherever he was at the time—he had been entertaining the troops—and we ran the film in the theatre at Denham. Afterward, the lights went up and there was Noël, Noël's back getting bigger and bigger by the second. I couldn't bear the silence any longer and said, 'Well, Noël, what do you think of it?'"

Coward turned to the back of the room and replied to Lean, "My dear, you have fucked up the best thing I ever wrote."

Lean replied only, "I'm sorry. I did warn you. I said I didn't know anything about high comedy."

Lean adds, "I suppose that I must've felt terribly hurt, but I never let things like that show. I probably went through a black period about it later. I was a rather frightened rabbit in those days.

"Anyway, years later [in 1956], I was in New York and Noël had just done *Blithe Spirit* for television, with himself in the Charles Condomine role that Rex had

played in the film version, and I met Noël afterward. It was really rather terrible, and Noël said, 'Well, my dear, what did you think of it?' I told him, 'You have fucked up the best thing you ever wrote.'"

Both laughed. At the time of the first unceremonious preview, Lean says, Coward "was really awfully nice about it. We went back into an office at Denham afterward and I said, 'Well, Noël, that's the end of my doing high comedy. Any other suggestions?'"

"My dear," answered Coward, "I think we'd better go back to a bit of real life."

"And we started talking," Lean remembers. "Noël said, 'I've got a little one-act play called *Still Life*. I shall write the script and I'll do it very quickly because I know the play backwards.' And he did it in about ten days. Enormous.

"So Noël wrote this script," says Lean, "and it was perfectly good. It was a sort of blowing up of the stage play. In other words, when they went out into the street, you showed the street. It started in the beginning, where they met in this waiting room, and went through to the end.

"And this, you see, was *Brief Encounter*."

In the midst of a séance. "David set up a stage set and just photographed it," complained Rex Harrison. "Four of us got up in line and then Margaret Rutherford would walk down the middle, pulling faces."

57

Written and produced for the stage in 1935, *Still Life* ran forty-five minutes and took place in a single setting, the refreshment stand of the fictitious Milford Junction train station. Here, according to Coward's script, "Laura [Gertrude Lawrence], an ordinary, respectable married housewife, and Alec [Noël Coward], a married doctor, have met briefly before while awaiting their trains for their respective destinations."

Alec and Laura continue to meet this way, in the station, every Thursday, and over teas and buns they discuss their year-long affair. "An accidental meeting," says Alec, "then another accidental meeting—then a little lunch—then the movies—what could be more ordinary? More natural?"

"We're adults, after all," says Laura.

Brief Encounter, Coward's expanded film script of *Still Life,* shows in plain fashion these accidental meetings, the lunch, the movies, condensing the affair into six weeks, but, veering from a key plot point in the play, never permits Laura and Alec to consummate their passion. Instead, their romance takes the form of anguished yearnings. Still, this film becomes a love story to end all love stories, not only for Laura and Alec—played memorably in the film by Celia Johnson and Trevor Howard—but for Lean.

Brief Encounter epitomizes his lifelong fascination with and affection for trains. "I don't know why," says Lean, who shrugs off analysis, "but there are trains in most of my films."

In Which We Serve presents the introduction of Shorty Blake and Freda inside a second-class compartment, and they later honeymoon in a railcar. The heroine of *The Passionate Friends,* played by Ann Todd, contemplates suicide in front of a high-speed, underground train. Maggie plots out her fiancé's future business aboard a trolley in *Hobson's Choice.* In *Summertime,* it is a train with Katharine Hepburn and other Venice travelers on board that opens and

MILFORD JUNCTION
Brief Encounter
(1945)

closes the film. The very existence of *The Bridge on the River Kwai* is founded upon the need to link the Burma railway from the Bay of Bengal to Bangkok and Singapore. In uniting the Arab tribes, T. E. Lawrence systematically destroys the Damascus–Medina Turkish rail system in *Lawrence of Arabia,* and he is winged by an assassin's bullet as he celebrates a victory dance atop a locomotive. In *Doctor Zhivago,* revolution-weary Muscovites, including the story's leading characters, flee the city on a midnight train that takes them on a long, arduous journey into the snow-capped Urals. In the same film, the hero Zhivago first glimpses the love of his life, Lara, on a streetcar; years later, he takes his last look at her from a tram. In *A Passage to India,* Adela and Mrs. Moore embark upon an overnight

Above: "You know what's happened, don't you?" Alec (Trevor Howard) says to Laura (Celia Johnson).

Opposite: Lean follows Celia Johnson as she ponders whether she and the Trevor Howard character should consummate their affair.

Celia had the same feeling about trains. We did *Brief Encounter* in Carnforth [in Lancashire, on the edge of the Lake District; the station is now demolished], and the *Flying Scotsman* used to go through at over one hundred miles an hour, at something like ten minutes past eleven. Celia and I would go out on the platform, we'd be looking at our watches, because the *Flying Scot* would always be on time, and, oh, it was magnificent."

"The trains used to come through at night," said Celia Johnson, "and in those days they were lovely steam trains, and they screamed in the distance, a high-pitched scream at seeing our lights on the station, and then they'd come hurtling through, all lovely smoke and flame flying behind them. We used to stay up all night in order to hear this and see the Scottish expresses go through."

That sense of thrill remains with Lean. "Celia and I would stand there with our arms around each other. Sounds curious. There were no sexual connotations to it, or perhaps there were, I don't know. But trains have always given me a tremendous kick. I think they're wonderful subjects for movies. They're almost alive."

Brief Encounter was filmed in ten weeks. "With today's modern equipment," Lean speculated in 1970, after he had spent a year filming *Ryan's Daughter,* "we could have done *Brief Encounter* in eight."

The budget was "chicken feed," he said, £270,000.

The choice of Carnforth, Lean says, was made because "the war was still on and the railway people said, 'There may be an air raid at any moment and you'll have time to put out the lights in that remote part up in the north. We'll know when the planes are coming.' We were a blaze of lights from filming."

The film begins in early evening, during the winter of 1938–39, before the war. Af-

Above: Laura Jesson (Celia Johnson) and Alec Harvey (Trevor Howard) flee a dreadful picture, on the fourth of their six weekly meetings.

Opposite: Alec, escorting Laura back to the train station, begs that she come instead to his friend's flat.

train from Bombay to Chandrapore, and, during the fateful journey to the Marabar Caves, Dr. Aziz swings Douglas Fairbanks–style astride the twenty-seven cars of what is in fact an ancient passenger train on the Mettuppalaiyan–Ootacamund line. Lean dressed the train specifically for that film.

"I suppose it's the small boy in me," says Lean. "I had toy trains as a child. I don't know whether this is particularly English, I can't believe it would be, but, for instance,

ter introducing the stationmaster, Albert Godby (Stanley Holloway), as "somewhere between thirty and forty years old. . . . His accent is North Country" and the "buxom and imposing widow," Myrtle Bagot (Joyce Carey), behind the buffet counter, Coward's script provides this description: "In the far end of the refreshment room, seated at a table, are Alec Harvey and Laura Jesson. He is about thirty-five and wears a mackintosh and squash hat. She is an attractive woman in her thirties. Her clothes are not smart, but obviously chosen with taste. They are in earnest conversation, but we do not hear what they are saying."

Some six weeks earlier, the couple had met in the same suburban station after one of Laura's weekly Thursday shopping trips. On that occasion Alec kindly removes a piece of grit from Laura's eye, caught there when she goes outside to the platform, to watch the express train rush through the station. They are both middle class and married, they think happily, to other people. The next week they meet again, casually, and then again. Over tea in a boathouse after a minor rowing mishap on a park lake, Alec says to Laura, "You know what's happened, don't you?" They have fallen in love.

Against the musical background of Rachmaninoff's Piano Concerto No. 2, the story is told entirely in first-person flashback by Laura. Her initial excitement at knowing Alec, during which she fantasizes about their being together in Venice, gives way to disgust, and, eventually, to sad relief when Alec informs her that he has accepted a medical post in South Africa. After briefly contemplating suicide by hurling herself under a passing train, Laura returns, in body and spirit, to her adoring husband, Fred, and their two children.

Brief Encounter was Trevor Howard's third film and first starring role, after he had done minor parts in Carol Reed's *The Way Ahead* (1944) and Anthony Asquith's *The Way to*

Brief Encounter opens with a shot of the *Flying Scotsman* roaring through the station. "I remember what I wanted for the very, very beginning of the soundtrack," says Lean. "It's now quite a famous soundtrack, unfortunately, because everybody's used it since on all sorts of films."

Lean's requirement called for cooperation from every quarter, including the *Flying Scotsman*. "We were obviously on good terms with the railway people," says Lean. "On whatever night it was, I said, 'Please tell them to start blowing the engine siren a mile before they get into the station, and keep it going for half a mile after they've left. We were just doing the soundtrack at this point, and the driver of the *Flying Scot* did this, and it was a wonderful track. You hear the changing pitch as it gets nearer and it's gone past, and the sound changing again. It's not a question of volume. It's a change of pitch."

A discerning eye might also spot in the first frames of the opening sequence a tall slender figure that looks remarkably like the silhouette of David Lean. Is it? "Don't know," he answers. "I suppose it might be."

"That's how it all began," Laura (Celia Johnson) confesses in her on-going monologue, "just through me getting a little piece of grit in my eye." Assisting her in the train station refreshment room, Myrtle Bagot (Joyce Carey) and Albert Godby (Stanley Holloway).

the Stars (1945). Like Celia Johnson a graduate of RADA, Howard (1916–1988) began working on the stage in 1934. The *Brief Encounter* script had been forwarded to him by his agent, Eric Goodhead, and still remained unread by the time producer Anthony Havelock-Allan rang the actor's small flat in London's Pall Mall, to ask Howard to make a costume-fitting appointment that afternoon. Impossible, said Howard; he was taking his wife, the actress Helen Cherry, to the cinema to see Alan Ladd and Veronica Lake in *I Married a Witch*. Goodhead had failed to inform his client that the part in *Brief Encounter* was his.

Still no more the wiser when he did meet Havelock-Allan for lunch, Howard showed up inappropriately dressed—in corduroys and a lumberjack coat, according to the actor's biographer, Vivienne Knight. The actor thought only, before the meal, that he was "just meeting somebody in films."

Howard had been decided upon by the three men of Cineguild and by Coward, who retained final approval, after they had viewed the rushes at Denham of *The Way to the Stars*. "He had only one shot on an aerodrome," says Lean. "A plane came in over the field and did a victory roll. Trevor looked up and said, 'Lineshot.' It was wonderful. Just on that one word, the way he said it and the way he looked."

For Laura, Coward had from the beginning insisted upon Celia Johnson. "I remember Noël sending for me and reading me the play," said Johnson. "A wonderful part. But I really found the whole thing very different from any other film I'd done because being in practically every shot, one got to know much more about filming than ever before."

Johnson suggested that perhaps she learned more than she cared to know. On earlier films, she said, she steadfastly kept away "from technicians, who I think are always rather frightened of actors. In fact, actors are rather frightened of technicians."

"Celia was magical," Lean reiterates. "I remember she had a scene where the Trevor Howard character says to her, 'Look, I shall be at Such-and-Such's flat, waiting for you.' And she says, 'I can't,' and she goes to the railway station. The train comes in, she gets on, and I have a close-up of her in there. Then you hear the doors banging shut—*ch-tunk, ch-tunk, ch-tunk*—the train preparing to go. You hear the man blow his whistle, and from the train you hear the steam."

In the script Coward writes that Laura is in "a nervous state of indecision. The guard's whistle blows. After a second or two she suddenly jumps up." Laura has changed her mind and dashes out of the train and back onto the platform.

"This is in long shot," says Lean, "because she came out of the foreground, and she made her way for the exit, to the rise that takes people off the platform, and on her back you could read her thoughts. 'I've done it,' 'I shouldn't be doing it,' 'Have I got the courage?' And all this thinking is transferred into the physical."

Lean provides this as a perfect casebook example of movie acting.

"To a certain extent," he says, "I presume the same is true for stage acting, but movie acting is thinking, which a lot of people don't understand. If you're thinking right, it changes the way you walk, the way you put your head, and is all completely subconscious, because the thought just makes you walk or put your head or whatever it is in the correct way."

Once Celia Johnson had reached the end of the platform and Lean said, "Cut," he told her, "Celia, you're just wonderful. How did you work out how to do that?"

"I didn't work it out," said Johnson. "She would just do that, wouldn't she?"

Beyond the high marks he awards Celia Johnson, Lean's personal feelings toward what is regarded as his early masterpiece are equivocal. "I saw it a couple of years ago," he says, "and I thought, 'This is pretty awful,' but, funny, I saw it again the other day, and it seemed rather good."

Much of Lean's opinion was permanently colored by the unpleasant memory of the film's first preview. Forced to take place before a boisterous audience in Rochester because Lean was on location there with his next film, *Great Expectations,* the preview yielded a damaging response.

"Very rough neighborhood, Rochester," recalls Lean, "but we took the first print of *Brief Encounter* to the manager of the nearby cinema and said, 'Look, could you run a new film, call it the premiere, and we'll have a first look at it?' He did, and during the first

love scene, someone down front, a woman, with a terrible laugh that I'll never forget"— Lean mimics a high-pitched whinny— "begins to laugh, and one or two others turned and said, 'S-h-h,' but then, some other people in this audience started to laugh with her. And each time a love scene came on, more and more people started to laugh. The whole audience, by the time it was over, rocking with laughter. I was so ashamed of it. I remember going back to my hotel room that night, thinking was there any way I could break into the lab at Denham and burn the negative?"

The critical notices in England, he says,

Top: Filming Alec and Laura in the "Milford Botanical Gardens" (actually, Carnforth).

Above: Celia Johnson checks the set-up.

Calthrop, was meant to be rather out of date, to show that Celia was sort of a provincial housewife. Now, of course, people say, 'Oh, that hat. It dates the film. Well, it was meant to.'")

In Germany, the film was received with boos and catcalls. A London newspaper reported a jingoistic explanation from a British Military Government spokesman: "Some Germans profess total inability to understand the moral scruples on which the plot hinges."

Those in attendance that first night in Rochester had trouble grappling with the same issue. Shouted one restless patron at the screen for the benefit of the others, "Hisn't 'e hever goin' to 'ave it orf wif 'er or hisn't 'e?"

That is a question that does occasionally crop up. Reviewing the videocassette of *Brief Encounter* for *The Daily Telegraph* in 1987, the historian Jeffrey Richards noted, "It was fashionable to the swinging nineteen-sixties to mock the well-bred anguish of the lovers and the film's exaltation of restraint over unbridled passion, duty over indulgence, and concern for others over immediate self-gratification. But in the AIDS-conscious nineteen-eighties, when fidelity and monogamy are the flavor of the decade, *Brief Encounter* may not seem quite the antique that its 'liberated' detractors claimed. Irrespective of the whims of fashion, *Brief Encounter* remains both documentarily and emotionally true."

Lean contends that, even with the contemporary freedom of expression, were he to make *Brief Encounter* today he would still keep Laura and Alec out of bed. "Otherwise," he says, "it just wouldn't work at all."

"I don't think *Brief Encounter* will be everybody's film," said C. A. Lejeune in 1945, "but I'm sure there'll be people here and there who find it immensely moving. Personally, if I were collecting desert-island films, it would be one of the first I should choose, because it seems to me to catch, in

Lean with Trevor Howard and Celia Johnson. "She was magical," says the director.

"were fairly good. I don't remember. The movie did well in America, but there were several places it went very badly. I remember being told that they had to take it off in Turin, Italy, after three days." Lean later learned that the Italians were put off by Trevor Howard's looks.

"The French went for it," Lean concedes, remembering that he once saw a dubbed version, "and it was quite funny watching Trevor and Celia speaking very quickly in French." Dilys Powell, veteran critic for *The Sunday Times,* said that the reason the French liked the movie was that they were happy to see that a man could fall in love with a woman who wore such a silly hat. (Lean notes, "The hat, designed by Gladys

words and pictures, so many things that are penetratingly true."

Lejeune and Lean are of one mind about the leading lady. "Miss Johnson's face and her walk and her eyes can tell a story or impart a mood or reveal a confidence without the help of any narrative," said Lejeune. "Good wine needs no bush. Good acting needs no explanation." The critic hailed the film for capturing so rightly the English personality, in the same manner as Marcel Pagnol was able to create a perfect reflection of regional France with his 1938 *La Femme du Boulanger.*

The Cannes Film Festival named *Brief Encounter* Best Picture; Celia Johnson won the Best Actress award from the New York Film Critics Circle; and David Lean became the first British director in history to be nominated for an Academy Award.

"It became a sort of cult film," says Lean, "and then it entered Bible country." Two years after its original release, Lean wrote in a film journal: "We defied all the rules. There were no big-star names. There was an unhappy ending to the main love story. The film was played in unglamorous settings. And the three leading characters were approaching middle-age. A few years ago this would have been a recipe for box-office disaster, but this wasn't the case with *Brief Encounter.* The film did very well in [England] in what are known as 'better-class halls,' and it is having a similar success, but on a smaller scale, in New York. The film was put on there at a small cinema called the Little Carnegie, and it has had almost unanimous praise from the New York critics."

And what about Noël Coward's opinion, especially after his disappointment with *Blithe Spirit*?

"Well, Noël, you see," says Lean, "he looked at *Brief Encounter* and said, 'My dear, I must tell you. You're the most resilient young man I have ever met.'"

Adds Lean, "And I can sort of pick myself up every now and then."

By the late 1930s, the British film industry again entered the doldrums. Alexander Korda's London Films, formed after the international success of his 1933 *The Private Life of Henry VIII,* went belly up in 1939, and with it, his four-year-old Denham Studios. This left the exuberant, Hungarian-born showman to leave for Hollywood and a brief period of retrenchment.

To take up the slack, Yorkshire flour heir J. (for Joseph) Arthur Rank (1888–1972) entered the field in 1935, and within a few years was operating a virtual English film monopoly, of theatres and production, including Denham. To some, Rank's control, which was to last a quarter of a century, posed an economic and artistic threat. Lean found it otherwise. "He was a great big tall man with a slight Yorkshire accent, a very keen Methodist by religion, and very strict," Lean says of Rank. "He was called 'Uncle Arthur' by everybody and that was not a mistake. He was like a wonderful uncle to us all. He used to say, 'David, have you found what you want to do next?' I'd say 'Yes' or 'No.' And he'd say, 'That sounds interesting.' He never questioned it. Never queried a script. Never interfered with casting. He trusted us."

Writing in the *Penguin Film Review* of October 1947, Lean detailed the war and postwar era and the subsequent launch of the innovative plan financed by Rank and initiated by his former colleagues Michael Powell and Emeric Pressburger after their successes with *49th Parallel* and *One of Our Aircraft Is Missing.*

"These two men," Lean reported, "approached J. Arthur Rank and asked for financial backing and studio space to make the films they wanted to make in the way they wanted to make them. Rank agreed, and Independent Producers was formed. Under their company name of Archers, these two produced *The Silver Fleet, The Life and Death of Colonel Blimp, I Know Where I'm Going, A Matter of Life and Death,* and *Black Narcissus.* Other producer-directors joined the group: Frank Launder and Sidney Gilliat (Individual Pictures), who made *The Rake's Progress, I See a Dark Stranger,* and *Green for Danger;* Anthony Havelock-Allan, Ronald Neame, and myself (Cineguild), who made *Brief Encounter* and *Great Expectations;* Ian Dalrymple (Wessex Film Productions), who is now preparing *A Woman in the Hall, Esther Waters,* and *Far From the Madding Crowd.*"

Cineguild was formed between the time of *Blithe Spirit* and *Brief Encounter,* signaling a parting with Filippo del Giudice's Two Cities. Funding for Lean's next four pictures came from Rank.

CHARLES DICKENS
Great Expectations (1946)

"I never had read *Great Expectations*," says Lean. "The only Dickens I ever knew was *A Christmas Carol*, although I should think *Oliver Twist* I had read as a boy. Dickens's plots are damn good basically, but they get awfully sentimental and, of course, the women are all difficult. They become frightfully empty-headed when they fall in love."

Yet, taken either separately or as a pair, Lean's two Dickens movies, *Great Expectations* and *Oliver Twist,* enthralling to the imagination and dazzling to the eye, are perfect encapsulations of the novels by England's once most popular author. All other Dickens screen adaptations, of which there have been several, suffer in comparison.

Asked why Lean decided to turn to Charles Dickens (whose "criticism of society is almost exclusively moral," according to George Orwell) after the "bit of real life" the filmmaker had just created with *Brief Encounter,* Lean says, "I'm afraid I just did them, more or less as a change from the Noël Coward thing."

"We decided we had to prove ourselves apart from Coward," explained Ronald Neame at the time the former cinematographer was promoted to producer of *Great Expectations.* "We like Noël very much, and we sincerely hope to work with him again, but any Noël Coward film must primarily be a Noël Coward film, and we wanted to try our own wings."

Pip (Anthony Wager) returns to the marshes with pork pie and brandy for Magwitch — only to find another escaped convict, Compeyson (George Hayes).

"You're not afraid of a woman who has never seen the sun since you were born?" Pip is asked by Miss Havisham (Martita Hunt), shown here in Satis House.

Although they would never work together on another film, Coward and Lean remained great friends. The desire to fly the nest, as Neame had put it, seems perfectly understandable in light of the fact that the critical notices for the four Coward-Lean collaborations focused their main, if not entire attention on the contributions of the playwright.

For his version of *Great Expectations,* Lean wrote the script with Neame and Havelock-Allan; Kay Walsh and Cecil McGivern supplied additional dialogue. Lean played the action by the book, losing only minor subplots while cinematically heightening actions and characters in the process.

Great Expectations provided Lean his richest plot to date. Set amid the tangled judicial system and insurmountable class distinctions of 1840s England, the Dickens novel is the five-hundred-page biography of the orphan Philip Pirrip, commonly known as Pip. Seven years old when the story opens, the boy is startled one Christmas Eve in the churchyard while visiting his parents' grave. An escaped convict, Magwitch, scares him into returning with food; Pip obediently complies, a kindness Magwitch does not forget, even once he is recaptured.

Soon after, Pip is summoned to the rotting mansion Satis House to play with the pretty, upper-class Estella, the haughty ward of the reclusive, man-hating Miss Havisham. Pip is to love Estella the rest of his life, despite her training to wreak revenge on all men for Miss Havisham's having been jilted on her wedding day.

At the age of twenty-one, Pip learns that he has "great expectations" from an unidentified patron, who he assumes is Miss Havisham. Pip settles into the life of a London snob, until Magwitch shows up on his doorstep one stormy night. It is the felon—escaped once again—who turns out to be the benefactor, and Pip, at first repulsed, later proves his devotion to Magwitch by assisting in what is ultimately their unsuccessful escape from England.

"In the late summer of 1939, temporarily out of work, I made a [stage] adaptation of *Great Expectations,*" Alec Guinness wrote in his 1985 memoir, *Blessings in Disguise.* Having been a reluctant trainee in a London advertising firm, the then-twenty-five-year-old Guinness, with his Dickens play, hoped to form a small theatrical troupe. He enlisted support from some fellow performers and called it The Actors' Company. "Martita [Hunt] was to play Miss Havisham," said Guinness, "which was almost hand-tailored for her, Marius [Goring] was to be Pip, and George [Devine] was to direct. London was blacked out; we rehearsed at any old pub room we could find, and we opened at Rudolf Steiner Hall [33 Park Road, Baker Street], which suited us admirably once we had managed tactfully to disguise its anthroposophical atmosphere."

Great Expectations ran six weeks and was

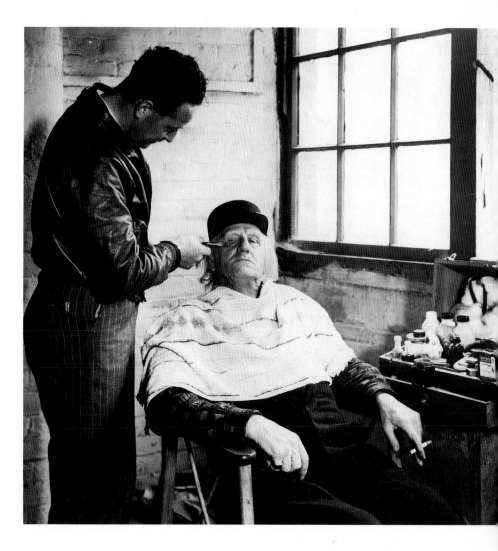

scheduled to move into the Shaftesbury Theatre in the West End when, as fate would have it, a German bomb landed there and destroyed the site.

Guinness remembered that during the Steiner Hall engagement, "It happened that David Lean and Ronald Neame saw the production and decided to make a film of the book as soon as the war ended, and they used Martita as Miss Havisham and me in my old role of Herbert Pocket."

The role marked Guinness's screen debut and the birth of a lasting association between the actor and David Lean, culminating in a thirty-eight-year collaboration that at various times has run both hot and cold. "I have worked with him in six films," Guinness says in his memoir. "On three we got along swimmingly and on three we had our differences."

Finlay Currie (1878–1968) being made up for his best-remembered film role, that of Abel Magwitch.

"Yes," agrees a cautious Lean, before adding, "How very good of Alec to print that." (The three happy circumstances were *Great Expectations, Oliver Twist,* and *Lawrence of Arabia,* which obviously leaves *The Bridge on the River Kwai, Doctor Zhivago,* and *A Passage to India* to be judged as something entirely different.)

On a separate occasion, Guinness, who admits to "a great fondness" for Lean, says that originally in his career "my love was the theatre and I didn't care whether I was asked to do films or not. The only time I'd done in a film studio was as a crowd artist." Guinness played an extra in the 1933 *Evensong,* a Gaumont-British musical. He complains, "We were treated like idiots. It was

such misery that I swore I'd never have anything to do with films. It was David Lean who kind of persuaded me [otherwise]."

Lean, in turn, credits Guinness for inspiring *Great Expectations.* "I wouldn't have done the film without seeing Alec's stage version. It exerted tremendous influence. I think I happened to read in the newspaper that it was on, and I remember it was in this tiny hall. It was wonderfully done, and, above all, I thought Alec was wonderful. That's why I picked him."

Once that was accomplished, Guinness remembers, "I learned an awful lot about films from David. He used to destroy a shot he didn't like by waving his hand in front of the camera lens and saying, 'Cut.' He said if he didn't do all that, some fool editor might use it."

As an actor, Guinness considered himself "like putty in [Lean's] hands. He was extremely helpful and 'simpatico.' I believe David made me rely on thinking, instead of just grimacing through a role."

Lean recalls Guinness as being "terribly nervous—very good but nervous. We had him in a blond wig." Lean smiles, remembering the sight of the young Guinness bounding up the flight of stairs in his first scene. "And Johnny Mills, of course, as Pip," adds Lean. "Johnny's an angel."

"We both lived in the same village, where I still live, in Buckinghamshire," John Mills recollects, "and David called one day and said, 'We're making a picture of *Great Expectations,*' and would I like to be in it? And that's how it happened." As a proviso to his own offer, Lean did warn Mills that Pip was a somewhat plain "coat-hanger" role, on which Dickens draped all the colorful characters. Mills would not be dissuaded. "*Great Expectations* was one of my favorite stories," says Mills, "and the film, I think, is a classic. It cost over £385,000, if I remember, and it stands up to time absolutely, doesn't it?"

As the young Estella, Lean hired Jean Simmons, who at sixteen was too young to take over the role as the heroine matures. Valerie Hobson played the older Estella. That she was married to Havelock-Allan may have figured in the casting.

"David," recalled cinematographer Guy Green, "made you feel part of a team. You wanted to do your best for him, and he showed his appreciation, especially to the technical people. He was not invulnerable. I've seen him on the set when he didn't know what to do. But the qualities he had were in inspiring everybody. One wanted not only to do a good job for him, but to top oneself for him."

Besides their work together on *One of Our Aircraft Is Missing,* Green had also served Lean as camera operator on *In Which*

We Serve before temporarily breaking off the working relationship. "I left to go with Carol Reed on *The Way Ahead,*" says Green, "on David's recommendation. We were working on *This Happy Breed* when Carol ran into trouble, and David very generously gave me leave to help him. David and Carol were best friends. Naturally there was some rivalry, they were our two top directors. But they were best friends at the same time."

Regarding any differences in the working styles of the two directors, Green says, "Carol was very much friendlier with the actors than David. David was inclined to be interested with pictures, using actors as part of the design, which I suppose can sometimes upset the actors."

John Mills says that was not the case with *Great Expectations.* "We had a wonderful time on it," he says, "a really marvelous time."

Six months of filming began September 1945 at Denham and in what still existed of

Mealtime on St. Mary's Marshes, site of Joe Gargery's forge. Facing Lean is Bernard Miles (Joe); on his side of the table, from left, producer Ronald Neame, Eileen Erskine (Biddy), Lean, Freda Jackson (Mrs. Joe), Anthony Wager (Young Pip), and Hay Petrie (Uncle Pumblechook).

"Dickens country," an inaccessible stretch of marshland fringing the Thames estuary and running inland to the Old Dover Road. An isolated road on St. Mary's Marshes, a mile inland, was selected for the site of Joe Gargery's forge, where Pip grows up.

The company went to London to shoot Pip's arrival by coach directly outside St. Paul's Cathedral, but returned to a desolate stretch of Thames coastline along St. Mary's Bay for the escape sequence with Magwitch. At high tide, John Mills and Alec Guinness enacted their arrival and departure by rowboat.

The story's most exciting sequence, the interception of their craft by the Rotterdam Packet Boat, was filmed on the River Medway, which was less congested than the Thames. The actual paddle steamer, which had crossed the channel in the 1840s, was discovered by the film's art designer, John Bryan, in Weymouth, where it was being used as a sightseeing ship. Bryan dressed the vessel with a forty-foot funnel, oversized paddle wheels, masts, topmasts, yardarms, the necessary rigging, and a clipper bow with figurehead.

"The sets for a lot of *Great Expectations* and *Oliver Twist* were built in forced perspective," says Lean. "*Citizen Kane* did that, as did a lot of early German films. They used unreality. Today, more and more, we use reality, which is a bore."

As one critic wrote of Bryan's work, including his lively contribution to *Great Expectations* (which was inspired by the illustrations of Gustave Dore): "His way of distributing and accentuating light and shade and his exaggerated perspectives manifested his disdain for convention."

While praising John Bryan, John Box, who would later design Lean's *Lawrence of Arabia, Doctor Zhivago, A Passage to India,* and *Nostromo,* explained his predecessor's technique. "Everything was built low and forced down as it came into the picture," says Box, noting that this is what accounts

for the characters appearing larger than life and the action so full that the screen seems about to burst from so many images. "David's influence, I'm told, was *Casablanca.*" Another source cites *King's Row.*

"Not sure which picture it was," says Lean, "but among the things that the Americans learned very early on was how to present stars, and one of the tricks in presenting the star is—in my opinion—to have some good, well-lit close-ups with well-focused lenses, because as you well know, unlike painting, photography gives everything equal prominence. One of the ways of beating it is to use a long-focus lens, with very little depth of focus, to telescope what you wish to present."

Another visual technique, says Lean, involves tracking shots. "When you begin making pictures," he says, "you're very inclined to shoot for the rushes. Say you have a scene and you shoot into a close-up. It looks good for rushes, but what you really should be doing is panning or tracking, but that doesn't look so good in rushes."

"The opening scene was a mixture of exteriors and studio shots," says Guy Green of the faithful reenactment of young Pip's running along the marshes on what Dickens called "a memorable raw afternoon towards evening."

"The marshes were exteriors," says Green, "the cows and the graveyard were interiors. It was a real mix, done in bits."

"Painted clouds, by John Bryan," says Lean as he watches that scene flash across the television screen in his sitting room. Soon comes a shot of an ominous-looking, anthropomorphic tree in the cemetery. "John Bryan, again," says Lean.

Quickly, from behind, Magwitch sneaks up on Pip and grabs the boy by the neck. Pip screams. Magwitch demands, "Keep still, you little devil, or I'll cut your throat."

"Worried terribly about that," says Lean. "I knew I had to shock the audience, grab their attention, as it were, once they'd settled into the cinema." His original challenge, he says, was "to convey Pip's fright to the audience. The best way to do that, the only way, was to frighten the audience as well."

The first time Lean watched the picture with an audience was at the press showing. "I was sitting in the back of the theatre," he says, "and I remember when Finlay Currie [Magwitch] came out, the entire audience went back in one big wave.

"And I sort of knew I was halfway there."

The British Board of Film Censors found the churchyard scene too intense for young viewers, depriving the picture of a "U" rating (for universal audience) in favor of an "A" (for adults). One of the several paradoxes concerning this decision was that at the time this same group saw fit to issue a "U" to *The Outlaw,* Howard Hughes's much-publicized Western starring Jane Russell, so suggestive that it had been widely banned in the United States. In the case of *Great Expectations,* the censors protested Magwitch's attack on Pip as well as Miss Havisham's death by flames.

"The censors also objected to the judge's black cap in the death-sentence scene," Ronald Neame told the press, "but that we easily cut out." Neame made the additional comment that by this time children had been subjected to much worse in cinemas, graphic war newsreels "of battles, bombing, destruction, and death."

"It is no more frightening than the book," *The Manchester Guardian* assured its readers. "Children as well as adults should enjoy greatly this notable product of a British studio." The same critique, though offering a few reservations (among them, bewilderingly, the characterization of Miss Havisham), asserted that *Great Expectations* "must certainly be called the best Dickens film yet made. To an astonishing degree the director, David Lean, catches and communicates the humor, the sentiment, and the

melodrama of the tale . . . we are miles away from the too-common insipidities of the photographed costume piece."

Some social historians view the climactic scene of Pip's tearing down the curtains of darkness on Satis House as a shedding of light on British life after the abysmal gloom of the war years.

Looking back to the original issue, Lean says, "I think the film came off rather well, actually, especially the first half. I went out on a Sunday night and saw, outside the cinema, a queue winding around the block.

"That was terribly exciting."

Inside Denham, shooting close-ups of the older Pip (John Mills) and his attempt to save Magwitch from drowning under the paddlewheeler. The exteriors had been shot using the Rotterdam Packet Boat, on the River Medway.

73

Oliver Twist (1948)

"I remember our doing the first scene of *Oliver Twist,* on the moorland with the pregnant woman making her way to the workhouse," says cinematographer Guy Green. "It was night, and it was stormy. In many ways it was similar to the opening of *Great Expectations,* and I had a pretty elaborate arrangement in the studio to create shadows as she was going across the marshlands."

Green and Lean then viewed the rushes. "I thought they looked great," Green remembers.

"No good," said Lean. "We'll have to do it again."

"What's wrong?" asked Green. "I think it looks terrific."

"Too romantic," said Lean. "I want it rougher."

Lean says that it would have taken approximately ten hours for a scene-by-scene adaptation of the Dickens novel. "The curious thing," he remarks, "people see the film and think they're seeing the whole book. I suppose some of that has to do with wanting to capture my first impressions as I read it, the main events, as it were."

For their faithful condensation, which at 116 minutes ran slightly longer than most features of its time, Lean and his cowriter Stanley Haynes (who also directed the film's second-unit locations in Beaconsfield) "read through *Oliver Twist* several times," and from that created an outline stripped of conversation and description and consisting of one-line summaries of each chapter.

In Chapter One, for instance, Dickens contemplates what the infant Oliver's fate might have been had he not been born in the workhouse, were he to have arrived in the company of loving relatives instead of the old pauper woman and surgeon who attend the difficult birth and ensuing death of Oliver's mother. In their outline, Lean and Haynes wrote, "Oliver is born."

The bulk of the film's episodes takes place in the workhouse; Sowerberry the undertaker's, where Oliver is sold into an unhappy apprenticeship for having requested a second portion of workhouse gruel; and Fagin's grimy den of young thieves. Oliver is lured there by the slightly older Artful Dodger (Anthony Newley), a filthy "snub-nosed, flat-browed, common-faced boy," according to Dickens.

Fagin, who fences for the sinister Bill Sikes (Robert Newton), is introduced by Dickens as he is frying sausages, "a very shriveled old Jew, whose villainous-looking and repulsive face was obscured by a quantity of matted red hair."

Alec Guinness says that in order to land the juicy part, he was the one to approach Lean, only to be told, "Alec, with all due respect, you're mad." Lean envisioned a more experienced film actor (Guinness's only previous film work had been *Great Expectations*), or "some heavier type of character. I suppose one always imagines [Sir Herbert] Beerbohm Tree, who did it on the stage and who, incidentally, happened to be the father of Carol Reed." Guinness persevered, insisting that Lean grant him a screen test—and that Lean not lay eyes

Fagin (Alec Guinness) attacks the Dodger (Anthony Newley) for letting Oliver out of his sight. Lean is in foreground, center.

upon him until he showed up for the camera, in full makeup.

"This extraordinary thing came on," Lean remembers of Guinness's Fagin regalia. Not only did the part go to Guinness, but the look he devised was basically kept for the film. This required him to be in makeup man Stuart Freeborn's chair at six A.M. every morning in order to prepare to shoot by eight-thirty.

For the role of young Twist, "We saw dozens and dozens of boys," says Lean. "Ronnie Neame finally came up and said, 'I

think Jack Davies's son would be marvelous. He has a wonderful face.' Jack Davies was a sort of film critic and gossip columnist. The boy's name was John Howard Davies, and now I understand that he holds an important position producing for BBC-TV. I haven't seen him since the film."

In contrast to haunts of London's underworld, the script provides the safe-haven home of Mr. Brownlow (Henry Stephenson), an upper-class, "very respectable-looking personage" whose heart was "large enough for any six ordinary old gentlemen

76

of humane disposition." Brownlow initially mistakes Oliver for a thief. Later, upon piecing together the puzzle of the past—and a locket taken from Oliver's mother—with clues provided Brownlow by Sikes's doxy Nancy (Kay Walsh), Brownlow discovers that he is the boy's grandfather.

Sikes bludgeons Nancy to death for speaking to Brownlow, and, when Sikes's own bull terrier leads an angry mob to the killer, is himself shot by police as he tries to escape over the rooftops with Oliver as hostage. Fagin is apprehended by the authorities (in the novel, he is shown on the eve of his execution beating his hands raw on the prison-cell door), and Oliver is united with Brownlow.

Oliver Twist opened at London's Odeon Leicester Square on June 22, 1948. "When the film came out," says Lean, "I didn't know what hit me. I was accused of being anti-Semitic. I wasn't anti-Semitic at all. I was just doing a Jewish villain."

So conscientiously did Lean and Guinness follow the work of Dickens's illustrator George Cruikshank that although the film never once mentions Fagin's background—Dickens in the text called him "a Jew" three hundred times—in September of 1948, *New York Star* columnist Albert Deutsch insisted after seeing *Oliver Twist* in London, "even . . . Dickens . . . could not make Fagin half so horrible." (To assuage outraged readers, Dickens later incorporated a good Jew as a minor character in his *Our Mutual Friends.*)

"On two successive nights the Jews and police fought with clubs, rocks, and firehoses around the Kurbel Theatre in Berlin's British sector," reported *Life* magazine March 7, 1949, under the headline, "Fagin in Berlin Provokes a Riot." The *Daily Telegraph* numbered the protestors at one hundred. The *Life* story went on to say, "Before riots ended, thirty-five Jews had been injured and three arrested. Seven policemen were hurt."

Bill Sikes (Robert Newton) kills Nancy (Kay Walsh) for speaking to Oliver's grandfather.

In America, the film's distributor, Eagle-Lion, which released all J. Arthur Rank productions in the United States through Universal, proposed that the Anti-Defamation League share the expense of test-screening the movie to determine whether the charges of anti-Semitism were well-founded. The League passed, but recommended that Eagle-Lion contact the twenty-six agencies of the National Community Relations Advisory Council. They too declined to sponsor the tests.

In the autumn of 1950, *Oliver Twist* was

presented to the Motion Picture Association of America, in the hope of receiving its Production Code Administration seal, guaranteeing the film could be played in the States. J. Arthur Rank submitted the script to code administrator Joseph Breen, who approved it after requesting eight minor changes, ironically none having to do with the character of Fagin. In a handwritten memo, however, Breen wrote, "We assume, of course, that you will bear in mind the advisability of omitting from the portrayal of Fagin any elements or inference that would be offensive to any specific racial group or religion. Otherwise, of course, your picture might meet with very definite audience resistance in this country."

The finished film never did receive the production seal; films that "unfairly represent" a race or nationality are denied one. When a test case was planned to release *Oliver Twist* without the seal, a Texas theatre chain suddenly withdrew its intention to open the picture.

"Then something terribly funny happened," says Lean, meaning funny as in peculiar. "It was just cut."

Twelve minutes were excised, or, in Lean's words (he had no hand in the deed), "butchered out of it." Removed were dramatized examples of Fagin's avarice, such as his counting jewels in a treasure box and his instructing the young boys in the techniques of thievery. Lean learned of the cutting—perpetrated, he was led to believe, by the American distributor—well after the fact. "I said, 'You've cut out all the humor. In fact, you've made it anti-Semitic.'"

The truncated American version opened in July 1951, prompting this observation from the *New York Times* critic Bosley Crowther, who had also been privy to the unscissored *Twist:* "The character of Fagin and the fact that he is a Jew (though that is never mentioned in the picture) are mere part and parcel of the whole canvas of social injustice and degradation, which is so bril-liantly filled out in Charles Dickens's great work. And it is this extraordinary canvas, this vast picture of poverty and greed which oppressed nineteenth-century England, that has been magnificently reproduced here."

It was to be another nineteen years before the complete *Oliver Twist* would be shown in America. The occasion was the 1970 world premiere of Lean's *Ryan's Daughter* and an accompanying retrospective of his work at New York's Museum of Modern Art. Viewing Guinness's portrayal of the obsequious, lisping ringleader in its much-maligned historical context, *The New Yorker*'s film critic Pauline Kael suggested that this Fagin would probably do more to offend militant homosexuals than Jewish groups.

In 1988, when the American videocassette of *Oliver Twist* went to market, it appeared in its full, uncensored version, a selling point noticeably absent in the advertising and publicity materials. This oversight can no doubt be attributed to the fact that, by all except the principal parties, the issue of censorship and *Oliver Twist* seems to have slipped from collective memory.

"We had already started work on *Oliver Twist* when I received news of my Oscar," recalls Guy Green, who won the award in Hollywood for his cinematography on *Great Expectations.* "I remember, in fact, we were shooting the first scene, on the marshlands, when I'd heard." Green had not even realized he had been nominated but learned later that Jean Simmons collected the golden statuette on his behalf. Within weeks it was presented to him during a small party at London's Dorchester Hotel.

In all, *Great Expectations* received three Oscars, one for Green's black-and-white photography and two for John Bryan and Wilfred Shingleton's art direction and set decoration. Lean was nominated as Best Director as well as for his screenplay (with

Neame and Havelock-Allan), and the film was in the running for Best Picture. It lost that top award to *Gentleman's Agreement,* a contemporary drama about anti-Semitism.

Asked his opinion of the Academy Awards, Lean, who has won twice and been nominated seven times, says, "If you have no hope of getting one, they're despised. But if you have, they're very important." Later, he adds, "I must say, they do count for something."

Oliver Twist, as painstakingly produced as *Great Expectations,* was far less popular and failed to be nominated in a single category. Of all the stories to emerge from the Dickens canon, few are as dark as *Oliver Twist,* and Lean would not inject into it any uncalled-for sentimentality. This, however, proved not the case with the splashy color musical adaptation of *Oliver Twist,* called

Oliver! In 1969 it won six Oscars, including Best Picture.

"Have you seen the musical?" asks Guy Green. "There are an *enormous* number of similarities to our film." Indeed, though ostensibly based on the 1960 London stage musical by Lionel Bart, the movie version, which delivers Fagin as a lovable rogue and allows him to escape (and which inexplicably names Brownlow as Oliver's uncle instead of grandfather), is more of an uncredited adaptation of the Lean film in story line and look than of either the Dickens novel or the Bart stage show. Coincidentally, the movie musical was cowritten and directed by Carol Reed, who received the Oscar for it.

Oliver! is for Lean "very difficult to talk about." He admits to having seen the musical but declines further comment.

Fagin (Alec Guinness), Bill Sikes (Robert Newton), and Nancy (Kay Walsh). In 1987, at a salute to Guinness by Lincoln Center's Film Society, no clip from *Oliver Twist* was shown. "I didn't want it," said Guinness. "It's one of David's best, but it created such a furor—people thought it was anti-Semitic— I was afraid that it might spoil the evening."

Above: Lean outside the soundstage with Josephine Stuart, Oliver's mum.

Opposite: Preparing for Oliver's arrival in London; Lean with John Howard Davies.

Shortly after *Oliver Twist* had opened as a hot potato in London, J. Arthur Rank rang Lean on the telephone. "Harry Cohn is at Claridge's and wants to see you," Rank said. "He wants to put on *Oliver Twist* in America."

Founding head of Columbia Pictures, Cohn (1891–1958) was the archetypical crude, tyrannical mogul, a reputation he carried to the grave. Forty years after their meeting, Lean says of Cohn, "No laugh, I liked him. Wish there were more like him around today. I know he used to give Frank Capra a terrible time, but at least the man loved film."

Lean arrived at Claridge's and knocked on the entrance of the appropriate suite. Cohn himself answered, saw it was Lean, took a bow so low that his face nearly touched the floor, and said, "I salute the work of an artist."

"He was very impressed that we had made *Oliver Twist* for under four hundred thousand pounds and were still able to come up with the quality we did," says Lean.

"I think I know what's wrong with the picture," says Lean, mimicking Cohn's Lower East Side accent. "It's da schnoz." Cohn pantomimed the shape of Fagin's exaggerated proboscis. To make the film palatable, Cohn advised Lean to reshoot all Guinness's close-ups, first giving him a new makeup job with a tiny nose, and to redub Guinness's dialogue, eliminating the singsong Yiddish inflection.

"I'm afraid that is not possible," replied Lean. "The way we devised Alec's makeup, that schnoz is visible even in long shot." Besides, Lean averred, it was no longer feasible to reenact Guinness's numerous scenes with the young John Howard Davies, who since completing *Oliver Twist* had, in Lean's words, "shot up a foot and a half."

Cohn, disappointed but still wishing to show his admiration for Lean, summoned the director to the hotel suite's kitchenette. "There," says Lean, "he opened the door to the refrigerator and took out six enormous beefsteaks. There was still the meat shortage on in England, but Harry Cohn told me to stick out my hands, and he counted, 'One, two, three, four, five, six,' and gave me the six beefsteaks. 'A young man like you,' he said, 'has to keep up his strength.'"

Lean remained eternally grateful, although he was not to work for Harry Cohn until another eight years had passed. And then, the hand that had once fed him turned around and slapped him.

"I didn't learn this until much later," says Lean, "but six weeks into making *The Bridge on the River Kwai*, we were already in the jungles of Ceylon, and Harry Cohn wanted to stop the picture.

"He said it was because there were no white women in it."

Set during the Boer War, the 1913 H. G. Wells novel *The Passionate Friends* deals with a love triangle and the strains it places on a marriage of convenience.

According to Wells's son Anthony West (whose mother was Rebecca West), the work was the summation of the author's affair with Amber Reeves, "the embodiment of my father's ideal of what a liberated woman should be." In 1922, the ubiquitous Maurice Elvey directed a silent version that, to please the censors, laundered the passions but remained faithful to essentials of character and plot. By 1948, adultery remained a favorite target of motion picture boards' blue pencils, a factor that was not to hinder screenwriter Eric Ambler in adapting *The Passionate Friends* for modern dress.

"The important thing," Ambler told C. A. Lejeune, "is the situation, and that could happen at any time. The story is so slight that you could write it on a postcard."

Asked to write it on a postcard, Ambler began with, "Poor young man." He crossed that out and substituted, "Poor brilliant Steven. Loves rich intelligent girl." Another change. "Rich intelligent Mary. He wants to marry her. She knows the marriage would spoil his career and marries instead a rich man. Steven and Mary meet again after several years and fall in love again. Rich man discovers and forgives, but forbids future meetings. War. [Lejeune noted that Ambler X-ed out the word "war" from his postcard, as well as reference to it in his script.] After war, Steven, now happily married, meets Mary by accident. Now he no longer loves her; but rich man hears of meeting, assumes worst, and brings divorce proceedings. Mary commits suicide."

Ann Todd was to play Mary Justin; Trevor Howard, Steven Sutton; and Claude Rains, Howard Justin, the banker husband. Production was well underway when, displeased with the results, J. Arthur Rank called Lean into his office and asked that he take command of the picture. Lean pro-

CINEGUILD TO KORDA
The Passionate Friends (1949)

tested, but Rank stood firm. "I think you owe it to us," said the head of the studio.

Despite his reluctance, Lean inherited *The Passionate Friends.* Production shut down for two weeks while the forces regrouped.

"I sat down with a friend of mine, Stanley Haynes, who worked on *Oliver Twist* with me," says Lean. "We worked day and night and we redid the script, kind of sharpened it up a bit, and I took over shooting. It was very unhappy. To this day, if the same thing happened to me, I don't know what I would have done. I don't think I did wrong."

"We met for the first time in the Albert Hall, where I had been a student and later played the Rachmaninoff Concerto for *The Seventh Veil,*" said Ann Todd in her 1981 autobiography. "It was an enormous crowd scene, everyone in fancy dress."

Todd recalled dancing with Claude Rains. "David as director was in the roof of the hall to film the whole scene," she said. "Then on 'Action,' strapped to the camera crane, he swooped down out of the darkness like Jupiter on Leda into a close-up of me. It was sudden, dramatic, and possessive—and my introduction to David Lean."

"I didn't know she'd written a book," says Lean, "but, yes, that's right. The scene at the Chelsea Arts Ball. I remember that." He adds, "And I married her."

Ann Todd started acting on the British

Above: Lean, who reluctantly took the helm of *The Passionate Friends.*

Opposite: Ann Todd as the enigmatic heroine Mary Justin: "Why can't there be love without this clutching, this gripping?" she asks.

stage in 1928, but it was her West End leading role in the 1943 *Lottie Dundass* that brought her attention. At one time considered a blond Garbo for her model's looks and icy detachment, Todd was a perfect casting choice for the traumatized concert pianist in director Compton Bennett's 1945 *The Seventh Veil,* the film for which she is best remembered (her autobiography was entitled *The Eighth Veil*). Prior to *The Passionate Friends,* she costarred as Gregory Peck's wife in producer David O. Selznick's *The Paradine Case,* directed by Alfred Hitchcock.

"This was my first film after returning from Hollywood," she said of *Passionate Friends.* "It is usual for the director to meet the stars before starting to work, but for some reason David didn't meet me—I think he imagined I would be conceited and grand after the success of *The Paradine Case.*"

After achieving stardom with *Brief Encounter,* Trevor Howard worked for director Sidney Gilliat in two 1946 comedy-thrillers, *I See a Dark Stranger* (with Deborah Kerr) and *Green for Danger,* and, in 1947, he played an RAF veteran drawn into black marketeering in *They Made Me a Fugitive* and a kindly doctor in *So Well Remembered,* a James Hilton melodrama directed by Edward Dmytryk.

Claude Rains (1889–1967) first appeared on the London stage when he was eleven, and made a career of playing suave character parts throughout his professional life. His film debut was the title role in Universal's 1933 *The Invisible Man,* for which he supplied only his voice and, in a few scenes, his bandaged-wrapped frame. By the time he returned to his native England to do *Passionate Friends,* Rains had received four Academy Award nominations as Best Supporting Actor: *Mr. Smith Goes to Washington* (1939), *Casablanca* (1943), *Mr. Skeffington* (1944), and *Notorious* (1946).

"Claude Rains and Bill Holden," says Lean, "were my favorite actors in working.

Professional, a joy. If there was an argument, we'd stop and discuss it. One side would see the other's point, and concede it. No problems."

After *The Passionate Friends,* Lean and Rains were not to work again for another twenty-two years, when Lean cast him as the cynical diplomat Mr. Dryden in *Lawrence of Arabia.* "Never had the parts," Lean explains. "You had to cast him very carefully. Interesting story about *The Passionate Friends.* Claude had arrived from America and we went straight into the scene where Trevor and Ann come back into the room and Claude knows they haven't been to the theatre, as they've said, and there's a cat-and-mouse scene. Claude says words to the effect, 'Enjoy the play?'

"They said, 'Yes.'

" 'Good,' said Claude. 'Care for a drink?' And the first hint you, the audience, get that he knows, is when he turns to one of them and says, 'Ice?' The way he says it, 'Ice?' You know he's on to them."

The scene was rehearsed, says Lean. "This is the first time I'd ever worked with Claude, and he said, 'Would you care for a drink?' and so on and so forth, then, 'Ice?' And I stopped it. 'Mr. Rains,' I said, 'I think you misread this scene.' "

"What?" asked Rains, astonished and perhaps a bit embarrassed.

"I said, 'You're playing a rather elaborate cat and mouse with them. For instance, "Ice?" has to have a cutting edge to it, which makes the wife think, 'Oh, Christ, he knows!' "

"Good God," said Rains. "I crossed the Atlantic to play this scene like that, and it's wrong."

"Look," said Lean. "I'm terribly sorry, but don't you see? You're playing it as an injured husband instead of being on top of it and playing Trevor and Ann."

"Yes," conceded Rains, "I'm a fool. I've misread it."

"Terrible silence," Lean remembers.

"Claude said, 'I won't be able to shoot this today. I'll go straight back to the hotel and I'll be ready in the morning.'

Rains returned the next day. Lean called for a fresh run through.

"And the rehearsal," says Lean, "was just more or less what you saw on the screen. The best scene he did in the picture."

The Passionate Friends was retitled *One Woman's Story* for the United States. "Don't know why they do these rechristenings," says Lean. "Mickey Powell's *49th Parallel* in America was called *The Invaders*. I don't know why they changed it, because *49th Parallel* is a wonderful title, and *The Invaders* is fairly commonplace. And I think Mickey's *A Matter of Life and Death* is a damn good title, and that was changed to *Stairway to Heaven*, not nearly as good. I mean *Stairway to Heaven* doesn't compare. It's all sentimental and sort of lousy."

While on the same track, Lean notes that his own *Summertime* was renamed *Summer Madness* for England. "The producers," he says, "thought that if it was called *Summertime*, people might think it was a Gershwin operetta. Can you imagine anything so ridiculous, Kate Hepburn in a Gershwin operetta?"

As it happened, *The Passionate Friends* was forced to undergo a name change because the American Production Code forebade the use of "Passionate" on a marquee.

"I have not the smallest doubt that *The Passionate Friends* will be more popular than *Brief Encounter* because the heroine is richer, younger, and more glamorous, the characters wear dressier clothes and move in smarter settings, and the story has what may be called a happy ending," wrote C. A. Lejeune in her otherwise disapproving review. Her prediction proved false.

The critic for *The Manchester Guardian* showed greater telepathic prowess in stating that it seemed "as if the story must have been wished on the director and not chosen

by him." The critic then wondered why the heroine and the film were bathed in "the kind of glamour of photography and of setting which is more usually associated with the demi-goddesses, the palaces, and the unrealities of Beverly Hills."

Location filming took place in scenic Switzerland (there are brief shots on a lake of Lean piloting a speedboat for Howard and Todd, necessitated by the lack of space in the vessel for both a pilot *and* a cameraman, so Lean served as both). "That was the trouble," thinks Lean. "We were playing sort of cumulus-cloud love scenes against cumulus clouds and beautiful mountains. *The Passionate Friends* was too much playing with the scene. It's much better, really, to play that sort of thing against dirty streets and subways, like *Brief Encounter*.

"But Claude was terribly good."

Lean scales the scenic terrain of Chamonix, Switzerland; looking back, he now feels that the glamorous backdrop detracted from the final picture.

Madeleine
(1950)

"Noël saw *Madeleine*," says Lean, "and he said, 'I'll tell you what I think is wrong with it. I don't think you can end the film not knowing what the end really is. I mean, did she kill him or didn't she? Somehow you've got to tip the scales a bit one way or the other.'"

Madeleine was set in Victorian Glasgow and based on the true story of Madeleine Smith, who in 1857 was charged with the arsenic poisoning of her French lover, Pierre Emile L'Angelier. After a sensational trial, the jury delivered a verdict peculiar to Scotland—Not Proven, leaving open entirely the question of her guilt. In showing the events leading up to the trial, the totally objective script does not present a viewpoint regarding her guilt but hints only that Smith might have considered killing the troublesome L'Angelier.

"It's like something that Somerset Maugham once said," quotes Lean. "'Real life frees the imagination, and then places it in a straitjacket.'"

While its lack of story clarity leads *Madeleine* to be widely viewed as Lean's least typical film, two of its sequences foreshadow scenes in his later movies. The first is the Highland dance attended by Madeleine and Pierre, filled with underlying sexual intensity, a precursor to the highly charged merrymaking of the guests on the night of Rosy's wedding in *Ryan's Daughter*. The other is the parade of taunting spectators who jeer Madeleine on her way to court, a frightening sequence that is repeated when Adela Quested goes to give evidence against Dr. Aziz in *A Passage to India*.

Asked what circumstances had brought the unlikely pair of Lean and Madeleine Smith together in the first place, he replies, "Ann. She always wanted to play it. It had been a very famous case." In a coolly re-

ceived West End stage version of the Smith story, *The Rest Is Silence*, Ann Todd had starred as the accused murderess. Madeleine's plight enthralled Todd, who possessed some of Smith's letters and owned the sunshade she wore in court.

"Ann was terribly stuck on this idea," says Lean. "It *was* a good real-life story, this nonproven verdict, and she was mad keen on it. In the end, I succumbed and said, "All right, I'll do it. But it wasn't really my cup of tea. Looking back, I don't think I should have done *Madeleine*."

Above: Madeleine Smith (Ann Todd) with lover Emile L'Angelier (Ivan Desny).

Opposite: Ann Todd and Lean; by now, husband and wife.

Page 88: No. 7 Blythswood Square, Glasgow; Madeleine mixes the arsenic.
Page 89: Madeleine stands trial for murdering her illicit lover. But did she?

"After *Madeleine*," says Lean, "the whole J. Arthur Rank thing with the production of films broke up. I think it was the influence of John Davis, an accountant who got more and more control over Arthur Rank and the Rank organization. It was a shame, because Rank was a very nice man who had a true belief that he wanted to make films that would entertain the people. With Davis, we felt the weight of the front office, so in the end Independent Producers was completely disbanded and I went to Alex Korda. Rank got in Sidney Box to head production, and he made the *Carry On* films, which appeared to be much more box office than ours."

Further changes were to be instituted. Without Lean's consent, against his wishes, and with no forewarning, Cineguild had dissolved.

"Ronnie Neame and Tony Havelock-Allan went to David one day," recalls a long-time colleague, "and just like that they told him that they had discussed something serious over dinner the night before. 'What's that?' David asked, very worried, because he could tell by the tone of their voices that there was something he didn't know. And then they told him that they had come to this decision that the three of them could no longer work together. They said, 'Look, David, we've decided that while your films will bring us prestige, it is our films that will make the money.' And David didn't have the slightest idea what to say. He was absolutely shattered."

"It was a terrible wrench," says Lean, "because we had all had a wonderful time at the Rank studios as independent producers, and I think we really did some good pictures between the lot of us. But then I went to Shepperton Studios, where Alex Korda was."

In the three years following the war, J. Arthur Rank attempted to build a solidly based British film industry, only to fail because of a variety of circumstances. Among them, the government had failed to rescind a wartime Entertainment Tax of 38 percent, which dug into box office earnings to such an extent that bankruptcy was inevitable. At the same time, Rank's detractors accused him of extravagance, citing most particularly the £1.3 million he permitted Gabriel Pascal to spend on adapting Shaw's *Caesar and Cleopatra*. In all, by 1949, Rank's losses on general film production reached £3.35 million.

"John Davis, an astute accountant and tough businessman, now emerged as the man who would save something from the wreckage," wrote George Perry in his historical overview, *The Great British Picture Show*. "Already the recklessly extravagant Filippo del Giudice had been swept away by the Davis broom. The talents of Carol Reed, Powell and Pressburger, Launder and Gilliatt, Ian Dalrymple, Anthony Havelock-Allan, Ronald Neame, and David Lean—the creative force of Independent Producers—one by one fell away, most of them joining Korda, who by now seemed to represent a beacon of artistic resurrection."

89

The Sound Barrier (1952)

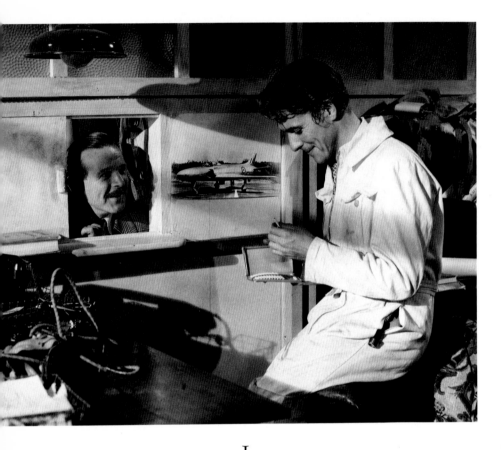

Pilot Philip Peel (John Justin), only moments after successfully breaking the sound barrier.

In March 1950, *The New York Times* reported that Lean and Ann Todd were headed for Noël Coward's Jamaican home to enjoy a belated honeymoon and that, despite the poor choices of material with *The Passionate Friends* and *Madeleine,* "Nothing has happened to Lean's talents. He is still second to Carol Reed among British directors." The story went on to say that before leaving London for Jamaica, Lean had been scouting locations around the Thames Estuary in preparation for his next film, an adaptation of the H. E. Bates novel *The Cruise of the Breadwinner.*

"A *wonderful* story," Lean remembers. "It was about a shorer, the *Breadwinner,* going out during the war, with a young boy

and an engineer. There was a German fighter plane knocked down in the sea, and they go to rescue it, and the German dies on board. I went to Charlie Laughton, but he wouldn't do it. It was a wonderful part for a great, big, blustery captain, perfect for Charlie, only he refused, explaining, 'I was out of England during the war and the British press would tear me to bits if I took on a role like this.'"

Lean never did the picture. Another consideration was the Mary, Queen of Scots story *The Gay Gaillard,* which provided a role attractive to Ann Todd, but neither did this reach fruition. Three other stories, each having to do with man's exploration into new realms, also presented themselves, according to Lean: "David Livingstone's journeys into unknown Africa, the story of Mallory and Irving, who were last seen climbing into the clouds near the summit of Everest, and the Scott expeditions to the South Pole. The trouble with all these ideas was that they were dated. They were all great stories of human courage, but the mystery had gone out of them."

In contrast, Lean's interest was sparked by something he had learned in 1946. "One evening," he recalls, "I picked up a newspaper called *The Evening News* and became intrigued by a story. It said that Geoffrey DeHavilland was killed over the Thames Estuary and the plane he was flying broke up in the air. Then there were two or three lines questioning whether he was exceeding the speed of sound, which it was thought could break up the plane."

Lean took the newspaper article to Alexander Korda, and the seeds were planted for what was to become *The Sound Barrier* (in the U.S., *Breaking the Sound Barrier* and even *Breaking Through the Sound Barrier*). "I said, 'Look, Alex, I think this is a bloody good idea for a movie,' and he said, 'I think it is, too. Why don't you go and do a bit of research into it,' and I did. I spent quite a time at Rolls-Royce in the aero-engine division, and met people there. That's where I got the idea of the designer [played in the film with proper eccentricity by Joseph Tomelty]. He was actually the chairman of Rolls-Royce, called Lord Hives. I thought he'd be a wonderful character, because he always had a cigarette in his mouth. The bloody ash went all the way down his waistcoat and he didn't seem to mind about his clothes or that sort of thing."

Lord Hives shared with Lean plenty of stories about company founder Henry Royce. One was Royce's theory of using only quality components in constructing a product that was meant to last forever, a practice Lean says should be equally applied to making movies. "That might stop the flood of rubbish that has taken over," says Lean, who coincidentally continues to drive the same special-edition Rolls-Royce he bought at the Paris Auto Show in 1964.

"I met a whole lot of test pilots," Lean says, "marvelous young men, not the sort of people one would suspect, and I took this information and wrote a diary of all these times, about forty pages, I suppose, and I showed it to Alex. He said, 'I think this is terribly good, and I know who can write this, Terry Rattigan.' Mesmerizing, Alex. He could take any subject and talk on it for twenty minutes. You can't imagine how wonderfully exotic I found him, especially after my being around Quakers."

The connection was made. "He got Terry on the phone," says Lean, "and said, 'Terry, I've got David Lean here, and he's got an idea, with a certain amount of research he's done on flying faster than sound, and I'd love you to write the script.'"

According to Rattigan's biographers, Michael Darlow and Gillian Hodson, the playwright thought Lean's and Korda's proposal "sounded dangerously like a film of ideas rather than character. He turned them down; he knew nothing about jets."

Dauntless, Korda convinced Rattigan, who during the war had been an RAF pilot

officer air gunner, to accompany Lean to the Farnborough Air Display. There the writer was charmed by the speed of the aircraft and the unassuming nature of the youthful test pilots.

"Terry wrote the script, and the pleasure of working with him was bloody good," says Lean, who ended up having to write for Rattigan the screenplay's domestic scenes between the Ann Todd character and her husband (played by Nigel Patrick). "Terry said, 'Here, David, you have more experience at this sort of thing than I.'" Rattigan was a bachelor.

It was also Lean's device to convey the sense of thrill on the London-to-Cairo test flight by cutting between shots of the air-

Susan (Ann Todd) set to confront her father, aircraft pioneer John Ridgefield (Ralph Richardson), over the death of her husband.

91

Testing the *Prometheus*. Lean acknowledges that it was an American, Chuck Yeager, who first broke the sound barrier. "There was a line about that in the film," he says, "only I'm afraid it was cut."

flight is reminded by Ridgefield that Prometheus was the Greek titan who stole fire from heaven.

"He came to a sticky end, didn't he?" asks Tony.

"He did," replies Ridgefield, "but the world got fire."

The patriarch also forces his only son (Denholm Elliot) to his death, when he crashdives on his first solo flight, undertaken during a futile attempt to prove himself to the patriarch.

"Father, answer me a question, will you?" says Ridgefield's daughter Susan (Ann Todd) after losing her husband and brother to what she calls her father's evil vision. "Is the ability to travel at two thousand miles an hour going to be a blessing to the human race?"

"Well," contends Ridgefield, "I'd say that's up to the human race."

Ralph Richardson (1902–1983), a mainstay of the Old Vic theatrical company during the 1930s and 40s, permitted his film career to take a back seat to his stage work for five decades. Nevertheless, by the early 1950s, he had achieved some recognition in Hollywood, and, for his role of Olivia De-Havilland's domineering father in William Wyler's 1949 *The Heiress,* with its shades of Ridgefield, he was nominated for an Academy Award.

His first picture for Korda had been the 1930 *The Shape of Things to Come,* and from then on the two were lasting friends. "His manner to me," Richardson said of the zesty Hungarian, "was mostly one of ironic weariness. He gave me the impression that I slightly bored him—very likely I did—but at the same time he drew me toward him." Though their ages were similar, Richardson said he regarded Korda "in a way as a father, and to me he was as generous as a prince."

"Alex said, 'I think Ralph Richardson would be wonderful in this part,'" says Lean. "I said, 'But Alex, I think he's so dull

borne vapor trail and the ground-level shots (of the Alps, and of antiquities in Greece and Egypt), all the while continuing the engine roar on the soundtrack. Rattigan's most significant contribution was the fleshing-out of strong characterizations and the difficult relationships between the protagonists, especially the father-daughter conflict portrayed by Ralph Richardson and Ann Todd.

For all its aerial splendor, the focal point of *The Sound Barrier* remains the ruthless character of Sir John Ridgefield (Richardson), a self-made aircraft manufacturer consumed by his insistence that his company be the first to build a plane to fly faster than sound. The test craft is called *Prometheus,* and among its victims are Ridgefield's son-in-law Tony, who before the fatal

on the screen,' and, quite honestly, I thought he was. I told Alex, 'I think he's wonderful on stage, but in movies he looks like a blather of lard.'"

"Ralph is a much better actor than you think," countered Korda. "He doesn't have to be dull, and this is a spectacular part. If Ralph plays this frightening tycoon, I think you'll be very surprised."

Korda pressed a meeting between Lean and Richardson, after first priming Richardson, going so far as to dress him in a proper tycoon's outfit and to add one last grooming detail. Revealing it embarrasses Lean slightly.

"I used to wear my . . . well, I have them clipped now, but I used to have these long eyebrows and I would brush them back," says Lean. When Richardson arrived for the

meeting, his bushy eyebrows were similarly coiffed.

"I bow to you," Lean told Korda.

"I'm glad I did," says Lean. Richardson won the New York Film Critics Award as Best Actor for *The Sound Barrier.*

"I think it's one of the best screen performances Ralph's given, actually," says Lean. "Anyway, the film was a huge success in England, and now it's never played for some reason. I thought there must be something terribly wrong with it. Probably one of the reasons it's no longer shown was that it's a bit of history that no one's interested in right now. People thought it was about jet engines and that sort of thing. But the BBC played it not long ago and I recorded it."

Lean's verdict? "I was absolutely staggered at how good it looked."

Tony (Nigel Patrick) and Susan Garthwaite (Ann Todd); Lean, sprawled out, took over writing their domestic scenes from playwright Terence Rattigan.

"Alex came to me and said, 'Look, do you know *Hobson's Choice*?'"

Lean did not. Korda had already dispatched two producers to adapt Harold Brighouse's 1915 stage comedy of a provincial King Lear for what was to be its third movie incarnation. In 1920, Percy Nash directed a silent *Hobson's Choice* with Arthur Pitt as Henry Hobson, the imperious Lancashire bootmaker, and Joan Ritz as his assertive daughter Maggie, who runs Hobson's shop *and* Hobson. In 1931, director Thomas Bentley's talkie starred Jimmy Harcourt and Viola Lyel in the same roles, and Frank Pettingwell as Will Mossop, the boothand whom Maggie fixes to marry. (The expression "Hobson's Choice," which means, in effect, no choice, is derived from Cambridge businessman Thomas Hobson [1544–1631], who, in renting horsedrawn cabs, offered his clients the horse standing next to the stable door or no horse at all.)

In orienting Lean, Korda demonstrated Hobson's comic walk, a tentative gait that is a reflex of the character's perennial state of inebriation. Remembers Lean, "Korda said, 'It's a very good play, but the screenplay that these two producers have done of it, quite honestly, I think they missed the point. It wasn't for them and it's my fault. I shouldn't have cast it to them. Now, don't read what they've done. Think of how you would do it.'

"So I sat down with a writer of Alex's, called Wynyard Brown, and I wrote most of the script and he wrote the new dialogue, and the film was wildly successful, in England particularly."

Besotted Henry Hobson—his downfall is drink, not romance—is intent upon maintaining his "rightful home comforts," in his case keeping in tow his three marriageable daughters. They organize the widower's domestic life and his better-grade bootmaker's shop while he partakes of the pleasures of the Moonrakers pub.

CHARLES LAUGHTON
Hobson's Choice (1954)

To escape her father's tyranny and his decision that at thirty she is too old to marry, eldest daughter Maggie summons from the cellar her father's chief craftsman, the unassuming Will Mossop. With a proposal of marriage and a vow that a better chance will not likely spring along—this from Maggie's mouth, not Will's—Will opens his own shop, to be run on Maggie's acumen, Will's craftsmanship, and the financial backing of one of Hobson's well-to-do customers, Mrs. Hepworth, who will have her boots made only by Mossop.

At first, Will is fearful, as shy as Charlie Chaplin's little tramp (whom he closely resembles), but then the confidence settles in. Hobson, however, is outraged by his daugh-

Above: Director Lean and star Charles Laughton.

Opposite: Charles Laughton, shown as Henry Hobson, enjoyed "working with David Lean," said wife Elsa Lanchester. "He was a kindred spirit and Charlie felt at home with him." Likewise Lean.

ter's elopement, no more so than when his business falls to nothing as the Mossops prosper, and Maggie must again intervene in the old man's salvation. The fade-out provides a family reconciliation and a business merger between Mossop and Hobson.

In September of 1952, Alexander Korda wired Charles Laughton's agent Paul Gregory in Hollywood to inquire whether the actor would be interested in coming to London for ten weeks to star in a film for David Lean. As it turned out, Laughton was well familiar with *Hobson's Choice,* because as a mature-looking teenager in his native Scarborough he had played the leading role at a community playhouse.

Korda's relationship with Laughton (1899–1962) had gotten off to a flying start in 1933 when *The Private Life of Henry VIII* put both of them on the map. Laughton, a graduate of RADA who had been acting in the West End since 1926, won the Best Actor Oscar playing the boisterous, rotund monarch. He followed with several other colorful roles, including a memorable Captain Bligh in M-G-M's 1935 *Mutiny on the Bounty,* before he made *Rembrandt* for Korda. Though hardly in the same league as *Henry VIII,* this biography, too, was successful.

In 1937, Korda embarked on an adaptation of the Robert Graves novel *I, Claudius,* and disaster struck. An insecure Laughton stalled production by searching for his character; the director Joseph von Sternberg, brought by Korda from Hollywood, antagonized the cast; and the leading lady, Merle Oberon, who later married Korda, was injured in an automotive accident. That last turn of events proved the final straw, and Korda aborted the expensive production, one-third of the way in.

During the intervening years, Korda had experienced other ups and downs, and Laughton became a Hollywood character star. In February 1953, on a reading tour in San Jose, California, Laughton received a telegram directly from Lean saying that the just-completed *Hobson's Choice* script was on its way and that it had been written specifically for Laughton. Laughton wrote Korda with his own demands: a house near the studio—Laughton abhorred hotels—two servants, and expenses for his companion.

Korda replied that provisions had been made for Laughton to live at a hotel on the studio's grounds. This displeased Laughton, even after being assured that Jennifer Jones was comfortably accommodated in the same location when she was in England.

According to his biographer, Charles Higham, *Hobson's Choice* was not a happy time for Laughton. He feared the script contained too many drunk scenes. Although Laughton liked Lean, he quarreled with his agent, felt infuriated that Korda was ignoring him in favor of a proposed (never made) movie about the building of the Taj Mahal, hated costar Brenda DeBanzie, the actress playing Maggie Hobson, and, "convinced that his marriage to Elsa [Lanchester] had finally come adrift, he was never more miserable." In addition, the tabloid press raked him for his having "deserted England in her hour of need."

"A quiet beach was chosen close to the Royal Hospital for the scene in which Willy Mossop is courted by Hobson's daughter Maggie," reported *The Manchester Guardian* on September 9, 1953, from the River Irwell in Salford. "On the river bank a bench was set beneath a property lamppost and cinders were scattered to make a path by its side, the camera was manhandled down the bank into its correct position at measured distance nose to lens, makeup was used, electric power switched on. Everything and everybody were playing the parts assigned—except the Irwell.

"First its banks were bathed in sunshine—warm bright September sunshine—when

Opposite, above: Maggie Hobson (Brenda DeBanzie) is courted by Willy Mossop (John Mills) on the banks of the Irwell.

Opposite, below: Lean with Laughton, once Hobson takes a drunken spill into the open cellar door of Beenstock & Son.

Will's former fiancée, Ada Figgins, gapes at Maggie as her mother gives Will grief. From left: Brenda DeBanzie, Dorothy Gordon, Madge Brindley, and John Mills.

Charlie," says Lean. "I probably should have held him down, but I couldn't. The terrible thing was, he put me in the position of being the audience. Instead of my saying, 'Come on, now, Charlie, tone it down a bit, would you?,' I'd roar with laughter and just let him go."

"That was rather interesting," recalls John Mills, who played Will Mossop. "David had never worked with an international star before, and he was rather in awe of Laughton. Laughton was very nice, and I think David handled him very well indeed, but there was this awe. I remember this one scene, a formal wedding, Charlie had to come in and there was a big scene at the table. And, at lunchtime, Charlie had said to me, 'You see, dear fellow, I see this comedy scene as starshells and rockets.' And I said, 'Yes—starshells and rockets. Very nice.' Then David said, 'Yes, yes, yes, yes.' But I didn't know what Charlie meant. I'm not sure David did, either."

Mills actually served as a last-minute addition to the cast. "Robert Donat was supposed to have played the part," he says, "but then he got asthma very badly, and I was called in. Because it was David, I didn't ask to see the script, I just said, 'Yes.' I was having a holiday in the south of France with Rex Harrison and [my wife] Mary, and a cable came: 'COME HOME QUICKLY HOBSON'S CHOICE URGENT.' So I took the next plane home and they were already in rehearsal."

"I'll tell you why I cast Johnny," says Lean. "Very funny. I remember when we were doing *Great Expectations* and we were on the Thames, the scene with the paddle steamer where Magwitch was killed because the paddle steamer runs down his rowing boat. We were waiting for the steamer to appear in order to get going, and Johnny was in the rowing boat with Finlay Currie and Alec Guinness, and while we were waiting, Johnny had us all in stitches by pretending to be seasick."

the script called for murk and gloom. Mr. Lean called for murk and gloom and they appeared as smoke and sulfurous fumes from fireworks and piles of burning motor tires drifted over the cameras and the 'stars' on the bench. Black distemper was splashed over the cinder path lest it appear too bright in the sunshine, and the property lamppost was smeared quickly with grime in case it looked more Shepperton than Salford.

"All now was murk and gloom, but Mr. Lean was still not happy about the Irwell. To him it seemed too like the Windrush."

While Lean managed to harness the Irwell, he admits with unbridled affection for his leading performer that he was unable to do the same with Laughton. "Dear old

Lean motions his own head back and forth. "He was terribly funny, and when Bob Donat dropped out, I thought who the hell do we have? And I suddenly remembered Johnny's seasick business. I thought, he's very funny, and Willy does have to be clumsy."

"David frankly admitted to me that he saw Willy at first as a largish, awkward, shambling sort of man, and he thought Bob was much better casting than I," says Mills, who, injury to insult, was given a pancake makeup pallor and a bowl haircut extending high above the ears.

"The key to Willy," says Mills, "was that he was a simple soul, utterly truthful, and he made no pretense about anything. No gimmicks to him at all. You just believed in Willy and it really worked. The thing was, not to think that he was funny.

"David," says Mills, "trusted me to come up with a performance. I just had to get it in my brain, how I was going to try and do it, and then left the rest to David. He presented it wonderfully—always very helpful that way."

The film's notices were mostly enthusiastic. "Delightful and rewarding," said *The New York Times*'s Bosley Crowther. Dilys Powell in London's *Sunday Times* applauded the attention to detail. "For once," she wrote, "the characters in a film about the past appear to belong to their period."

Laughton gave some reviewers difficulty. John McCarten of *The New Yorker* found him "singularly unattractive" and lacking the necessary sympathy for his clown role. *Time* magazine thought he "smirks, pouts, bug-eyes, belches, quivers his wattles, sleeve-wipes his nose, and generally golliwoggs to a degree he has not attained since *The Private Life of Henry VIII*. Too much Laughton leaves the audience feeling that there has been too little Brenda DeBanzie and John Mills."

"A dear chap, Charlie," Lean repeats.

"Will fulfills the dream of every man," says John Mills, "to rise up and tell off the boss." Here, Will tells off Hobson before daughters Maggie, Vicky, and Alice. From left: Brenda DeBanzie, Charles Laughton, Prunella Scales, Daphne Anderson, and John Mills.

"There used to be this pub besides the Thames, don't know if it's still there, and we used to go around and have drinks together." Lean takes in a deep breath. "Brenda was very good, too," he adds. Of her many character roles, including that in 1960's *The Entertainer*, DeBanzie was never better than she was in *Hobson's Choice*.

"She's dead," says Lean. "Charlie's dead. Charlie hated her. Don't know why. He thought she'd gotten the wrong end of Maggie playing the part. I said, 'Look, Charlie, why do you carry on about Brenda like this?' He said, 'I'll tell you why. Marvelous part, that part of Maggie, and Maggie is a real cunt—only Brenda doesn't understand that sort of thing.'"

"Now, most people," explains Katharine Hepburn, "if they have a wonderful piece of linen, they think they need to embroider it." Most people, she emphatically states, are not David Lean.

"Life's imprint on him is so strong," she says. "I mean, I know from my friend [editor-director] Tony Harvey, that if you sit in a cutting room long enough, it has a very strange effect on you, because you're all alone and you form your own point of view. You can try something as many different times as you want, and you always come out right. So you develop a sort of habit of always being right. That's David."

Katharine Hepburn and Lean worked together on *Summertime,* based on the 1952 Arthur Laurents play *The Time of the Cuckoo.* In the original Broadway production, Shirley Booth starred as the visitor to Venice, a middle-aged spinster who in her tormented American fashion refuses to succumb to a brief encounter while on holiday. In the film version, coadapted, "equally," says Lean, by Lean and the novelist H. E. Bates (*The Cruise of the Breadwinner*), the heroine, after some reluctance, falls for the charms of the city and her newly found lover.

"The man who finally produced the film, Ilya Lopert, had bought the play *The Time of the Cuckoo,* written by Arthur Laurents, who incidentally hated the film," says Lean. "And I think it was Lopert who suggested Katharine Hepburn. She was such an enormous star. Certainly in those days I wouldn't have dared approach her. I wouldn't have thought she was interested."

"I knew," says Katharine Hepburn, "that David was going to throw out the whole script to the play, and instead of having a lot of details about this and that and the other thing that *The Time of the Cuckoo* was about, he would just concentrate on a sort of forty-year-old secretary going to Venice for the first time and being flirted with across the Piazza San Marco and reacting to it in the most enthusiastic way, and then leaving

VENICE
Summertime (1955)

because it was totally impractical. And he was going to keep it just that."

Such simplicity, says Hepburn, was born of artistic necessity. "If the essential subject of a story is of interest to everyone, and that one is, then all you need are the circumstances, don't you?"

Whereas "most people make a situation so complicated that they would louse it up," continues Hepburn, "David is clear, simple, and straight." She credits much of that ability to his utter lack of sentimentality.

"I think most of us quarrel with ourselves," she says, " 'Oh, should I be more this or more that, what is and what should be?' David doesn't feel what should be.

"Take that fire." She points to her living-

Above and opposite: Jane Hudson and Renato De Rossi (Katharine Hepburn and Rossano Brassi); she finds his charms—and those of the city—too potent to ignore.

Above and opposite:
Katharine Hepburn and
David Lean. "She's just about
my greatest friend," he says.
"I love her."

geon, her mother a strong activist for women's rights), Katharine Hepburn studied dramatics at Bryn Mawr College. The day after she was graduated in 1928, she found her first professional job on the stage. Playing summer stock and Broadway, she gained a reputation for being outspoken (directors were not excluded from her comments), and was hired, fired, then rehired for her breakthrough leading Broadway role, in *The Warrior's Husband* (1932). RKO Pictures hurriedly paid a backstage call with the offer of a West Coast contract, one which Hepburn attempted to thwart by asking an enormous price. The studio met her terms.

Hepburn's first film was *A Bill of Divorcement* (1932), with John Barrymore, and she continued at RKO, routinely playing young independent-minded women of means. When those roles ran their course, and audiences tired of her in them, she returned to Broadway in Philip Barry's brittle romantic comedy about a spoiled society girl who does not know her own heart (or even if she has one), *The Philadelphia Story*. The 1940 M-G-M film version—Hepburn owned the movie rights to the play—brought her back to Hollywood and a contract with that studio.

"She was jolly good in *The Philadelphia Story*," says Lean, proffering his ultimate compliment. "And she looked smashing."

At M-G-M, among her most memorable films were a series of literate battles between the sexes starring herself and Spencer Tracy, including her immediate predecessor to *Summertime, Pat and Mike*, directed by George Cukor. She played a talented athlete to Tracy's cantankerous coach.

"I can remember my first meeting with David," says Hepburn. "I went over to London, I met him, and I thought, 'Oh, you're a charming man.' Then I met his wife, who was Ann Todd, and I could see that Ann Todd quickly asked me to tea, to see

room fireplace. "Now, David can look at that fire and describe that fire absolutely. He would say, 'This is what I think. And that is what I would do.' Meanwhile, most people are saying, 'What would Joe think if I did that? And Mary, she'll be thrown for a loop.' But not David."

The daughter of a distinguished New England family (her father was a noted sur-

whether I was going to fall in love with David. Because everyone fell in love with him.

"But," insists Hepburn, "I was in love with Spencer, so I had the most impersonal feelings toward the male sex."

Hearing her own statement, she laughs so heartily as to make her next remark nearly indistinguishable. Asked to repeat, she calms down and says, "So we became great friends, David and I. And we have remained, for years, friends."

Of their working relationship, Hepburn says, "I quickly kind of smelled out what David was like, because I was brought up in the generation that always tried to please people, though you'd never guess it, I suppose." Again with the laugh. "So I would try to figure out what a person's personality was. With David, I was absolutely thrilled with what he knew about film, and he and I just really hit it off. I know he can be tough, because he's absolutely direct. You do something and he'll say, 'What do you mean by that?'"

"She came to London and she was just wonderful," remembers Lean. "She's been, well . . . I don't know, I suppose she's just about my greatest friend, even now. I love her. I mean, she had the same sort of expertise as Celia Johnson. Celia and Kate, the two of them, are the great actresses I've worked with. Just, just wonderful, both of them, no trouble at all, always easy. I remember being with Kate in Venice. We had a set, high up overlooking the canal, in which I said, 'Look, Kate, I'm afraid I can give you no excuse for it, but, having done this and that in the middle of the room, you've just got to walk to that window, and I can give you no reason for doing that.' And she said, 'Yeah, well, that's what I'm paid for.' And she did it. And it looked as if the only thing for her to do was to move to that window so she could look out. Just wonderful. I do admire that professionalism. It's like the actress who once asked Alfred

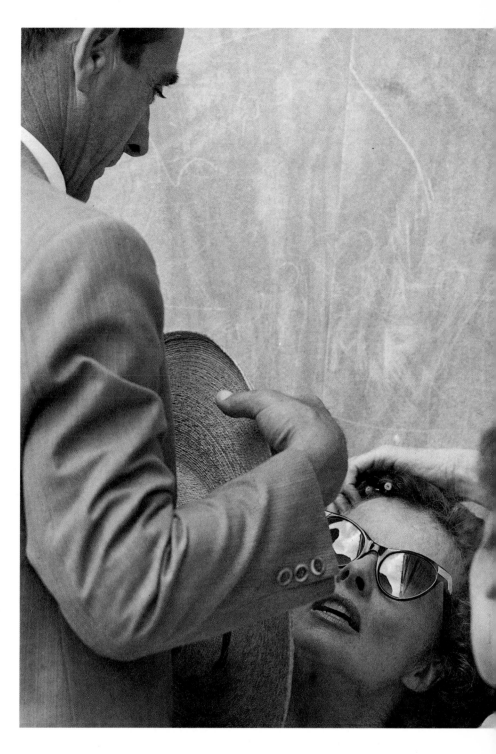

Hitchcock, 'What's the motivation for this scene?' and he said, 'Your salary.'"

"It sort of became a mad game to me," admits Hepburn. "David has a preconceived idea of what he wants out of a location, so I figured he probably had a preconceived idea of what he wants out of the actor. He would say something like, 'Now, in this scene, when the sun gets there, you've got to burst into tears, and you'll have

said, 'What are we going to do? I might as well shoot myself.'"

"That was awful," says Lean after hearing that Hepburn has told all. "I'd picked Isa after I'd seen her in a French movie playing a world-weary woman who'd obviously known a lot of men in her time. Then she showed up in Venice looking sort of glamorous, all wrong for the role, and I had no idea what could have happened to her. It was her hairdresser who tipped us off. He saw her scars and said she'd had a facelift."

Hepburn attempted to make the best of the situation. She recalls saying, "David, why don't you let me direct her scene?"

Lean permitted Hepburn to do just that. And what sort of a director was Katharine Hepburn? "*Very* dictatorial," says Lean, mimicking Hepburn's commands of, " 'Now, look here, Isa.' " This time it was Lean's turn to laugh. "She was very tough."

"I was," Hepburn admits proudly. "I hit her. I slapped her, because I knew that's what David wanted to do. I really tortured her, sort of beat her up. And finally she played the scene quite well.

"Isn't that funny?"

Above: De Rossi's shop window and the goblet that draws her inside.

Opposite: Hepburn and Isa Miranda (Signora Fiorini); Lean could not direct Miranda in the scene, so Hepburn tried her own hand.

Overleaf: Shooting in the Piazza San Marco. The year of the film's release, tourism in Venice doubled.

to do this and that, otherwise we'll have to come back here another day and do it again.' That's a terrible responsibility, but it didn't bother me, probably because I was so anxious to please him."

Hepburn unearths an old secret: that there was another performer on the film not so adroit, or fortunate—the Italian actress Isa Miranda (1909–1982), who played the owner of the *pensione* where Hepburn's character comes to stay. "David picked her out," says Hepburn, "and when she came to make the picture, she'd lost weight and had her face lifted. Well, David just went mad, because he'd picked her looking the way she did, with just reason. And any time she tried to do a scene, he nearly had a stroke. He just

Filming took place during the summer of 1954, with Venice largely taken over by the cast and crew. Lean, who relished this shooting on foreign location—*Summertime* even looks like his brightest film to date—was stationed in the Danieli Hotel. Hepburn was in the Bauer Grunwald, Rossano Brazzi in the Gritti Palace, and the art director, Vincent Korda, in the Grand.

Noël Coward paid a visit, spending five days with Lean and Hepburn. Despite his longstanding fondness for both parties, Coward did not enjoy his holiday. "I will never go to Venice in August again. It was like being shut up in a hot wet box and noisier than all hell," Coward jotted in his diary. "I coughed my lungs out every night and might well have expired like Camille if Kate hadn't given me some codeine."

Above: Jane Hudson of Akron, Ohio, and Mauro (Gaitano Audiero), the spinster and the street urchin.

Opposite: Getting an eyeful. Lean refuses to accept full blame for Hepburn's subsequent ocular infection.

Shooting *Summertime*'s most famous scene, in which she takes a Chaplinesque fall into a canal, Hepburn developed medical symptoms of her own, although Lean refuses to take the full share of the blame that she continues to ascribe to him.

"When David said, 'You have to fall into the canal,'" says Hepburn, "I said, 'Then, what the hell, I'll fall into the goddam canal.' Anything to please David."

"Nobody in his right mind would risk coming into contact with the water in Venice's canals," wrote Michael Korda, the son of Vincent, in his 1979 family saga, *Charmed Lives.* Telling of his boyhood visit to the set of *Summertime,* Korda reported, "The health authorities of Venice were anxious to avoid the scandal that would be caused by Miss Hepburn's succumbing to typhoid, skin diseases, or dysentery, and suggested that the scene be shot in a swimming pool. Miss Hepburn herself, having taken a good look at the water in the canal, was anything but enthusiastic about the prospects, but neither Vincent nor David Lean was willing to compromise with realism."

When chlorine chemicals were poured into the water, Korda said, bubbles erupted, sending suds everywhere within camera range. Just when it appeared the day's shooting would have to be abandoned, Vincent Korda suggested that a wind machine blow clear the area. Michael Korda remembered Lean's framing the scene with his hands.

Came time to walk the quay backward into the water, Hepburn was already smeared in Vaseline in order to protect her skin.

"I thought of everything except putting drops in my eyes," she says, "and I've had one of those terrible infections in my eyes ever since. Staphylococcus. And when you've got rusty hair and freckles as I do, the eyelids are weak."

How many times did Hepburn have to take the plunge?

She flashes Churchill's Victory sign. "Twice," she says. "The first time, somebody rushed in and tried to rescue me. Ruined the take. Can you imagine?" The would-be hero was a passing gondolier.

"I know Kate blames me for her eyes," says Lean, "but it's just not true. She was absolutely mad. Every day when we broke for lunch, she would make some remark about the terrible way she thought I was going to spend the hour, and then off she would go with members of the crew rowing ahead of her in a boat to clear a path. She'd be swimming the canals."

When Lean's claim is repeated to Hepburn, she goes silent, then takes both hands, clasps them firmly under her chin, and declares *sotto voce:*

"I am a fool."

Above: Hepburn, with Brassi. "If the essential of a story is of interest to everyone," she says of *Summertime*, "then all you need are the circumstances."

Opposite: With fans on the island of Burano, outside Venice.

"Toward the end of shooting," says Lean, "Lopert began to think that we were spending too much time and said he was going to take away my cameras." Lopert made good on his threat, and Lean was forced to finish with his own hand-held Bolex.

"It's nothing, really," says Lean. "Producers are always doing something like that."

The critics soon assured Lopert that he got his money's worth. "Imagine a cross between *Brief Encounter* and *Three Coins in the Fountain*," suggested C. A. Lejeune, who wondered, after seeing the film, how the original stage play could have been set entirely indoors.

"Few actresses in films could equal Hepburn's evocation of aching loneliness on her first night in Venice as she wanders, forlorn and proud, like a primly starched ghost in a city of lovers," said *Time*. "The Eastman Color and the camerawork by Jack Hildyard are superb." Critics also compared the lilting original musical theme by Alessandro Cicognini to the moodiness of Rachmaninoff.

"As a movie, *Summertime* does what movies were supposed to do when Edison first invented the darn things," wrote Lee Rogow in *The Saturday Review*. "It brings to you through the magic of the camera all the glory of a famous city thousands of miles away." Rogow further stated that movie audiences in the past had usually been cheated, believing that they were on location with stories when in reality all they were seeing were a few establishing shots photographed by second-unit crews, edited into Hollywood studio work.

As a result of *Summertime*, the tourist influx into Venice doubled. In contrast, the financial fortunes of the British film industry slumped toward disaster, partly due to the growing acceptance of television, and what little movie production that did take place in England was inevitably backed by American money. Hollywood producers such as Sam Spiegel and his Horizon Pictures Corporation set up London offices merely to take advantage of England's tax benefits and low production costs. Seeking greener pastures, British directors, among them Carol Reed, flocked to Hollywood.

For Lean, who never gave any thought to working in America, Venice cast a stronger spell. After finishing *Summertime*, he was to return there at every available opportunity.

"Kate once saw me off at the airport in Los Angeles," Lean remembers, "and at the gate she said she had a surprise for me, a friend who was also going on the flight."

"The only thing you must know is," Hepburn said at the time, "my friend is very shy." It was Greta Garbo. She and Lean did talk some in flight, although he said that for the most part she was "pretty quiet."

Among the things that intrigued Lean about Garbo was that she traveled so rarely. Did she, he asked, like Venice? "That would be impossible," she told him solemnly. "The crowds."

"Oh, come on," chided Lean, as though avoiding his favorite city for any reason was the most ridiculous thing he had ever heard. "Not go to Venice?!"

Summertime premiered in the open air of Venice on May 29, 1955, in the eighteenth-century Palazzo Grassi on the Grand Canal. Invited guests, following their arrival by gondola, entered the Palazzo through a high marble hall decorated by Longhi. Placed dead center over the movie screen was the constellation of the Plough.

The opening was an international event thrown by Ilya Lopert, who played host to journalists from the United States, France, Germany, Sweden, Denmark, Belgium, Britain, and Rome, as well as Gloria Swanson and the Algerian Kerima. Noticeably absent were David Lean and Katharine Hepburn.

Public events were never either's forte, before or after. Both were nominated for Academy Awards for *Summertime*, but neither attended the ceremony—although Lean did collect his Best Direction citation from the New York Film Critics Circle, and, starting in 1958 when *The Bridge on the River Kwai* was in the running, he began attending Academy Award nights those years he was nominated (1963, 1966, 1985).

Katharine Hepburn does not attend the Oscars, nor does she watch them on television. "And wouldn't you know," she remarks after receiving a phone call from the *Guinness Book of World Records* people concerning the storage of her four statuettes, "I've won more of the things than anybody else." She has been named Best Actress four times.

In May of 1988, Lean was to be saluted by the Film Society of Lincoln Center in New York, a gala event from which he eventually was forced to withdraw owing to a scheduling conflict. While the event was still pending, Hepburn pondered speaking publicly on her friend's behalf, something she reluctantly had done ten years earlier when the Film Society so honored George Cukor.

"I don't know," she said, "I should think I'd probably have to. I'd be forced." After a moment's thought, she adds, "Why did David accept the goddam thing? What is it?"

Told that it is a matter of selection by the Film Society, she said, "They picked me, too. I turned them down. I said, 'No, thank you.' And David hates that kind of thing. Oh, he's a fool."

Further proof of Lean's aversion to bringing attention to himself is that it took him nearly three years before he happened to see a television documentary about his career and his making of *A Passage to India*. When told this, Hepburn responds, "Isn't that terrible? But you see, he's just like me."

Qualifying her statement, she says, "To have a terrible, false vision of yourself is a form of ego that is so deep that you can hardly even look at a picture, that is what I think it is. I mean, I ask myself, 'Why have I never been to the Academy Awards?' And I say to myself, 'It has to be because I'm afraid I'm not going to win it.' It has to be. That is the only logical reason for a person not to go to the Academy Awards.

"Now, if I were an honest person, which I'm obviously not, I would refuse to compete. I would not allow my name to be entered. I would make a statement and say, 'As I do not believe in Academy Awards'—and I don't believe in Academy Awards—'I do not wish to compete.' But I do say to myself, 'I wonder if I'm going to win it.'"

Hepburn sees that this indeed presents a dilemma. "I mean, it's all false," she says. "Now, David is much more honest about these things. He says, 'Oh, Lincoln Center wants to honor me? I don't know what wicked thing this dinner is, but I think it's wonderful.'

"So you see, he's much more honorable than I am."

Above: Lean accepts his Best Director plaque from the New York Film Critics for *Summertime*. Also on hand were, from left: Hal Wallis, accepting the Best Actress award for Anna Magnani; Ernest Borgnine, named Best Actor for *Marty;* Abe Weiler of the *New York Times;* and Harold Hecht, producer of the Best Picture, *Marty.*

Opposite, above and below: Venice provided a perfect backdrop.

At the time of the Venice premiere of *Summertime,* Lean was laying the groundwork in the Far East for his next project, adapting the Richard Mason novel *The Wind Cannot Read.* Having found location shooting so delectable on the Hepburn picture, Lean's life, both personal and professional, was never to remain the same.

"He has celebrated his first independent production by quitting his normal domicile in London and betaking himself to India, via Japan and Hong Kong, with the likelihood that he will not be back for the better part of the year," reported Stephen Watts of *The New York Times,* on June 19, 1955. In fact, Lean was not to return to a London home for a full thirty years.

Michael Quinn, the hero of the novel, was, like Mason himself, an RAF pilot posted to India in 1943. There Quinn falls in love and marries Sabby, the woman who teaches him Japanese. Captured in Burma, Quinn is sent to a prison camp, where word reaches him that Sabby is dying of a brain disease. Against all odds, he escapes to see her one last time.

Lean was set to meet Mason in Hong Kong to consult on the script, with the expectation that they would establish production headquarters in Bombay. Alexander Korda envisioned Kenneth More as the lead, and Lean and Mason were to determine whether to remain faithful to the book's ending—and kill off Sabby—or provide a happier finish.

"In the end," says Lean, "it really didn't matter. The whole thing just collapsed. Korda died and that was the end of that." (In 1958, the Rank Organization produced a version of *The Wind Cannot Read,* starring Dirk Bogarde. Ralph Thomas directed from a script by Richard Mason.)

Coincidentally, a British soldier trapped in a Japanese prison camp in Burma also served as a principal element in Lean's next film. After *The Wind Cannot Read* fell through, Lean found himself in New York,

SAM SPIEGEL I
The Bridge on the River Kwai (1957)

in dire need of a project, when his agent in London informed him that the producer Sam Spiegel owned the rights to a novel by Pierre Boulle—and needed a director. Lean had read the book—*The Bridge Over the River Kwai* (1954)—and told the agent that if Spiegel were planning on filming a faithful adaptation, then Lean would be interested. The two future collaborators met at the New York home of their mutual friend Katharine Hepburn.

"I met Sam through Kate," says Lean, "after every director in Hollywood—including Willy [Wyler]—had turned down his lousy script for *The Bridge on the River Kwai.*" Others who declined Spiegel's offer included John Ford and Howard Hawks.

Above: Eight months to plan and build (with 45 elephants to drag its 1,500 tree trunks into place), the bridge stood 90 feet high and 425 feet high. Total cost, $250,000.

Opposite: Shears (William Holden) with military nurse (Ann Sears); Columbia Pictures chief Harry Cohn insisted upon her inclusion.

William Holden's arrival, with Alec Guinness's back to camera. "At the time," Lean says of Holden, "he was the top star in pictures." The actor also earned the film's top salary, $300,000 (nearly double that of Lean), as well as 10 percent of the gross box-office receipts. Says Lean, "He was worth it."

"Sam had this book," Hepburn recalls, "and he asked me who I thought might direct it, and I said, 'You should get David Lean. He's the best director in the business.' So Sam and David met here at dinner." Hepburn is referring to her Manhattan townhouse, where she has lived since the 1930s. "And they came back here three times. Sam did all the talking. David never said a word. He's so hopelessly shy, especially when he's supposed to be talking about himself."

"Finally," Lean says, "I asked Kate, 'What am I to do?' and she said, 'Look, David, you might as well do it. You'll learn a lot from Sam, and there's a lot he'll learn from you.'"

Lean's first lesson came in the form of advice from his old friend William Wyler. "Willy told me," says Lean, "to do with Sam Spiegel what he did with Sam Goldwyn—become equal partners, fifty-fifty on everything. Equal credit. Equal money." Spiegel easily agreed. Only Spiegel kept the books.

David Lean has never quite forgiven Sam Spiegel.

"They were a great team," says Betty Spiegel, widow of Sam, talking about her late husband's illustrious—and notorious—partnership with Lean, a collaboration that arguably produced both men's greatest works, *The Bridge on the River Kwai* and *Lawrence of Arabia.* "They were at odds most of the time," says Mrs. Spiegel, "but when they got together they could do no wrong. It's a shame they didn't do more pictures together."

"We *were* a great team," agrees Lean when told of Betty Spiegel's sentiment, "but I couldn't go on with Sam. I couldn't trust him."

"Oddly enough," says Mrs. Spiegel, "Sam and David usually seemed to agree on casting. David was never as earthbound as Sam. I'm not saying David is drifty, because, while he may be ethereal, David's very focused. I always felt that David only lived when he was working, although he does have a personal life, which he keeps personal. It's difficult to get to know David—difficult, but not impossible. He doesn't spill over, which is the understatement of the century."

Sam Spiegel, on the other hand, says his widow, "was always concerned with the budget. This would leave David to say, 'What budget? I've got to do this shot.'"

A middle-European refugee from Hitler—which did little to inhibit him from selling Hollywood films to Nazi Germany soon after he emigrated—Sam Spiegel (1901–1985) eked out a colorful (some would say "checkered") early existence in the motion-picture business. "Armed only with charm and a talent for languages—he was ultimately conversant in nine—Spiegel took on the world," John Gregory Dunne wrote in *The New York Review of Books,* March 17, 1988. "His dimensions were that of an altar votive candle, half-melted, the flesh cascading from him like cooled wax; his voice came from the esophagus, a low rumble, like thunder on the horizon."

At times in legal trouble with the governments of the United States and England, Spiegel invariably managed to keep one step ahead of creditors and the law as he worked in a most suitable arena, the movie business. Beginning in the 1940s, Spiegel, who had been desperately eager to produce films, put together various projects under the adopted name S. P. Eagle, and it was that credit which appeared on his first genuine success, the 1951 *The African Queen,* starring Hepburn and Humphrey Bogart, and made on location in Uganda and the Belgian Congo. In 1954, when he produced the significant drama about labor racketeering, *On the Waterfront,* Spiegel reverted to his original name, prompting the show-business newspaper *Variety* to report, "THE EAGLE FOLDS ITS WINGS."

Equally lofty was the reputation Spiegel built for himself. He was a scholar who never went to university, although he claimed he did. He was a generous host who ensured the glass of every New Year's guest—his parties were legendary—was filled to the brim, although he was loath to pay the liquor bill. He could sweet-talk a creative artist into doing practically anything, although he believed that the best creative atmosphere on a movie set was one of heavy conflict, which *he* would create.

Why Spiegel relished causing such difficulties remains a mystery, as direct questions put to Sam Spiegel were never met with direct answers. Yet those around Spiegel—and there was invariably an entourage—found him charming. "He had an *enormous* personality," Lean concedes.

"He used to like to surround himself with really sophisticated society people. And I used to sit and watch them and think to myself, 'Wouldn't you all be surprised to know what Sam had been doing only an hour ago.'"

Lean heaves a studied sigh. "You know," he says, "it really was a love-hate relationship, Sam and I." He throws his hands in the air. "I really couldn't resist Sam." Lean sounds as angry at himself now for the lingering weakness as he was at Spiegel once the film was completed. "It was after the last argument we had on *Lawrence,* having to do with money, I'm sure, and I said, 'All right, Sam. I've caught you once and for all. You've cheated me for the last time. This is it. I'm

On the bridge, Lean, Sam Spiegel, and visiting dignitaries, friends of the producer. Notes Spiegel's widow Betty, "We weren't on what you'd call the beaten path."

117

Lured out of retirement to play Colonel Saito, Sessue Hayakawa, born in Japan, had been a star in Hollywood silents from 1914 to 1923.

never speaking to you again.' And a few days later he rang me up. He knew I used to like to go to the grill at the Berkeley in those days. And he said, 'Come on, baby. Let me take you to lunch. Let's patch this up.' Of course, the film was just about to open. I suppose he thought the producer and director should be speaking."

And? "I went to lunch. We patched it up."

"I told Sam I would do *The Bridge on the River Kwai* on the condition that he threw

out this terrible script he had by Carl Foreman," says Lean, who takes issue with the awarding of a 1985 posthumous Oscar to the writer for his contribution to the *Kwai* screenplay. "There isn't a single word of Foreman's in the picture," says Lean.

Foreman (1914–1984) had been a Hollywood screenwriter since the 1940s, when he collaborated on a number of low-budget Bowery Boys films, and rose to prominence in the next decade with his scripts for *Young Man with a Horn, Cyrano de Bergerac,* and *High Noon.* The last assignment had been completed just prior to Foreman's being blacklisted by the studios for his having taken the Fifth Amendment before the House of Representatives' Un-American Activities Committee, which from 1947 to 1957 staged a witch hunt in Hollywood for those suspected of being Communists.

Like several blacklisted writers, Foreman moved to London and took to writing pseudonymously. In 1954, he optioned for three hundred pounds (against a purchase price of three thousand pounds) the Pierre Boulle novel about British prisoners of war forced to build a link in the Burma railway for the Japanese. In his adaptation, Foreman downplayed Boulle's protagonist, the blimpish Colonel Nicholson, in favor of a rascally American he added to the story. It was Foreman's desire that Humphrey Bogart play the Yank and that Carol Reed direct.

Spiegel picked up Foreman's script after Alexander Korda rejected it outright on the grounds that the novel's British colonel "is either insane or a traitor." That is where the project stood when Spiegel and Lean met at Hepburn's house.

"The script was no damn good," reiterates Lean. "The whole thing started in an American submarine that was being depth-charged. It had nothing to do with the story at all, and I said, 'Look, Sam, this is hopeless.'" Spiegel believed he was helping Lean when he brought in Calder Willingham, whose novel and play *End as a Man,* about

118

brutality in a Southern military academy, had been turned into a 1956 flop entitled *The Strange One* and produced by Spiegel.

"He's a very good writer," says Lean, but the director nevertheless did not approve of Willingham's work on the *Kwai* script. "It had this line of dialogue in it, 'You, sir, are a bounder, sir,' and I said, 'Look, no one speaks like this.'"

Spiegel gave Lean his usual catch-phrase, "Don't worry, baby," flew Carl Foreman to Versailles, and practically locked him in a room with a copy of Boulle's book and a typewriter. Lean found the second Foreman version no better than the first. The only solution was for Lean to leave for Ceylon, where the film's quarter-of-a-million-dollar bridge was already under construction, and create the script there himself.

"I wrote it all, start to finish," says Lean, "the beginning, the entrance to the camp, the men whistling as they came in. I had trouble with the part of the American, which wasn't in the book, so I said to Sam, 'Look, you must get me some help.'" Spiegel enlisted the services of Michael Wilson, who won the screenplay Oscar for the 1951 *A Place in the Sun* (adapted from Theodore Dreiser's *An American Tragedy*), but who, like Foreman, had fallen victim to HUAC.

"Mike was a nice man," says Lean, acknowledging too that in the case of Wilson's posthumous Oscar for *Kwai* (the writer died in 1978), the award was deserved.

"Now," says Lean, relishing—and recoiling from—another Spiegel story, "comes time for the screen credit. I said, 'Sam, now look, I think it should say 'By Michael Wilson and David Lean.' So what did Sam go and do? 'Screenplay by Pierre Boulle.' He did not write a single word of the script, I can assure you." More to the matter, Boulle barely spoke a word of English. "*Sam's* idea," gasps an exasperated Lean.

(It was also the director's unpleasant discovery to find in the December 15, 1957,

announcement ad in *The New York Times* the Sunday prior to the premiere of *The Bridge on the River Kwai* that their fifty-fifty venture was now being presented by "Sam Spiegel Productions." According to the letter of their contract, the advertising copy should have read "Presented by Sam Spiegel and David Lean."

"Sam," recalls Katharine Hepburn, biting her lower lip to stifle a guilty laugh, "was always taking credit away from David in the most awful ways.")

"Comes the Oscars," says Lean, "and the award for Best Screenplay is being announced. The winner? Pierre Boulle! And who gets up to accept it? *Sam Spiegel!*" Moments later, Lean collected his own award, for direction. Facing the press afterward, Lean was asked to clarify his film's screenplay credit. "You tell *me* that," Lean shot back, "and you've answered the sixty-four-million-dollar question."

Lean's reply was not appreciated by Spiegel, who was still hovering in the press-

The prisoners arrive. Says Lean, "Sam wouldn't pay for British extras." The solution: Singhalese natives, done up in whiteface.

teenth time to an interviewer on television, Lean commands, "That's it. Shut the damn thing off.")

Lean believes the source of Guinness's contention is Laughton's wife, Elsa Lanchester. "Elsa," says Lean, "had written that Charlie was going to do *Bridge on the River Kwai*—when, in fact, she must've been thinking of *The Cruise of the Breadwinner.*"

Although Lean's *Hobson's Choice* star was never in the running, Guinness was neither the first nor only candidate for Nicholson. "On Tuesday," Noël Coward wrote in his diary on Sunday, December 22, 1957, "Sam Spiegel gave me and the company [of Coward's *Nude With Violin*] a private showing of *The Bridge on the River Kwai,* a really magnificent picture. Brilliantly directed by David and acted superbly by Alec, James Donald, Jack Hawkins, Sessue Hayakawa, and Bill Holden. Really satisfying. I rather wish now I had done it."

"Noël as Nicholson?" says a quizzical Lean. "Not to my knowledge. At least Sam never told me. I suppose it's quite possible. I remember Sam wanted Cary Grant. I had lunch with Cary. Completely wrong. We also offered it to Olivier. He turned it down." (Laurence Olivier chose instead to direct and star with Marilyn Monroe in *The Prince and the Showgirl,* stating for the record that it seemed a rational decision to play love scenes with her rather than disappear into the jungles of Burma.)

room. Hearing his director, Spiegel began a physical duel with Lean, who immediately parried to his own defense.

Their weapons were their Oscars.

"David," says Alec Guinness, who played Colonel Nicholson, "didn't want me for the part. I'll never forget his greeting me at Colombo Airport and saying that his choice had been Charles Laughton."

"Absolute rubbish!" fumes Lean. "I never went to the airport. I never said a word about Charlie Laughton. The whole thing is in Alec's dream department. Imagine anything so ridiculous as Charlie Laughton as a starving prisoner of war." Lean feels that Guinness's version lives as an undying plague. (Seeing Guinness tell it for the ump-

There were other would-be recruits. "Sam came over and tried to persuade Spencer to do it," says Katharine Hepburn. Spencer Tracy as Colonel Nicholson? "Yes," says Hepburn, "and Sam kept coming back. But Spencer, who read a great deal, had read the book and he said, 'It has to be played by an Englishman. You can't have me do it.' And Spencer would have been wonderful."

Guinness, at best, was hesitant about accepting the role of the obsessed military

120

man. Jack Hawkins, who played Major Warden, leader of the commando squadron (a special unit of Mountbatten's) sent to destroy the bridge, claimed that when Guinness heard that Hawkins was willing to take a part, Guinness rang him—twice—to express his own uncertainty.

Guinness told *Focus on Film* interviewer Gene Phillips that he had seen Foreman's script and considered it "absolute rubbish—filled with elephant charges and that sort of thing." Then Spiegel paid Guinness a second call, with the revised script. "I turned it down a second time," said Guinness, "because I found Colonel Nicholson to be a blinkered character. I wondered how we could get the audience to take him seriously." A third call from Spiegel came in the form of an invitation to dinner. "He is a very persuasive character," said Guinness of Spiegel. "I started out maintaining that I wouldn't play the role and by the end of the evening we were discussing what kind of wig I would wear."

Eight months of filming began in October of 1956. William Holden, who was signed to play the role of the raffish American, Shears, was scheduled to arrive in December. A preliminary scouting expedition revealed that the real River Kwai was nothing more than a trickling stream, and not very photogenic, to boot. Malaya was no good, due to some guerrilla activities, and the Golden Triangle on the frontiers of Siam and Burma provided less than expectations. The company finally settled in a tiny village in Ceylon called Kitulgala, a two-hour drive from the Colombo Airport, through rice paddies, tea plantations, and elephant herds. To reach the site, where the Indian Ocean joins the Arabian Sea, one traveled first to Rome, then over the Ionian Sea and the Dardanelles to the minarets by the Golden Horn. From Bombay, the route spun north to Delhi and Karachi, to Bangkok, over Northern Malaya, and across

the Bay of Bengal to Colombo.

Though Spiegel had erected a compound consisting of bungalows, plumbing facilities (including a water-filtration system), and catering service (whose quality degenerated as Spiegel made weekly budgetary cutbacks), no one found it a picnic—except for Lean.

"David was like a kid in a candy store," says Betty Spiegel, who, like Sam, usually found it too hot to venture outside their air-conditioned suite at Colombo's Galle Face Hotel. "I think David is at his happiest living in an adverse environment, and he flourished like an orchid in Ceylon. It was hot, it was humid, people were dropping like flies, and he was happy."

"Material comforts didn't mean a thing to

"Sam," recalls his widow, Betty Spiegel, "was always concerned with the budget. This would leave David to say, 'What budget? I've got to do this shot.'"

121

David," says Geoffrey Horne, who played the neophyte Lieutenant Joyce. "At one point we were all forced to live in almost a dormitory. David never complained about it. He was very content."

Of his own participation, Horne, who was then twenty-four and a member of the Actors Studio (he had played a cadet in Spiegel's *The Strange One*), says: "I remember getting to Ceylon and thinking the whole thing extraordinary. The accommodations were a swell arrangement. There were these tin shacks around this villa. I shared mine, with a net between the beds, with this Major General Perowne, who'd been hired as a technical advisor. He wore a monocle and used to get letters from his wife in England about the flowers in their garden. Boy, was I thrust into another world."

Jack Hawkins found that his happiest moments were in watching the elephants that worked on the building of the bridge. "They were mainly female elephants," said Hawkins, "and seemed to have some kind of trade union of their own, because about every four hours, just as though someone had blown a whistle, they would drop whatever they were carrying in their trunks and lumber into the river for a long swim and a soak, followed by a good feed."

Came time for relaxation, Betty Spiegel recalls, "David was always on the sidelines. I remember once we were all sitting around a veranda. Sam had built chalets around a tea plantation and he flew in a chef. We ate very well. Anyway, one day Holden acquired this mad, wild monkey that he was trying to tame, and had chained it to a tree on a long lead, because Bill loved animals." The leash provided access to the human members of the party, and the monkey suddenly was attracted to Sam Spiegel.

"Sam," announced Holden, "there's a monkey on your back."

"Don't anyone move," came the petrified command from Spiegel. In telling the story,

Betty Spiegel imitates the monkey's plucking a hair off Spiegel's bare chest and nibbling it. Jack Hawkins suggested someone get a gun.

"Don't anyone shoot!" ordered Spiegel. "You may hit me."

"It had already bit two people," says Betty Spiegel, laughing at the story. "They finally coaxed it away with some food and sent it back into the jungle."

"Bill was a wonderful man," says Lean, "but he used to love pulling these wild schoolboy pranks." The old smile returns to Lean's face. "He nearly set fire to the bridge in front of Sam."

"Bill made a balloon once," says Betty Spiegel. "He had seen the natives make balloons out of old newspapers, and he made one with a bucket attachment of oil-stained rags. The arrangement was, you lit it and it rose and floated off to wherever it went."

The moment of ascension was one night during a party to celebrate the next day's blowing up of the bridge for the seven CinemaScope cameras—and everyone's going home. "Up the balloon went," says Betty Spiegel. "It was very colorful, everyone oohing and ahhing and applauding Bill for being like one of the Wright brothers. We were watching, riveted, when suddenly we realized the balloon was heading toward the bridge."

" 'Sam,' I said," says Lean in a goading voice, " 'take a look at that.' "

Spiegel was horrified. "Bill," he threatened, "if that balloon lands on the bridge, you had better be on it."

"I always like to make sure that it's possible for actors to do a scene," says Lean, "and I remember one scene: it was supposed to be night, when Holden was taking wires down a small waterfall to connect with the detonators for the bridge. I sent everybody to lunch so that I could run through the scene myself, and, as I was going down the waterfall, I looked up at the bridge and there was Sam.

His silhouette was always easy to recognize: these thin legs, his hat, and his walking stick. And I could see that Sam was *furious*. I said, 'What's the matter with you, Sam?'

"He said, 'You're taking a terrible risk.' I told him I was just working it out for the actors. 'You're *what?*' said Sam. And he said, 'What do you think would happen to *me* if you broke your leg?'"

Finished with the anecdote, Lean folds his arms across his chest and pronounces it "Typical Sam."

To Horne, Lean, who was then forty-eight, "was like a stern father, but a loving one. I later met Rock Hudson on a film, and what he said about his father-son relationship with George Stevens was the same as I had with David." Asked for a specific example of Lean's direction, Horne recalls, "Once, he really liked my timing in a scene, and when it was over, he said something about it reminding him of Celia Johnson in a railway station."

Horne remembers Sessue Hayakawa (1889–1973), a veteran of the silent screen who had been coaxed out of retirement to play the sadistic Japanese Colonel Saito, as "very old, very quiet. He did everything he was told and rarely spoke."

"My relationship with Mr. Lean was particularly good," Hayakawa told an interviewer in 1962. "Of necessity he is something of a solitary traveler in his profession. In his role of director he sees not only the fragments which, woven together, make the whole composition of a film, but the entirety as well. We never found ourselves in opposition, but he was less than slightly beloved by some of his associates being boiled by the hot sun and infernal humidity."

"People used to think David was going mad," says Horne. "He used to sit by himself on a rock, hold his cigarette straight in the air, and stare." Hayakawa recalled one member of the technical crew shrieking, "Lean! The bloody perfectionist! He shot thirty seconds of film a day and then sat on a rock and stared at his goddam bridge!"

"There was a tense scene on the set one day," says Horne. "David started to castigate the entire crew for their inefficiency and lack of interest in the film, like some local preacher scolding the community. He said everybody was guilty, and Freddie, some carpenter, shot back, 'Everybody, boss?' And David said, 'No, not you, Freddie.' And not Eddie Fowlie, of course, David's property man. Eddie could do no wrong. But the rest all hung their heads in shame."

The real dust-up came between Lean and Guinness for their differing interpretations over Colonel Nicholson. "David and I did not see eye-to-eye on the way Nicholson should be played," says Guinness. "I saw him as a much lighter character, played with some humor. Not that it mattered." (Guinness has also said in interviews that he never particularly cared for Lean's loud rhapsodizing over the talent and masculinity of William Holden.)

At dinner after arriving in Colombo, Guinness asked Lean how he saw the colonel, and Lean responded with, "Alec, if you and I were having dinner with him now, we'd find him a complete bore.'

" 'So,' said Alec," according to Lean (Guinness confirms the story), " 'you're asking me to play a bore?' And I said, 'In a way, I suppose I am. But, in the context, he is not a bore.'

"Well," says Lean, "Alec got mortally offended and said, 'I'll pay for my air fare and go home.' I said, 'Don't be ridiculous. It's a marvelous part,' but he refused to believe it. And he continued to refuse to believe it. That's why, later, he didn't go to the Oscars. He didn't think he'd win."

Guinness did win, as Best Actor for his Colonel Nicholson. It was also not long afterward that he was knighted.

"But," says Lean, "after the film was over and Alec saw it put together, typical of Alec,

"It sounded like a little pop gun had gone off," Betty Spiegel says of the dramatic dynamite explosion of the bridge. "A bunch of us were busy talking when I said, 'Hey, what's that noise?' Then I looked up and realized, 'Oh my God, it's the bridge.'"

Lean says that Guinness informed him in no uncertain terms, "Now look here, I haven't cared for the way you've directed a single scene of this picture."

"Good," Lean retorted. "If that's the way you feel, you can jolly well pack up and fuck off." For extra measure, Lean threw in that Guinness should feel free to take the British crew home with him.

This did not promote harmony on the set.

A solution arrived in the form of William Holden, set to begin shooting his role as Shears. Before Holden could so much as extend a hand of greeting, he heard first-hand the crew's complaints about their "genius director," who they felt had grossly insulted them and created this standoff.

Holden instinctively took matters into his own hands. In the manner of a locker-room pep talk, he told those assembled, "Now, just hold it. You've got a great script here, a really good story, and a director who knows what he's doing.

"So, come on, you sons of bitches, let's get to work."

The Bridge on the River Kwai was David Lean's first epic, and his first film for the wide screen—in this case, CinemaScope, an anamorphic process that effectively doubled both the width and the effect of the standard movie-screen image. "Before shooting," says Lean, scoffing, "Sam said, 'You've got to see a lot of CinemaScope films.' I told him, 'I don't need to. If you've an eye for composition, you can fill out the corners.'"

Lean obliged Spiegel, taking in one CinemaScope picture. "I remember going to see a very good Otto Preminger film, set in an army camp." It was *Carmen Jones,* the folksy Americanized version of the Bizet opera.

As for the magnified scale of his story, Lean cites two Spiegelisms. "Everyone commented on how large a cast of British army extras we had in the camp," says Lean,

he was absolutely charming and sent me a lovely letter. Two, in point of fact."

On the set, the fighting was not over. Eight weeks into shooting, Guinness insisted upon a close-up in the scene taking place on the bridge the night before the explosion, when Nicholson reminisces about his career, with Saito in the background. Lean felt the scene played better with the point of view over Nicholson's back shoulder.

"The coolness with which each man regarded the other was almost solid enough to be seen," said Hayakawa.

"Poor old Spiegel," says Lean. "Alec went to him and demanded the close-up. And I gave it to him."

This involved an exchange of words.

about to explode that myth. "What British extras? Sam wouldn't pay for them. What we had were Singhalese natives, done up in whiteface."

Regarding the length of the film, two hours and forty minutes, Lean says, "I remember going to Sam when I finished the script, because everyone thought this was going to be a small prisoner-of-war picture, and I said, 'Sam, this is going to be bigger than you think.' And he said, 'Don't give me that, baby.' In the end, Sam took the camera away from me, so I was left with an Arriflex to go shoot scenes myself [the vistas, establishing shots of the landscape], blow them up to CinemaScope, and use them to fill out the picture, to give it its proportions."

The final cost of *The Bridge on the River Kwai* came to three million dollars. On its first issue, it grossed thirty million dollars, its reception buoyed in part by the tremendous popularity of the theme song. The film was rereleased in 1964, on the heels of the success of the second Spiegel-Lean collaboration, *Lawrence of Arabia.*

When shown on American network television in September 1966, *Kwai* attracted a record sixty million viewers. By legitimizing feature movies as a prime-time staple, it also permanently altered video programming.

Lean mentions that he saw the film not long ago in Hong Kong, and that the love scene between William Holden's character and the nurse that was forced upon Lean by Columbia Pictures chief Harry Cohn "didn't detract too much." Overall, the director felt, three decades later the film looked "pretty good."

"There's an old adage that I've always thought pertains to David," says Betty Spiegel. " 'Never explain and never complain.' He's never done either. He's the only person I know who never complained— except when Sam wouldn't give him more time.

"But that wasn't complaining. That was David fighting for his art."

Pierre Boulle's novel on the futility of war and the folly of heroic intransigence, *The Bridge Over the River Kwai,* is a work of total fiction, with partial grounding in some actual persons and events. Nicholson was based on Philip John Denton Toosey, a senior British officer in command of prisoners, who had been a Territorial Officer since 1927. Toosey was initially sent to the Continent and evacuated from Dunkirk. Posted east and captured by the Japanese in 1942, Toosey possessed the reputation of an officer who could handle the enemy and ease the conditions for his men. In 1945, he was awarded the Distinguished Service Medal for bravery against the Japanese in Malaya, and he was later made an Officer of the British Empire for his conduct as senior officer in the prison camp.

Unlike the book, the film's plot climaxes with the blowing up of the bridge. That, says Lean, "was everyone's idea from the start. In the novel, there's only the *idea* of blowing up the bridge. You can't present that in a movie and then not do it." As for the question—left unresolved in the film—of whether Nicholson actually played a hand in destroying the bridge by deliberately falling on the dynamite plunger, Lean says, "The film's ending was too ambiguous. The colonel does realize his mistake and is trying to blow up the bridge when he is killed."

The tune that Lean originally had wanted the British soldiers to be whistling in the prison came was "Bless 'Em All," which he remembered hearing as a boy during the 1914–18 war. Its actual lyrics had been replaced, he recalls, by the soldiers' saucy *"Fuck 'em all, the long and the short and the tall . . ."*

"Sam came to me with a long face one day," says Lean, "and said that the rights to 'Bless 'Em All' would cost too much. So I remembered another song from my childhood, 'Bollocks, and the Same to You.' That turned out to be 'The Colonel Bogey March.' "

Permission was first secured from the elderly widow of the tune's composer, Kenneth J. Alford—he had been a director of music in the British army. She insisted upon knowing the circumstance of the song's use in the film. Conscious of the soldier's ad hoc lyrics about bollocks, which had not been the composer's intention, the filmmakers informed the widow that the tune would be whistled.

"She was very poor, and ended up with a percentage of the film," says Lean. "She was originally South African and had always wanted to go back and visit." This she did, with her royalties from *Kwai.* "She went," says Lean, "then came home and died."

With his earnings from *The Bridge on the River Kwai,* Sam Spiegel purchased the five-hundred-ton yacht the *Malhane,* which he anchored off the Riviera. Spiegel's fifty-fifty partner David Lean took a rest. Ceylon and the rigors of filming had dehydrated him.

In the wake of his Oscar win for *Kwai,* Lean received several offers, none to his particular liking. The producer-star of one, *Spartacus,* Kirk Douglas, says he personally invited Lean to direct. "I suppose he did," recalls Lean, "but look, it's just never any good, when a group of people are already set to do something, for me to join them. It's like . . . well, it's like trying to jump on a running horse." William Wyler, preparing his 1959 remake of the biblical spectacle *Ben-Hur,* also approached Lean with an offer he refused: "to direct the chariot scene," says Lean, "with full credit—'Chariot Scene Directed by David Lean.'"

Lean nearly bit at an offer from Spiegel, to adapt another novel by Pierre Boulle, *The Opposite Side of the Coin.* "Then I found out while I was reading it, that Sam's old rival Otto Preminger had gone and bought it himself. He then had the nerve to ring and ask me to direct it. I told him, 'You can get yourself lost.'"

What had fascinated Lean about the book was the prospect of working in India, introduced to him a few years earlier when Alexander Korda had underwritten the research trip for *The Wind Cannot Read.* Lean's own idea was to film a biography of Indian political and spiritual leader Mahatma Gandhi. To that end he had hired Emeric Pressburger to fashion a script. "He spent some time in India," Lean says, "and when we talked afterward it was really a marvelous discussion. He had great ideas for the script. And then he wrote it. I don't know what happened in the meantime, because the script was just awful." Lean's next candidate for screenwriter was French novelist Romain Gary, who could not be drawn into Lean's enthusiasm. The next hope, ex-

SAM SPIEGEL II
Lawrence of Arabia
(1962)

istential writer Albert Camus, died with Camus in a car crash.

Lean's final push to do *Gandhi*—with Alec Guinness playing the martyred leader—was aborted in the late 1960s, after Lean read the script by his *Lawrence of Arabia* and *Doctor Zhivago* screenwriter Robert Bolt. "Robert did a forty-page treatment that was just wonderful," says Lean. The final script was not. (Attentive to the project's history, Richard Attenborough says that before he began production on his 1982 Academy Award–winning *Gandhi* starring Ben Kingsley, he asked Lean if he still fanned his own hope of pursuing his by then twenty-year-old idea. "David told me, 'No, go ahead,'" says Attenborough, who

Above: T. E. Lawrence (Peter O'Toole) contemplates his fiery adventure.

Opposite: Peter O'Toole and Omar Sharif became international stars due to *Lawrence.* Of their later work, "I very much liked Peter in *Goodbye, Mr. Chips* [1969]," Lean says, "and Omar was very good in that Willy Wyler musical." He means *Funny Girl.* Here they are as Lawrence and Sherif Ali Ibn el Kharish.

127

Top: Lawrence searches for a miracle that will take Aqaba.

Above: Auda Abu Tayi (Anthony Quinn); "a wonderful bandit," says Lean.

made his film from a script by John Briley. Lean has not seen that film.)

While still on the trail of *Gandhi,* Lean was approached by Sam Spiegel to do the story of Thomas Edward Lawrence (1888–1935), the controversial military figure who led the Arab revolt against German-allied Turkey during World War I. Lean did not immediately snap at Spiegel's offer; the director, taken by the colors of India, was uncertain whether the desert landscape could provide him with the canvas he had already created in his mind. But then he began looking into the life of Lawrence. He spent the next three months reading everything he could about the enigmatic soldier, statesman, scholar, and egoist.

Spiegel was not the first to envision a film on the life of Lawrence. "Years ago, before the Second World War," says Lean, "Alex Korda wanted to do a *Lawrence* with Leslie Howard." Korda was dissuaded by his brother Zoli, "partly," Michael Korda quotes his uncle as saying, "because of Palestine, and Churchill was very worried because he felt it was important to have the Turks as allies when the war came." Alexander Korda did think, however, that "Olivier would have been wonderful as Lawrence."

As late as 1958 Anthony Asquith was set to direct Dirk Bogarde in *Lawrence of Arabia* from a script by Terence Rattigan, produced by Anatole de Grunwald. The British government's 30 percent entertainment tax was blamed for the death of the project. Rattigan converted his script into a stage play called *Ross,* after one of Lawrence's numerous postwar pseudonyms, and a blond-bewigged Alec Guinness starred in a 1960 West End version.

When Spiegel announced his *Lawrence,* to be adapted for the most part from *Seven Pillars of Wisdom,* T. E. Lawrence's privately published account of his own exploits, Herbert Wilcox tossed his burnoose into the ring, saying that he had purchased the screen rights to *Ross* for £100,000. Production on his film was set to start in March 1961, and Laurence Harvey would star, said Wilcox, who then left for New York to find a director.

Spiegel, who had yet to sign anyone, including his director, countered Wilcox's publicity with his own, claiming that his *Lawrence* would begin in January. He faced only two problems: no star and no script.

"Cary Grant will probably play General Allenby," Spiegel told the *Daily Mail,* "Jack Hawkins will be Colonel Newcombe, Horst Buchholz will portray Sheik Ali, and I am negotiating with Sir Laurence Olivier to appear as Sherif Feisal." Of these, only Hawkins would be signed to do the movie.

For the title role, Spiegel announced that the job would no doubt go to a newcomer from Lancashire, twenty-five-year-old Albert Finney. "He did a superb test for me," said Spiegel, "and one of the big advantages is that this boy really looks like the portraits of Lawrence."

"Finney worked four days, then quit," says David Lean. "He told me he wasn't interested in becoming a star." In 1963 Finney became an international film star playing the title role in *Tom Jones.* "I think what it was," Lean ventures, "was that he didn't want to be tied to some awful five-year contract with Sam Spiegel."

The next choice of both Lean and Spiegel was Marlon Brando. Their selection of an American to play the British military man was criticized by many, including his surviving brother, Professor A. W. Lawrence, who remarked, "It seems a mistake. I think it will almost inevitably mean that the film will be a flop—in [England] at least." Brando proved unavailable; he was shooting overtime and over budget the 1962 remake of *Mutiny on the Bounty.* Lean regrets to this

"Nothing is written," Lawrence tells Ali after rescuing another man, Gassim, from his fate. Ever after, Lawrence is "El Aurens."

129

"It really was a love-hate relationship," Lean says of working with Sam Spiegel. So notable—and notorious—was their creative marriage that this belly-to-belly photo hangs in the offices of many filmmakers.

Lawrence. Again Lean and Spiegel concentrated on American actors. "The fact is," Spiegel told one journalist, "we considered every possible British actor, but it requires a big international name. After all, the film is going to cost twice as much as *Kwai.*" He also said they would have asked Alec Guinness "if he were fifteen years younger."

Many more unlikely names were in the running. "Montgomery Clift used to ring me weekly in Madrid, where I was living," says Lean, "begging to play Lawrence." Anthony Perkins was also considered. "I had also thought of Richard Burton," Lean continues. "He would have been marvelous."

Finally, Katharine Hepburn recommended Peter O'Toole, a twenty-eight-year-old Irish actor whom she had seen in the stage play *The Long and the Short and the Tall* at London's Royal Court Theatre. O'Toole played a loud-mouthed Cockney. Says Hepburn: "He had a big nose, Peter O'Toole, and he was just great. And I suggested him to Sam Spiegel." (O'Toole dismissed the frequent reports that he had enlisted a plastic surgeon to reshape his nose after that of T. E. Lawrence as "fairy stories," but Hepburn, who costarred with O'Toole in the 1968 *The Lion in Winter,* persists: "Oh, he had his nose fixed, all right. What's wrong with having your nose fixed?" All Lean says is, "The one thing about Kate is, she never lies.")

David Lean first saw the young Irish actor "playing this rather ridiculous Englishman, in a small picture called *The Day They Robbed the Bank of England* [1960]. I'd never heard of him before, of course, but there was something about him. I said, 'Fine, I'll go for that.'" When O'Toole's film tests were screened, Spiegel and Lean did that rare thing. They agreed.

The casting of Lawrence solved, the problem of the script remained. Lean assigned the job to Michael Wilson, largely as a way of thanking him for his work on *Kwai.* A year and a half later, the finished script

day never having worked with Brando—the "finest screen actor of our time," the director states unequivocally, explaining that his admiration stems from the way in which Brando allows a character to exist within himself. (Brando was later slated to play the part of the wounded soldier-lover in Lean's *Ryan's Daughter,* originally written as a man missing one arm, and had all but signed the contract when he rang Lean to report that he could not master disguising his limb.)

With both Finney and Brando out of the picture, the search continued for the lead in

arrived in Jordan, where Lean was already scouting locations.

"It was awful," Lean remembers of Wilson's script, and he refused to move ahead unless another was written. (In 1964, Wilson petitioned the Writers Guild for credit for *Lawrence,* on the grounds that such is due when an author contributes at least one-third of a script; the Guild upheld his claim, although neither the studio nor the producer acted upon the decision.) With no suitable script, again the director and Spiegel butted heads. The setting this time was Spiegel's yacht, the *Malhane,* as it was moored off Aqaba.

"Sam," reports one observer, "who did not relish being in Arabia in the first place, or spending all the money that David's perfectionism would require, told David, 'Forget it. There's no script, there's going to be no picture.' That was all David needed to hear. He grew red hot. He stared down Spiegel, then said, 'Now look, Sam. We went fifty-fifty on *Kwai.* I came away with one million dollars and you came away with three million. And when this one's done, I'll come away with three million and you'll come away with nine million. So let's stop this fucking around and get on with the picture.'"

Spiegel left for London, where he went to the Globe Theatre to see *A Man for All Seasons,* Robert Bolt's play about the relationship between Henry VIII and the sixteenth-century ascetic Sir Thomas More. Bolt (born 1924), a former history master and BBC radio-play author, was soon after hired to do the *Lawrence* script—an odd choice, it might seem, but both Spiegel and Lean saw the need for an intelligent script that could evoke not only Lawrence's actions but also his thoughts and feelings. "Sam and David," says Betty Spiegel, the producer's widow, "always thought that films were made down to the public, and they refused to be a party to that." She remembers that when *Lawrence of Arabia*

Albert Finney as T. E. Lawrence. The actor worked four days before quitting.

entered its gestation phase, "Sam and David just assumed that everyone knew who Lawrence was, knew where Aqaba was, and knew a bit of history."

Spiegel arranged for Bolt to work on the *Malhane,* but before the playwright could leave London, he was arrested for his participation in an antinuclear rally in Trafalgar Square. While Spiegel went to work behind the scenes to spring his writer, Lean and *Lawrence*'s production designer, John Box, returned to Jordan to scout more locations.

The desert proved to be as starkly beauti-

ful and challenging a landscape as Lean could have hoped. "I can understand," says Lean, "how most of the great religious leaders came out of the desert, because, when you're there, you feel terribly small and, in a strange way, also very big. Because this vastness ... it's a sort of pitilessness combined with enormous beauty."

"We had a marvelous guide, a man named Aloysh," recalls John Box. "With him, David and I got to know the desert. We took *Seven Pillars of Wisdom* with us, and we worked out how Lawrence described the battles. We discovered the old railway lines that he helped destroy. They were still there, because the desert doesn't give out. Most importantly, we didn't find Lawrence's accounts wanting in any way, which was reassuring." The pair came across a fort looking exactly as Lawrence had described, and, according to Box, Lawrence's writings of "going up a hill to an amphitheater, where behind it were a waterfall and a fig tree" were confirmed when he and Lean, smothered in heat and flies, "found that precise spot. We didn't believe it," Box continues, "but this gave David a sort of faith in Lawrence, a faith in his integrity."

At the time, Lawrence's reputation was somewhat in dispute: was he a hero or merely a self-aggrandizing charlatan? Bolt himself found Lawrence to be "both a hero and a villain—a hero inasmuch as the Empire was heroic material, which I don't think it was." Even Lean was temporarily stymied. He recalls, "My favorite line about Lawrence belonged to Lowell Thomas, whom we called Bentley in the film so that Lowell wouldn't sue us. Thomas said of Lawrence, 'He had a genius for backing into the limelight.' Thomas hated the film, by the way." (The chief complaint of the journalist who had made Lawrence famous in America was that a six-foot-two actor was playing the five-foot-four military man.)

Working in Jordan presented constant challenges to *Lawrence*'s cast and crew. The logistics of moving equipment and personnel from London to the port of Aqaba, where the company established its headquarters, and from there to location sites sometimes as far as three hundred miles away posed numerous problems. And once there, the crew, actors, and hundreds of Bedouin extras and animals had to be fed and watered. In addition, the temperature in the desert sometimes rose so high that wet towels had to be draped over the cameras, and even the thermometers had to be cooled in order to prevent them from exploding in the effort to record it.

The political realities of the country proved no less difficult to surmount. The crew were allowed to shoot in Jordan only because of the intercession of Anthony Nutting, then Britain's Minister of State. Spiegel had met Nutting at the New York premiere of *Kwai,* and he approached him during the planning stages of *Lawrence.* "The next I heard was a message saying he'd like to work with me," Nutting told a *Daily Mail* reporter in 1960 regarding his involvement with Spiegel. "He clinched it by inviting me out to dinner and telling me, 'You're sitting at the very table where I persuaded Alec Guinness to play in *Kwai.*'"

According to Lean, "Tony Nutting went himself to see King Hussein and asked if we could do it." Nutting not only paved the company's way into Jordan, but also convinced the young king, descendant of Hussein of Mecca, Prince Feisal's father, to allow members of his army—which had done battle in Israel—to work on the film.

Regarding Spiegel's entry into territory that prohibited Jews, Lean says, "It was very brave of Sam, because it was no joke in those days." On one occasion Lean and Box were forced to run for cover as snipers' bullets were fired at them from behind rocks. Their guide explained the reason: "Arabs had been taught that anyone wearing trousers was Jewish." "I remember being on a hotel balcony with Sam," Lean continues, "and

his saying, 'Baby, where is Elat?' because, I think, that's where his mother lived, and I started to point when Sam hit me very hard on the hand. 'Don't point,' he said. He was very frightened that people might see and know he had connections with Israel."

Betty Spiegel confirms her husband's fear. "Sam was petrified. I remember putting Sam and David on the plane from Rome to Jordan, and Sam saying to me, 'Do you realize I'll be only six miles from my own mother and I won't be able to visit her?' Sam went with great trepidation." This was not, perhaps, entirely due to his fear of Arab assassins. "You can rest assured," he told his wife upon his departure, "that if it's David's location, it will be uncomfortable."

On one occasion, Spiegel caused Lean some discomfort of his own. "We were setting up a shot," Lean reminisces, "when suddenly some bullets bounced off a reflector. It scared me, I can tell you. Then I found out it was the soldiers protesting. Sam hadn't paid them."

Before he left London, Spiegel telephoned veteran cinematographer Freddie Young (born 1902) and said, "David Lean wants you to photograph *Lawrence of Arabia.*" Young did not hesitate. "David was already in Jordan," he recalls, "in Amman, having a recky [reconnaissance trip], and I joined him there. We had a chat and he told me various things, then sent me off on a recky with the art director." Lean was interested in capturing all the various terrains the desert had to offer, "unlike John Ford," notes Young, "whose different Westerns often used the one landscape. You would always see the same cactus sticking up."

One of the things Lean told Young was, "I don't know how in bloody hell we'll do it, but I want a mirage." The idea had been brewing for some time. "Everyone," says Lean, "had said that a mirage wouldn't photograph—it was an illusion of the eye. But one day while on a mudflat I took out my

Opposite, from top: Aqaba, about to be taken from the land. Faraj and Daud with their idol, El Aurens. Watching helplessly as Daud sinks in quicksand; this shot was accomplished by digging a hole in the ground and inserting a wooden box into which Daud could fall.

Overleaf: The massacre at Tafas.

133

Alec Guinness as Feisal. "His voice," Lean says admiringly, "reflects the right Arab nuance."

think he was very glad to dispose of it because nobody had been using it."

Upon his return to Amman, the cinematographer showed Lean his booty. "I told him I had the lens for the mirage," says Young. "I said, 'We'll be able to get a very effective close-up of this mirage by putting this long-focus lens on it, because a mirage is always a long, long distance away.' And David used it very cleverly."

The mirage does more than simply mark the entrance of Sherif Ali (Omar Sharif) as Lawrence and his Hashemite guide Tafas rest at the watering hole of the Harith: the three-minute, all-but-silent sequence creates a feeling of suspense and further underscores the mystery of the desert, for Lawrence and the audience.

Lean credits inspiration for the impact of Sherif Ali's arrival to advice given him by William Wyler. "Willy always said, 'If you're going to surprise an audience, first you must nearly bore them to death.' I remember asking him once, after Hitchcock's *Psycho* had just come out, if he'd seen it yet. He had. I asked him how the shower scene was, and he said it was very good. 'But,' he said, 'the three minutes before it, when nothing happens, they're *brilliant.*'"

This in mind, Lean and Bolt concocted some tedious activities with which Lawrence could occupy himself. Lawrence drinks, pauses, puts down his canteen, walks a few steps, stretches out on a sand mound next to a dry bush, removes his compass from a pocket, blows it free of dust, checks its needles, whistles a few bars of "The Man Who Broke the Bank at Monte Carlo," then daydreams. The peace is momentarily shattered when Tafas drops a water bag back down the hole, but all is becalmed by the time Lawrence begins to see on the distant horizon a small black dot approaching.

"It was a tiny pinprick," says Freddie Young. "We put Omar, oh, I don't know, about a quarter of a mile away, and David

Hasselblad and there it was, a mirage on the horizon."

Lean also informed Young that he intended to shoot *Lawrence* in seventy millimeter, and to that end sent him off on another "recky"—to Hollywood to choose the staff and the Panavision equipment. Young remembers that trip well: "As I was talking to Robert Gottschalk, who was president of Panavision then, I saw a long lens lying on a bench, and I asked Bob what it was. He said, 'Oh, it's an eight-hundred-millimeter lens,' and I got a hunch and said, 'Well, put it in with the other equipment.' I

Lawrence and his conquest: a Turkish train. When filming began, O'Toole was twenty-eight.

told him just to come riding toward the camera. We shot a thousand feet of him coming closer and closer and closer. It was fantastic watching him coming toward us, sort of this swirling wave. It looked like a sea on the desert."

"It seems to me it was something more like two or three miles," recalls Omar Sharif. "It wasn't terribly early in the morning. I think, nine or ten A.M. David needed a really high sun to capture what he wanted."

How many takes were required? Lean looks disappointed at the question. He holds up one finger.

"One take," echoes Sharif, "but a very long one, because of the distance I had to travel."

To frame the entrance, John Box and members of the crew scattered by hand tiny black pebbles across the sand, in the shape of a wide "V" that narrowed as it closed in on the feet of Lawrence. This, says Box, was symbolic of Lawrence's meeting a mysteri-

ous figure who would forever change his life. For added dimension—and to provide Sharif and his camel a sort of guiding track—Box spray-painted a straight white line on the sand. "Freddie didn't understand that, or like the look of it," recalls Box, "and started kicking it away with his heel."

"Omar rode right up until he got to the spot which had been designated," says Young, "and then he got off the camel. Fantastic introduction for Omar Sharif. But the sound was also weird because as he got close, the audience got the *clop, clop, clop,* of the camel's feet, and David kept cutting backwards and forwards to Lawrence and the Arab. They were apprehensive, and it made the scene more exciting, because you didn't know what was going to happen. Not a sound, except for this *clop, clop, clop.*

"And when it was shown in Hollywood," remembers Young, "everybody was absolutely knocked over by the mirage, which just goes to show you—when David says, 'I

137

Top: After the death of Daud. "Peter was uncanny," reports cinematographer Freddie Young. "The script would say what Lawrence was thinking, and Peter would capture that."

Above: The Arab Council disbands.

Opposite: Omar Sharif's entrance; he was first seen as a tiny dot on the horizon.

don't know how in bloody hell we'll do it,' you'll somehow do it."

Sam Spiegel's first choice for the part of Ali was the French actor Christian Marquand. "He spoke with a French accent and had blue eyes, and I think Sam had him signed to some sort of long-term deal," says Lean, who told Spiegel that Marquand was not right for the role and demanded to see photographs of possible replacements. Spiegel

delivered a series of postcards of Egyptian film stars, and Lean remembers that the second picture was of someone who looked perfect. On the back of the card was written the name Omar Sharif.

"My first meeting with David was most extraordinary," Sharif remembers. "He flew me out to the desert of Jordan, in Amman, the middle of nowhere, really, in this little plane. There was no landing strip or anything when I looked down, nothing except this lone figure standing in the desert. You can imagine how impressive this was to see from the air."

The lone figure was David Lean. "The plane taxied and landed," says Sharif, "and that was the first time I saw him. He took my hand and shook it, and as he was saying, 'Hello, Omar, so glad you could come out here' and so forth, I could tell that with his very piercing eyes he was closely examining my face and profile, and sizing me up. Then he took me by the hand to the costume tent and sent everyone out, saying that he could handle this by himself, and he started going through the costumes. He said, 'What do you think of black, Omar?' Then he took me to makeup, and he—himself—started fixing me up. First he tried a beard, and that wasn't right, so next he tried a moustache. I did not have my own then." Sharif has worn a moustache ever since.

"Gave him a screen test," Lean remembers of Sharif, "and he was very good." Sharif was tested with Christian Marquand, who soon after was sent home to France.

Filming began in May of 1961, and lasted twenty months. Peter O'Toole distinctly recalls Lean declaring to him on the very first day of shooting, "Pete, this could be the start of a great adventure." Confirming the actor's memory, Lean, in 1989, states unequivocally, "And it was."

"We'd work two or three weeks straight," remembers Box, "then take two days and go to Beirut, which in those days used to be

Omar Sharif agrees with Young's assessment: "It was very exhausting, but extremely exciting. I was enthusiastic, because this was obviously going to be something worthwhile."

"All told," Young continues, "we had about thirty tents. The crew called it the David Lean Camp. David actually had a caravan, he being the boss. I used to go into his caravan every morning and say, 'Good morning, David, sun's going to come out very shortly.' He would say, 'Come in and sit down, Freddie. Have a cup of coffee.' He wouldn't be hurried. And then he'd say, 'I'm worried about how we're going to do this scene, Freddie,' and we would talk about it. Sometimes he'd get out tapes of his conversations with Robert Bolt about the scene, just to refresh his memory about the characters and their attitudes."

Young also remarks that, despite Lean's reputation as an unstinting perfectionist, the director is in fact a most frugal filmmaker. "David shoots only what he wants. He doesn't leave anything for anybody to cut out afterward or prepare an alternate scene. In those days Hollywood was very fond of what was called 'coverage.' They would cover a shot—long shot, medium shot, over the shoulders, close-ups, reverse shots, overhead shots—meaning that the editor could really have a ball game with the fantastic amount of film to choose from. But David was very clever in that respect. He directed and photographed a scene so that it could be used in only one way. And, because of all his preparation, he very often had to shoot it no more than twice or three times. No alternative, you see. He was very economical."

Because of the high desert temperatures, the cans of film had to be stored in specially built refrigerator trucks, then shipped directly to London for processing. Spiegel did not allow Lean to see any of the rushes.

"Sam sent a cable saying that if we didn't speed up, he was going to have to come

marvelous. David once said to me, 'You know, John, we live the life of princes.' And he wasn't saying it to brag."

Young reports that though the conditions were grueling, morale was high. "We used to go miles into the desert. We'd go to one place where there was red sand and red rock, another where there were black mud flats, then another thirty or forty miles away for something else. One time we were in a quite nice hotel, but another time we were under canvas tents for about six months, hundreds of miles from anywhere. Still, we were happy. It was very well organized, and we had very good tents—double-clad, that sort of thing. And we had good toilets. Matter of fact, the roof of a toilet went off one day in a sandstorm. We never saw it again."

through with a big broom and sweep things clean," Lean recalls with a smile. "So I ordered the prop department to get me a big broom, and I shot a scene of myself in the desert sweeping the sand and then coming over to the camera, pointing a finger into it, and saying directly, 'Now look, Sam. We're going as fast as we can and we're doing a bloody good job.'"

The story seems perfectly innocent until Lean concludes it with a certain degree of self-satisfied relish: "I can imagine that Old Spiegel, sitting in a screening room in London, did not enjoy hearing that."

"Sam tricked me into finishing the script," Lean says, disappointed to this day that he was not allowed to return to some locations, and downright indignant not to have been permitted to shoot in the rugged terrain of Petra as Spiegel had promised.

"We had to have an eight-week layoff while Robert and I finished the second half of the script," says Lean, who, in tandem with Bolt, wrote the screenplay in continuity. "Sam said we could do the rest of the picture in Spain, but in the end we also had to go to Morocco, because there was no desert in Spain, and no Arab horsemen. Sam had to bring camels over from North Africa. I think they're still there, or their relations."

Sevilla doubled in the film for Cairo, Jerusalem, Deraa, and Damascus. The Moorish city also served as the site of the only set built for the whole of *Lawrence*—for the crypt scene in St. Paul's Cathedral (which, ironically, was excised from the print shortly after the film's premiere and not reinstated until its 1989 reissue).

The film opens with Lawrence's fatal motorcycle accident, proceeds briefly to his funeral, then flashes back to focus on four phases of Lawrence's career: the taking of Aqaba from the Turks; his physical and emotional debasement at the hands of the Turkish Bey in Deraa; the massacre at Tafas;

and the collapse of the United Arab Council in Damascus.

The first location was an area in southeastern Jordan known as Jebel Tubeiq, which borders on Saudi Arabia. Here was shot Lawrence's first look at the desert and most of the trek sequences, including those both to and from Feisal's camp as well as the caravan across the Nefud. According to John Box, Jebel Tubeiq's black basalt desert contained hundreds of years of camel tracks that the film unit needed to follow in order not to get lost.

The second location in Jordan offered the mudflats at Jafr—and the most frequent mirages in all the desert. Omar Sharif's entrance was filmed here, as was the "Sun's Anvil" segment in which Lawrence rescues

Above and opposite: Demonstrative David Lean. With gun, to show how Lawrence should assassinate Gasim (after he is caught stealing), and with another prop in reply to Spiegel's threat of coming to the film set "with a big broom."

Importing camels to Spain. "I think they're still there," says Lean, "or their relations."

presents Lawrence with the white robes of an Arab.

"John had a very good idea about the Lawrence costume," remembers Lean, who looks at Box across his dinner table at home and asks, "That was your idea, wasn't it, John?"

"The first time Lawrence is presented with the robes, they were to be made from the finest pure silk," says Box. "Then, as the film progresses, and he gets 'downer and downer,' the material gets thinner and thinner, so the costume becomes more like muslin, which also makes Lawrence seem more and more ephemeral. In other words, as the substance of the man disappeared, we also took it away from his costume."

Just a few weeks shy of his thirty-eighth birthday, Maurice Jarre was contacted out of the blue to become involved in the musical score of *Lawrence of Arabia.* "I had just finished the music for a French film, *Sundays and Cybèle.* It was a Columbia picture and Sam Spiegel was kind of influential at Columbia," says Jarre, who had scored various French films in the previous decade. "Spiegel really liked the music for this film."

Summoned to the George V, Jarre met "a film producer with a big cigar." This was Spiegel, who told Jarre, "I'm doing the biggest picture ever made."

"That's nice," says Jarre. "This," Jarre thought to himself, "was the pure simplicity of a Hollywood producer."

"I want three composers for this film," continued Spiegel.

"Very unusual," said Jarre.

"First," said Spiegel, "I want Khachaturian, to write the Arabic music."

"Very strange," thought Jarre. "A Russian to write Arabic music?"

"Then," said Spiegel, "I want Benjamin Britten, in London, to write the British music."

"That makes sense," said Jarre.

"And I want you," Spiegel told the

the lost tribesman Gasim. This was the hottest spot of the shoot, Box recalls, where temperatures seldom dipped below 100 degrees during the day and tended to hover around 120 — "too hot for even the camels."

Wadi Rumm, twenty miles north of the head of the gulf of Aqaba, is made up of "towering red cliffs rising two or three thousand feet from the pink, sandy floor of the desert," says Box. The backdrop served for Feisal's camp and the well where Ali

142

Frenchman, "to write the dramatic music."

"I'm very flattered," said Jarre, despite his uncertainty of what the arrangement might entail. Spiegel recommended that the composer come to London at the end of June, for further instruction.

This Jarre did. First thing one Monday morning in his office, Spiegel said, "I want to show you the film."

"I was very excited," Jarre remembers. The men adjourned to a small screening room on South Audley Street, near the Dorchester.

"From nine until twelve I saw this footage," says Jarre. "It made very little sense. I barely saw Lawrence."

When they broke at twelve, Jarre voiced his confusion. "Don't worry," Spiegel replied. "You'll see more after lunch."

Jarre was to learn that Spiegel had forty hours of film to show. "That was the rough cut," says Jarre. "I watched this for a week — without David Lean." This, too, Jarre thought "a little strange. But I was still very excited."

At one point, Jarre said to Spiegel, "This is very nice, but where is David Lean?"

"Don't worry," Spiegel assured him. "He's cutting the film."

Jarre later found out that Lean had set up a sleeping cot in the editing room and was living there around the clock, in sort of a race against the clock. "They had the premiere scheduled before the Queen in only a few months," says Jarre, "in December."

Despite the length of the rough cut, Jarre could sense an impressive film taking shape. "Every frame was gorgeous," he remembers. Thus inspired, after the week's viewing, Jarre began "to write a few things." The next day, the phone rang. It was Spiegel.

"I have bad news," said the producer. "First of all, Khachaturian can't come to England to record. And I have more bad news. Benjamin Britten is tied up for a year."

"I was smiling inside," admits Jarre, al-

though he kept a sad voice for Spiegel. Jarre still lacked a commitment from Spiegel and had not yet met David Lean.

Jarre's lingering bewilderment was met with another call from Spiegel, from New York. "I have good news," the producer said. "I now have ninety percent of the music. You will write ten percent and do the arrangement." Jarre suddenly looked upon the entire affair as "like a Hitchcock movie." He was not even sure David Lean existed.

"Will I go to New York?" Jarre asked Spiegel.

"No," said Spiegel. His American composer saw no reason to view the film. "He'll just need to see a few scenes."

"Very strange," thought Jarre. Might he ask Spiegel who was this American composer? "Certainly," said Spiegel. "Richard Rodgers."

More weeks pass. "Sam called again," says Jarre. "He said, 'Now we'll see the scene.' It's now mid-September." Spiegel booked a tiny screening room in Berkeley

Production designer John Box and assistant oversee the model that will convert Almeria, Spain, into Aqaba.

Overleaf: The Arab attack on that very Turkish stronghold.

143

chair. Later I learned that's David's way of getting angry."

Finally Lean broke his long dead silence. "Sam, let's stop this rubbish. You take me from the cutting room to play me *this?*"

"Maurice," demanded a short-tempered Spiegel. "Didn't *you* do anything for this movie?"

"I said, 'Sure,'" says Jarre, "and sat down and played what became the theme from *Lawrence of Arabia.* David came over and put his arm on my shoulder and said, 'Sam, this chap here should do the work.'"

The composer did not establish a personal relationship with Lean until after the picture was completed. He would score, arrange, and conduct the music of every film Lean would make thereafter.

The music for *Lawrence* was conducted on a sound stage at Shepperton Studios with the full London Philharmonic Orchestra. Only three microphones were used. Jarre had to sit idly by while Spiegel brought in Sir Adrian Boult to conduct Jarre's score—for full screen credit—when in fact Boult only conducted the overture, which Jarre then had to conduct again, for both the film and the soundtrack recording. (Jarre is billed as the sole conductor on the record, which has the same music as the film; Jarre had to fight Spiegel for this point, as it would have affected his royalty earnings.)

"Sam for some reason wanted Adrian Boult's name on the picture," says Lean, "but it's Maurice's work start to finish."

"Sam with David seemed a constant fight," Jarre recalls. "There was one sequence in *Lawrence,* a quiet night scene in the desert, for which they each wanted a different kind of music. Sam wanted something big and dramatic, but David said, 'No, I want something subtle, to reflect Lawrence's solitude.' I didn't know what to do."

Jarre's solution was to compromise, making the music soft but dramatic. "They both hated it," he distinctly remembers. "Then I

Maurice Jarre, composer and conductor of *Lawrence of Arabia*—and every Lean film since. The director's favorite Jarre score is the one for *Ryan's Daughter;* Jarre thinks, however, that the critics' harping about the overuse of the music in that Irish love story caused Lean to minimalize the score in their next film, *A Passage to India.*

Square, brought in a piano and a pianist. Jarre walked in and there were Spiegel and David Lean.

"First the pianist played Richard Rodgers's Arabian theme," says Jarre. "Really atrocious." He hums a few bars from memory. It sounds like bad Borodin meets *The King and I.* "Next came 'The Love Theme from *Lawrence of Arabia.*'"

This literally took Jarre's breath away. "I said, '*The Love Theme?*' I mean, there was talk that Lawrence was homosexual, but I didn't think this was shown in the film. I looked at David, and he was shrinking in his

did exactly what David wanted, and they fought again. We met about it another three or four times, and each time, Sam was very stubborn."

Eventually, Lean won out. In the final analysis, Jarre believes, the majority of the decisions to reach the screen—in all areas—belonged to Lean.

Lawrence of Arabia held its Royal Invitational Premiere on December 9, 1962, at the Odeon, Leicester Square. In 1988, looking at a photograph taken that evening, of himself bowing before Queen Elizabeth, Lean

points to Her Majesty and says, "She's a dear. Really nice."

The film opened in New York Sunday night, December 16, in the midst of a newspaper strike. Lean, however, still recalls *New York Times* critic Bosley Crowther taking to the radio airwaves to pronounce the film "as devoid of humanity as the parched desert sands it portrays."

Seeing Lean some time afterward at the Cannes Film Festival, Crowther extended the director a cordial hello. "Oh no you don't, Bosley," replied Lean. "Not after what you did."

The Royal Invitational Premiere, London, December 9, 1962. From left: Anthony Quayle (Brighton in the film), O'Toole, Lean, and Queen Elizabeth II. One month later, the epic was missing some footage.

147

Above: February 4, 1989: the epic is restored. At the New York gala premiere, Lean (here with O'Toole and Sharif) told the crowd at the Ziegfeld Theatre, "I hope you like it, and tell your friends to come 'round and see it." They did.

Opposite: After nearly two years of filming *Lawrence* on location, O'Toole said of Lean: "I've never seen a man so in love with the desert."

"Of the new movies," wrote *Life* magazine's Peter Bunzel for the 1962 year-end issue, "the most ambitious is *Lawrence of Arabia* directed by David Lean. It is a film of visual splendor—perhaps the most beautiful ever made. In one memory-burnishing sequence, heat waves rising from the desert make an oncoming camel-rider look like a squiggly mirage, then like an eerie specter skithering just off the ground. This phenomenon alone is worth the unusually high admission prices." (Spiegel set the *Lawrence* ticket at a then-record four dollars and eighty cents. His film cost thirteen million dollars.) The *Life* critic had one small carp (it was one of Crowther's largest). "At three hours and forty minutes," wrote Bunzel, "the film is too long."

"I remember walking up Fifth Avenue with David Selznick after *Lawrence* opened," recalls Lean. "He said, 'David, they're going to be at you to cut it. It's

exactly the same length as *Gone With the Wind,* and they were after me to cut that.' His final advice was, 'Don't do it.'"

In fact, Lean's film ran but one minute less than Selznick's 1939 Civil War epic, and this did prompt a request from Spiegel.

As Lean tells it, "Sam came to me and said, 'Look, baby, the film isn't doing well. It's performing all right in the cities, but outside, in the small towns, it's dying.' And I remember going with Sam into the projection booth of the theatre and my taking out ten minutes."

The deed must have been carried out the first week in January 1963, because on the ninth of that month, the *Evening News* reported that the public was being deprived of seeing the same film the Queen witnessed at the premiere. Lean was quoted as he left the airport for Paris, "I would defy anyone to spot where [the cuts] have taken place." Still, so great was the protest raised by the newspaper that Spiegel claimed in *Variety* that the shortened version would not run in London, only in America. What Spiegel failed to acknowledge—even to Lean—was that on top of the ten minutes approved and removed by the director, Spiegel had excised another ten.

For the 1971 rerelease, Spiegel made his most persuasive plea yet. "Sam told me," says Lean, " 'Look, baby, maybe if you take some more out of it, then maybe, maybe you can see some money.'" Lean obliged, although he was not to see a royalty check for *Lawrence* until 1978. By that time, the film was forty minutes shorter than the version seen by Queen Elizabeth.

In 1987, American restoration experts Bob Harris and Jim Painten (Harris helped to resurrect Abel Gance's hacked-up 1927 masterpiece *Napoleon*) set their sights on the missing footage from *Lawrence.* Gone was the shot of eye-goggles dangling from a tree branch after the motorbike crash, the first bit of dialogue in the picture (Colonel Brighton's remark questioning the propriety of burying Lawrence in St. Paul's), the build-up heralding Lawrence's arrival in Auda's tent, and numerous verbal exchanges regarding the motives of Lawrence between Feisal and Lawrence, Feisal and Bentley, Lawrence and his servants, and Allenby and Brighton. In particular, the second half of the picture was lacking coherence.

As the revival project was launched, Harris contacted Lean, Columbia Pictures, and the Spiegel estate. International film archives were combed, and the original negative finally turned up at the Technicolor lab in London. According to Harris, the negative looked to have very little life left, and some of the voice track had been destroyed.

Peter O'Toole, Alec Guinness (Feisal), and Charles Gray (who earlier had dubbed Jack Hawkins's voice once the actor, now deceased, had developed throat cancer; Hawkins played Allenby) met with Lean in a London recording studio in April 1988. "It was quite a sight," says Lean. "Peter walked right up to the screen so he could see how his lips moved, then walked back to the mike to recite dialogue perfectly." Arthur Kennedy redid some of his Jackson Bentley in a television station in Savannah, Georgia, the town where he lives, and Anthony Quinn (Auda Abu Tayi) ran through his lines in a New York sound studio.

In May 1988, introducing the by now totally complete *Lawrence* with its improved soundtrack—Lean hesitated over the new (to him) word "Dolby"—to a private audience of Columbia Studios staff and invited guests at the Samuel Goldwyn Theatre of the Motion Picture Academy in Beverly Hills, Lean voiced two regrets.

The first was that "the rats had gotten at the film" to begin with. The second was, "I'm sorry that my old sparring partner Sam Spiegel isn't here. Because, if he were, I'm sure he'd say, 'Baby, if only you could take out a few minutes, for the television version. . . .'"

Sam Spiegel suffered a fatal heart attack on New Year's Eve, 1985.

"I got a letter from David when Sam died," says Betty Spiegel. "It was a short letter, because David doesn't waste his words, and it said, 'I think we had the best years of our friend.'

"We did," she comments. "Certainly in terms of projects, David had the best of Sam. And I had it, in terms of age and fun and laughter and health. But David had some of that, too. I heard Sam remark once, when it came to having fun, he had laughed the most with David."

On April 8, 1963, at the Santa Monica Civic Auditorium in California, *Lawrence of Arabia* repeated the feat of *The Bridge on the River Kwai* by winning seven Academy Awards, including Lean's for Best Director and Spiegel's for Best Picture. (Lean had already won the Screen Directors Guild Award for *Lawrence* on February 9.)

In a letter from the Beverly Hills Hotel dated April 17, Lean recounted portions of the celebratory evening for John Box, who had won an Oscar for his art direction while remaining in England. Lean said that the film's snapping up of the early technical awards served as a fair tip-off that the night might go their way, although he felt badly for nominees Peter O'Toole and Omar Sharif, the latter in particular, whom Lean was watching the moment the supporting actor winner was announced—Ed Begley, in *Sweet Bird of Youth.* (O'Toole, not in attendance due to his starring in a London stage production of Brecht's *Baal,* lost to Gregory Peck in *To Kill a Mockingbird.*)

Joan Crawford presented Lean his golden statuette, and he thanked the audience by saying, "This limey is deeply touched and greatly honored."

"They've always been very generous to me here," Lean says in 1988, sitting in a hotel suite in Bel-Air. "Really," he emphasizes, "very kind." Had he ever wanted to make a picture in Hollywood? "The opportunity never came up," he says, "except that time I directed Claude [Rains] as Herod."

The week after winning his Oscar, Lean stepped in to direct "some glorified second-unit stuff" for George Stevens's arduous biblical production for United Artists, *The Greatest Story Ever Told.* In the letter to Box, Lean related, "Poor old George Stevens is in the usual trouble with budget and pressure and I found out he was in a terrible state because he was in a position where he had to hand over some dialogue scenes to a second unit or not shoot them at all. It was suggested, by Fred Zinnemann, that perhaps I

RUSSIA
Doctor Zhivago (1965)

could help him out and he said he wouldn't dream of asking but, oh, how wonderful it would be, etc. So I volunteered as sort of a return gesture to the directors.

"I'm doing it for minimum rates for a second director and handing it over to the Directors fund for widows. They are scenes with the old Herod (Claude Rains has volunteered!) and the young Herod (Jo Ferrer was already in the picture), so I am with at least a couple of old pals. [Ferrer played the Turkish Bey in *Lawrence.*] Will take me about a week and I am about as lost as I could be with an enormous bloody set and no ideas yet as to where to move the actors or put the camera. George is shooting out in the wastes of Nevada somewhere and I sit in

Above: John Box's early sketch for the hideaway at Varykino.

Opposite: The infidels Lara (Julie Christie) and Zhivago (Omar Sharif). "The trick," says Lean, "was in not having the audience condemn the lovers."

151

Locations were scouted in Finland and Yugoslavia before Lean chose Spain for the bulk of filming. Here, Finland simulates Siberia.

"I've had so many things offered to me but most of it doesn't appeal," Lean communicated to Box. "The current idea which is tickling me is *Doctor Zhivago.* [Producer Carlo] Ponti owns it and is very keen for me to do it. I read a very well done thirty-page synopsis and have just started on the book itself. It's very long and covers many years with the usual snags, but it's wonderfully written with great compassion and understanding for human beings. Best bit of writing I've read for I don't know how long. I like it because of its humanity. Enormous understanding for the passions, affections, and heartbreaks. Think I'm just about ready to tackle something like it. It's so beautifully done and so *true.* That's the great thing. Truth. I find I just can't take and am no longer attracted by the phony-for-dramatic reasons which I once was. Not badly, but I was. That's one of the great things about *Lawrence.* I think it notched us up a few standards.

"Wish you would read it—if you haven't," Lean concluded to Box about *Zhivago.* "Not for your opinion, but because I think you'll find Mr. Pasternak ringing all sorts of bells which you've only tinkled for yourself."

According to Pasternak's biographer, Ronald Hingley, "Toward the end of his threescore years and ten (1890–1960), the Russian poet Boris Leonidovich Pasternak emerged as the author of a renowned novel with a poet as its hero: *Doctor Zhivago.* He also became an important figure on the international political stage." Pasternak's sprawling portrait of war and the revolution in his native "martyred, headstrong, crackbrained, lunatic country"—and how those times affected a particular poet-doctor struggling with his own romantic nature—was originally announced for publication in 1954, then suppressed. The Soviet government found it, in the words of the official organ of the Writers Union, *Lit-*

his huge office plus madly efficient secretary, private dining room built by DeMille as designed as sort of Bounty dining saloon, and technicians and people I know only by screen credits. It's being shot in Panavision with an extra squeeze and will be shown in Cinerama. I'm mad, aren't I?"

Lean has never seen the finished *Greatest Story Ever Told*—which proved one of the great sanctimonious turkeys of all time, and, at four hours and twenty minutes, surely the longest.

The question still remained of what the director who had won Oscars his past two times at bat would undertake as his next assignment.

eraturnaya gazeta, "full of hatred of Socialism" and a "carefully thought-out ideological diversion." The manuscript was smuggled out of the country.

"*Doctor Zhivago* was first published in Milan in 1957," wrote Hingley, "and it helped to earn its author the offer, which came from Stockholm the following year, of the Nobel Prize for Literature. The announcement of the award, followed in quick succession by Pasternak's enthusiastic acceptance and sudden renunciation of it, provoked a global drama in which he figured as the hero and the Kremlin (except in its own version) as the villain." The biographer suggests that never before "in the whole history of literature" had there been "such a worldwide public stir."

The Milanese publisher, Giangiacomo Feltrinelli, sold the film rights to the Italian producer Carlo Ponti, who approached Lean with the project the week of the Oscars. On April 18, 1963, Ponti was quoted in *The Daily Telegraph* as saying, "We have just begun to work on the film. There are a lot of details to be worked out. For instance, we still have to decide who will do the screenplay."

Ponti did not name a director, but he did express hope that he would be allowed to film some scenes in Russia, given that since the book was published widely in the West—in twenty-eight languages, including Russian (by the University of Michigan)— the Soviet government might consider a movie version an inevitability. Ponti reasoned, therefore, that if *Zhivago* were filmed in its backyard, the Kremlin could possibly attempt to exert some control. (This was never to be. As it also happened, *Doctor Zhivago* was not to be published in the Soviet Union until January 1988, thanks largely to Mikhail Gorbachev's policy of *glasnost.* By then, the Lean film version— loudly denounced by Soviet officials at the time of its release—had yet to be screened in the U.S.S.R., although that ban also ap-

peared to be easing. In 1987, however, Lean was invited to the Moscow Film Festival, its officials informing him that they would be happy to show "any" of his films. "That's easy," he told them, "*Zhivago.*" Lean says, "They sort of stuttered and stammered, then said, 'We're afraid that's impossible. We plan to do our own version, you see.'" Another commitment preempted Lean's visit to the festival.)

In May of 1963, Lean set sail for Europe aboard the *Leonardo da Vinci,* his copy of *Doctor Zhivago* in hand. Reading it on the voyage, he recalls, "I was deeply touched, in tears, really."

Thus inspired, Lean demanded one final prerequisite from Ponti, who visited Lean at his hotel in Madrid that summer.

"Look here," Lean warned Ponti, "I know all about movie producers. If I should find that you have so much as *one finger* in the till, then that will be the end of it. I'll walk off the picture." As a gleeful postscript, Lean adds, "Next time I saw him . . . was the premiere."

"The story of *Doctor Zhivago* is very simple," says Lean. "A man is married to one woman and in love with another. The trick was in not having the audience condemn the lovers."

The central character of the story is the poet-surgeon Yuri Zhivago, idealistic in his art yet pragmatic in his profession. Orphaned as a child, he is sent to live with his mother's sister and her well-to-do family in Moscow, where he studies medicine. Following his schooling, Zhivago marries his cousin Tonya, though he is fascinated by the mysterious young woman Lara, herself engaged to the obstreperous student revolutionary Pasha. Fate, in the forms of World War I and then the Russian Revolution, plays each character a different hand. Zhivago is conscripted into medical military service, where he serves with Lara, now an army nurse. Her husband has since disap-

On the main Moscow set. Lean's hand-picked cast played the parts of, from left, Tonya, Lara, Pasha, Yevgraf, Gromeko, Zhivago, and Komarovsky.

whom Pasternak created as Zhivago's common-law wife.

Elsewhere in the book, Lara has an affair at age sixteen with her mother's lover, the corrupt lawyer Victor Komarovsky. The mother attempts suicide, which Lara and Komarovsky are ready to accept, as it means that their secret will die with her. Three years later, Lara goes after Komarovsky with a gun, to extract money from him. In Lean and screenwriter Robert Bolt's final version, Lara fears her mother's death, and her brandishing a pistol at Komarovsky not long after the suicide attempt is in Lara's defense of her own honor.

"I remember the first time Robert brought me his script," says Lean. "I said, 'Look here, Robert. It's no good. You've made Lara an absolute bitch.' And he said, 'Well, some people like that.'"

Bolt had another go at it.

"If you took the novel *Doctor Zhivago* as it stands and treated it as a shooting script incident by incident," says Bolt, "the resulting film would run at least sixty hours. Therefore, in the film you can only have one-twentieth of the book." This requirement, Bolt explains, entails turning the film "into something not merely shorter, but quite different. You have to take in and digest the whole work to your own satisfaction and then say, 'Well, the significant things, the mountain peaks that emerge from this vast panorama, are such-and-such incidents — moral points, political points, emotional points. And those are all I can deal with in dramatic form.' Another point is that you cannot take your dialogue from the novel to any extent. The characters have to become your characters — you make them your own, make them speak as you would have them speak."

In their four months scouting locations for *Zhivago,* David Lean and John Box traveled ten thousand miles by car. The journey began in Scandinavia, and the two were un-

peared, though he is to resurface during the Revolution as one of his country's more militant radical leaders. Zhivago's marriage disintegrates, not solely because of the ravages of the postwar Russia — Tonya eventually escapes to Paris with her father and Zhivago's two children — but because of Zhivago's affair with Lara. For the two lovers, life does not end happily. Zhivago, long since parted from Lara, suffers a fatal heart attack on a Moscow street, while Lara ends her joyless days in a Soviet workcamp.

To make the characters in the film more palatable than they appear in the novel, some of their individual traits are softened. The movie's Zhivago is less peevish than he is in the novel; likewise, the scenario drops the hero's third major affair, with Marina,

questionably sold on Finland until they learned that they would not be able to find available screen extras there, as no unemployment existed. Another stop was Yugoslavia.

"After a few days, we were thrown out of our hotel to make way for a Third World conference," says Box, who also remembers "prostitutes being brought in for these conferees. With all that free lust available, none of them would go home. David was furious." Upon leaving Yugoslavia, Lean declared he would give a free vacation to anyone who could shoot a movie in a Communist country. (In 1988, Lean was similarly disillusioned by Cuba, which he had hoped might supply the backdrop for *Nostromo*. "It was awful," Lean says of Havana. "The phones don't work, and we didn't know until half an hour before we left whether there would be a flight out of there.")

Box took one last look at Belgrade, this time in the winter, "to see," he says, "if we could shoot in the snow." It was obvious that they could not. "If we did," says Box in 1988, "we'd still be shooting."

It was decided to build the whole Russian

Moscow's "Street of the Elite," before the Revolution. John Box prepared it for eighteen months.

capital in the small Madrid suburb of Canillas. "Moscow recreated by John Box, after eighteen months of documentation, has two main streets: the Street of the Elite and the Street of the Poor," wrote Violette Leduc in *Vogue* magazine, September 15, 1965. "It can be seen from a long way off when one arrives by car, it is pale grey, it is so peaceful in the landscape, the snow on its roofs is as fine as tulle, as soft as flour."

Wandering in the shadow of three immense poster likenesses of Lenin, Marx, and Trotsky, the French journalist, a pro-

tégée of Simone de Beauvoir, reported (in the manner of a Russian poet): "The wind was blowing, the sun gave out no warmth, the revolution was becoming organized, Zhivago was no longer living in a palace but in a wreck of a palace. The snow which is no longer falling, which did not melt, was at once realistic and comforting . . . a desert padded with soft white cotton."

Two weeks' filming was done in Finland, the lumber town of Joensuu, four hundred miles north of Helsinki; Laplanders were imported to play Siberian refugees. Here

Lean shot the movie's epic train sequence along what was actually the winter railway that had been laid during the 1940 Russian invasion of Finland. Thirty-two state-owned freight cars were pulled by two wood-burning engines, as Lean's crew tooled about on bulldozers and motorized snow sledges.

"The rest," says Lean, "was done in Spain, except for some second-unit work in Canada." That singular shot can be quickly seen at the outset of the film's Part II, the first glimpse of a mountain as the train races out of a tunnel.

The film's well-known "Ice Palace," the house in Varykino where Zhivago and Lara seek final refuge before being forced to separate (and where Zhivago writes his love poem to Lara), took on several shapes in John Box's design sketches before he arrived at a final solution.

"David was in a meeting," says Box, "and I remember my interrupting to go in and show him this Russian stamp I had found. There it was, in the illustration, the house at Varykino."

Erected in the Spanish mountain region near Soria three hours' drive north of Madrid, the gingerbread wooden structure was draped with snow—of the white plaster variety—as a means to mold the genuine substance once the winter snow fell. The house went up in September, then Lean and company patiently awaited the delivery from the skies. And they waited.

Cinematographer Freddie Young remembers, "It was supposed to be the coldest spot in Spain. In preparation, we whitewashed all the trees and hedges within sight." Still not a flake.

"By March," says Box, "a real panic set in. It snowed, but it wasn't deep enough."

"Warmest winter they ever had," chimes in Lean.

"We had to use white marble dust," says Box. "Bob O'Brien, president of M-G-M, came to Spain. David was very apologetic."

O'Brien told Lean not to worry; the rushes spoke for themselves. The only issue raised by O'Brien was whether Lean might possibly have the film finished earlier than expected.

"Impossible," said Lean.

Zhivago was slated to premiere in March 1966, and the whole of the production had revolved around that deadline. (By shooting's end, Lean would have in excess of thirty-one hours of film to whittle down to three hours and twelve minutes.) O'Brien, with his eye on the Oscars he foresaw for the film, had theatres in New York and Los Angeles available the week of December 20 of that year (1965, and it was already March). The studio president made both facts evident to Lean, who stood by his first reaction, "Impossible."

Twenty minutes later, Box vividly recalls, "David came back. 'All right, Bob,' he said. 'We'll do it.'"

"Damn it, I'm going to use Omar," decided Lean. "He's easy to work with." M-G-M wanted Paul Newman.

159

Above: The "Ice Palace" at Varykino; paint and marble dust for snow.

Opposite: A scene of seduction: Rod Steiger and Julie Christie. The same year as *Zhivago*, she epitomized the swinging sixties in *Darling*, and won the Oscar.

Doctor Zhivago premiered at the Capitol Theatre in New York on December 22, 1965.

Critics compared the eerie, shimmering rooms of the "Ice Palace" to Miss Havisham's cobwebbed sanctuary at Satis House in Lean's *Great Expectations.* John Box says that the image could have been lodged somewhere in the back of his mind, as he clearly admired that design. "The inspiration for the interior of the Ice Palace was, in fact, a photograph I'd seen of Scott in the Antarctic, of him dead in this room, with a hole in the roof where the snow came in," he explains.

To achieve the frosted look inside the house, Box says, "Eddie Fowlie went 'round with a bucket of wax and flung it, and I followed him with cold water."

"Eddie Fowlie," says Lean, "began as my prop man on *Bridge on the River Kwai.* I don't know who hired him, but I remember it was so tremendously hot working in Ceylon, where the bridge was crossing a river valley that had no wind, that at the end of each finished shot, no matter how many takes we did, I'd always give ten minutes for everyone to go into the river."

Rising to the surface after one such plunge, Lean found himself face to face with this Eddie Fowlie, who termed their frolic "bloody millionaire stuff." Says Lean, "He's been with me ever since."

In fact, Fowlie's life is tied inexorably to Lean's films. That was his girlfriend's picture that adorns Saito's calendar in the colonel's hut in *Kwai* ("David was most intrigued by that," recalls Geoffrey Horne), and another of his girlfriends fell down the slop hole in the middle of the desert in *Lawrence.* Fowlie would later meet his wife, Kathleen, in Ireland during the making of *Ryan's Daughter,* and the couple settled in Almeria, Spain, where Fowlie remained ever since he first herded camels through the area for *Lawrence.* Fowlie is also responsible for having found, among other locales, a proper facsimile of E. M. Forster's fictive Marabar Caves in *A Passage to India,* the Central American backdrop for *Nostromo* (Almeria), and the photogenic Irish wooded glen—complete with bluebells— where Rosy and her soldier have their tryst in *Ryan's Daughter.*

"There was something extra in my pay envelope that week," Fowlie says of that last accomplishment, "because David was all set to pick up the company and move from Ireland to New Zealand."

"In movies," says Lean, "you go to places no tourist would ever go. I remember sitting next to someone while I was watching *Zhivago* and my saying, in an astonished voice, 'I was there.'"

160

Above: Rita Tushingham (daughter of Lara and Zhivago) and Alec Guinness (Zhivago's half-brother). The search of her background opens and closes the story.

Opposite: Sharif as Zhivago, once Russia's military struggle is to close.

Fowlie, listening to his friend tell these stories, blurts out in his cockney accent, "bloody millionaire stuff."

Doctor Zhivago was photographed in thirty-five millimeter, then blown up to seventy for its roadshow engagements. This was done as a budgetary consideration, and while Lean thinks the M-G-M lab did "a wonderful job," he regrets not shooting in seventy (actually, he reminds you, one shoots in sixty-

five, with the remaining five millimeters for soundtrack). The film's first cinematographer was Nicolas Roeg, who had served as second-unit photographer on *Lawrence.*

"I like Nick very much," says Lean (Roeg has since gone on to become a director in his own right), "but after two weeks I wasn't getting what I wanted."

Lean sat down with Roeg, assured him that no other cinematographer had been approached for the job, and the men parted ways. The director turned again to Freddie Young.

"*Zhivago* was my favorite film," says Young. "It gave me more things to do photographically than any other picture, like that scene in the house with Julie Christie [Lara], when her mother is ill, with Rod Steiger [Komarovsky] there. We had one shot where you would see him go past windows at night, and out into the solarium off into the snow. That was very difficult photographically, but absorbing to do when you've something exciting like that."

Much of *Zhivago* seems to have been shot through glass panes: Lara's boyfriend Pasha reading a letter from her, Zhivago studying germs through a microscope's lens, his looking through a window for signs of a winter thaw, a candle burning in the window on a Moscow street as Zhivago and his fiancée, Tonya, ride by in a sleigh. Lean recalls when he first started at Gaumont-British—where Freddie Young at the age of seventeen had also gotten his start, as a lab technician—he wandered into what appeared to be an abandoned structure.

"I remember this one studio was completely glass," Lean says. "That's what they did in the early days, they used the daylight to get exposure on the film. Then, when the lamps came in and got more refined, they painted over the glass with black paint. The weather had taken off some of it and so it had the most extraordinary effect. I remember looking up at it through the chinks, the bits of glass and sky."

Through a window pane: Komarovsky (Rod Steiger) is about to inform Lara (Julie Christie) that her mother's life has been saved.

George Cukor. He never looked through the camera. John Ford never looked through the camera.

"David looked through the camera."

Omar Sharif concurs. "With David, you would spend a great deal of time mapping out every movement and inflection. We never shot a scene the first day on a new set. We'd have tea in his caravan and discuss things, then he'd walk it over with the actors." The final step, Sharif says, "was for David to take out his viewfinder and figure out what shot he would make."

Sharif came to *Zhivago* after some behind-the-scenes negotiations between Lean and M-G-M. "Very difficult, casting," says Lean. "In general it always is. For *Zhivago* the great difficulty was that the main character is not very interesting."

Lean's original choice for the role of the doctor-poet was Peter O'Toole. A friend of the actor says that O'Toole was not prepared to endure the rigors of filming with Lean so soon after *Lawrence*—or possibly ever again. ("I'll bet," comments Katharine Hepburn.) O'Toole and Lean were not to speak again until 1988.

As it became evident that *Zhivago* was going to be a large investment (the picture's budget rose from five million dollars, to eight million, to eleven million, to, eventually fifteen million dollars), M-G-M recommended that Lean cast box-office names in the major roles. "The studio came up with all sorts of ideas," remembers Lean. "Paul Newman had just played a Nobel-winning writer in something called *The Prize,* so he was suggested for Zhivago. They said, 'Look, he can play a writer.'" Lean is still laughing. No small hint was given by M-G-M president Robert O'Brien that producer Carlo Ponti's actress-wife, Sophia Loren, be given the role of Lara. Lean delivered the message that he would cast her in the part "providing you can convince me she can play a seventeen-year-old virgin."

"Finally," Lean says, "I received a phone

"The thing I remember most," says Young of shooting *Zhivago,* "was the incident with the daffodils. The windows in the house [where Zhivago spent the winter with his wife] were all frosted up, and we took a pane of glass and put it in the icebox until it froze over, with all these frozen crystals on it. Then we rubbed a little patch away, and gradually the heat melted away a little pattern . . . and we saw a sea of daffodils."

Young—who has been billed on screen as Fred A. Young, F. A. Young, and Freddie Young—says, "I love working with David because he's one hundred percent behind me whatever I would try to be doing pictorially. Where another director would say, 'Oh, to hell with that, let's get on with it,' that is something I never heard from David. And I've worked with some great directors.

call in Madrid from Bob O'Brien, and he said, 'David, cast whoever you want in the picture.' And I thought, 'Damn it, I'm going to use Omar. He's easy to work with.'"

"I don't know what was going on with the studio," says Sharif, "but from my end of it, when I'd heard that David was going to do *Doctor Zhivago* I was doing a film in Yugoslavia called *Gengis Khan,* and I read [Pasternak's] book to see if there would be a suitable part for me. As an Egyptian I didn't think I'd be asked to play a Russian."

Sharif found such a part, the idealistic student who turns rabid revolutionary, a role that finally went to Tom Courtenay. Sharif informed his agent.

"I remember sitting in the lobby of the Hotel Metropole in Belgrade," says Sharif, "playing chess with Telly Savalas, and my agent called. He said, 'They've not offered you the part of the revolutionary.'"

Sharif's heart sank.

"They've offered you the title role."

Sharif spent two months preparing for *Zhivago.* During the shoot a surgeon was dispatched to instruct him in sewing medical stitches. This way he could pass for a physician. But could he look Russian?

"It was sort of a stretch," says Lean, "but in that part of the world, well, he could have been Manchurian. So we pulled his eyes back with tape, to take the orbs out of it, though Omar still has those large orbs. The critics liked making something of that. And we straightened his hair. Sort of made it look like mine."

"I wasn't aware of that," Sharif says about resembling his director. "But if you've seen photos of Pasternak, that's how he wore his hair. I also increased my forehead one inch, by waxing away my hairline."

For a key scene, Zhivago's politicization once he witnesses from a Moscow balcony the mowing down of protesting workers by the czar's horsemen, Lean repeated the device he used in *Great Expectations,* when Pip

peers out of Jaggers's office to view the public hangings in the square below. Rather than display the violence, Lean cuts to reaction shots of his protagonists.

"In preparation for that scene," says Sharif, "David told me to think of being in bed with a woman and making love to her." Sharif's face, Lean instructed him, was to look as it would "just before orgasm."

Shooting lasted from December 28, 1964, to October 7, 1965. "Nine months," notes Sharif. "It wasn't as rugged as shooting *Lawrence*—nor as long—because we were in Spain as opposed to the desert. I mean, we were in a small town in Spain, but at least there were restaurants."

Echoing Katharine Hepburn's first reaction to meeting David Lean, Julie Christie,

Tonya (Geraldine Chaplin) returns from her studies in Paris. She, too, peers through a window, a recurrent motif in the film.

who played Lara, calls him "a very endearing man." When Lean cast her for the female lead she was known only as an up-and-coming intense new actress. What sold him was her entrance in the 1963 film *Billy Liar*—"swinging her purse," he recalls.

"I remember an atmosphere of kindness and reassuringness," she says of working with Lean, "and, above all, David's ability to alleviate my fears by demanding clear and specific acting tasks of me."

Comparing Lean to filmmakers with whom she has worked before and since, Christie says, "David's presence on *Zhivago* was more paternalistic than that of many directors. The whole vision of the film was in *his* head, and he used us [actors] like colors on his painting.

"This," she adds, "admirably suited the very insecure young actress I was. I was never unsure of what he wanted, and I always *understood* what he wanted, which I've not always been able to do with other directors. When I couldn't come up with what he asked, he found a way of getting me to alter the emphasis to his satisfaction.

"The only time David's paternalism did not suit me was when I wanted to go off exploring Spain during a week or two when I wasn't needed. But he wanted to keep us under his wing, *in case*. Then I retreated like a sulky schoolgirl."

Rita Tushingham, who played the grown-up daughter of Zhivago and Lara, does not remember Lean ever displaying his temper. "The only thing was," she recalls, "most of us in the cast were so young, and youth is like cackling hens. David liked an air of concentration, and he feared we sometimes lacked that."

Others in the cast included such veterans as Siobhan McKenna, Ralph Richardson (working with Lean for the first time since *The Sound Barrier*), and Alec Guinness, who played Zhivago's half-brother.

Tushingham recalls laughing a lot with Guinness. "He loved to joke," she says, "and

he found humor in a lot of things." Of the others, Tushingham says, "Ralph Richardson had a parrot. It used to sit on his bed. He also had a hamster, or maybe it was a guinea pig. Whatever it was, the hotel got very upset because it ate its way under the carpet."

For the role of Zhivago's wife Tonya, Lean cast Geraldine Chaplin, the twenty-one-year-old daughter of Charlie Chaplin and Oona O'Neill and the granddaughter of Eugene O'Neill. Because of her celebrated bloodlines, Chaplin received the lion's share of the film's advance publicity—much to the displeasure of some of the other actors, according to a 1965 article in *Esquire* by Helen Lawrenson, who visited the set.

"I really can't remember," says Christie, looking back. "Because I had no scenes with Geraldine I never got to know her well."

What Christie does recall, "above all," she says, is that "I felt *safe*—safe with David at a time when I was particularly vulnerable. I also felt a closeness based on paternalism, and a kind of wistfulness in his character, which, he being so successful, was rather appealing.

"I felt he really did care for me, but that may be part of David's charm—to make people, particularly women, feel that."

"*Doctor Zhivago* got the most terrible reviews," says Lean, "worldwide, which people tend to forget now." Lean does not. "*Newsweek* said it had 'cheapjack sets' and 'pallid photography,'" he recites by heart, "and the sets and photography are precisely what won the Oscars."

Zhivago won a total of six Academy Awards, although the major awards went to another picture. "*The Sound of Music*," says Lean, "completely shut us out." The sugary musical won five Oscars, including those for Best Picture and Best Director, Robert Wise.

"Willy Wyler rang me up when the nominations came out," says Lean, "and said,

'You're not going to win it this time.' I said, 'I don't think so, either, but why do you think?' And Willy said, 'Because they never give it to you three times in a row.'"

Far more alarming, Lean underscores, were the reviews. "I remember the premiere in New York," he says, "a big dinner atop one of the grand hotels there, and I said, 'Why is everyone reading newspapers?' Then they told me. Everybody was reading the notices."

Judith Crist, one of the most influential New York critics of the time, wrote in *The Herald Tribune,* "It is merely spectacular soap opera, declaring that love and revolution make gloomy bedfellows."

Lean was crushed. At the premiere party, he says, "People sort of shook my hand and said, 'Well, David, *I* liked it,' that sort of thing. But nothing helped. The film was a disaster.

"Then I tell you what happened. Bob O'Brien, the boss, said, 'David, I think it is a very good picture, and I am going to spend another million dollars to advertise it.' And he did. The first week, you could have thrown rocks around the theatre and not hurt anybody; the second week, still completely empty; third week, business started to increase; and by the fourth week it was packed."

No small part of the draw was Maurice Jarre's "Lara's Theme," which the composer was forced to write hurriedly for the film once it was learned that the ancient Russian folk song Lean and everyone else had thought was in the public domain was, in fact, "not an old song at all," says Jarre. "Suddenly we were at it again, writing a score in September for a film that was going to open in December."

"We really took off with *Doctor Zhivago,*" says Lean. "It made more money than all my other films put together."

Doctor Zhivago has grossed more than two hundred million dollars worldwide. With the inflation rate taken into considera-

The New York premiere, December 22, 1965. With Lean are his wife, Leila, and the president of M-G-M, Robert H. O'Brien.

tion, it is outranked in the earnings game only slightly by *Gone With the Wind, The Sound of Music, E.T.,* and *Star Wars.* While this success provided Lean with a princely income to match his already princely life style, it also, apparently in some quarters, diminished his critical reputation, especially in his native England.

One need only cite—as Lean has—*Halliwell's Filmgoer's Companion,* a British publication, which begrudgingly admits Lean to its own Hall of Fame "for his understanding of the art of cinema, despite his final submergence of his sensitive talent in pretentious but empty spectaculars."

"What was I supposed to do," Lean wonders after reading the snub, "stop after *Great Expectations*?"

IRELAND
Ryan's Daughter (1970)

"There are so many staggering stories of that time in Ireland," says Sarah Miles, wavering between coyness and total candor in her recollections of starring in the original love story written by Robert Bolt and directed by Lean. "*Ryan's Daughter* wasn't just a movie," she says, "it was a way of life."

Told that Miles has related colorful stories about what is already a touchy subject, Lean, with a combination of abiding patience and dread, remarks, "Knowing Sarah, I am not the least bit surprised."

"When they were casting *Doctor Zhivago*," says Miles, who made her film debut in 1962 as the nymphet student who seduces Laurence Olivier in *Term of Trial,* "I'd never met David Lean or Robert Bolt, but later I learned that David had said to Robert, 'I think we ought to cast Sarah Miles. She'd be perfect. She does it all with her eyes.'"

The role was that of Zhivago's mistress, and Bolt adamantly opposed Lean's recommendation. "Robert," says Miles, "told David, 'No, no, no. She's just a North Country slut.' Then David said to Robert, 'No, you're wrong. You've just seen her films and believed her publicity.'"

Miles never received so much as a screen test for *Zhivago*. By the time she finally met David Lean, she was Mrs. Robert Bolt.

In 1968, David Lean was vacationing in Naples and Capri when he received from Bolt a script based on Flaubert's *Madame Bovary*. Lean did not care for it, and wrote Bolt a single-spaced, twelve-page letter explaining his reasons. He also said that with a good deal of reworking, and perhaps a change of setting to a more challenging backdrop, say India or Ireland, some sort of film might be possible.

The two men worked together in Rome the better part of a year. Anthony Havelock-Allan, Lean's producer from two decades before, "was also there at the time. He had just finished producing [Franco] Zeffirelli's

Above: The illicit lovers, Rosy Ryan (Sarah Miles) and British Major Doryan (Christopher Jones).

Opposite: On the schoolhouse set, Robert Mitchum, Lean, and Freddie Young, the cinematographer.

Romeo and Juliet with John Brabourne," says Lean, "and he showed me the rough cut." Lean in turn showed Havelock-Allan his and Bolt's work-in-progress. "I asked if he would like to come on it," says Lean, "and that is how he came to produce *Ryan's Daughter.*"

In that draft, then called *Michael's Day*, Michael served as the centerpiece of the story, which Bolt and Lean decided would be set in 1916 Ireland at the time of its "troubles." Michael is the village idiot in the tiny town of Kerry and ironically the only one who ever knows what is actually going on there. As this threw off the balance of the film, Lean and Bolt changed the focus to

169

Rosy, the daughter of town publican Thomas Ryan.

Viewing the finished film, one can still see the grounding in *Bovary*, insofar as the structural sense and characters are concerned: a young heroine who pays for her capriciousness (Emma Bovary poisons herself, while Rosy Ryan is publicly stripped and shorn); a learned but ineffectual husband named Charles (Charles Bovary is a medical doctor while Charles Shaughnessy is, as Bolt himself had been, a schoolmaster); and a virile lover who is the fulfillment of the heroine's fantasies (Flaubert's *Rodolphe* Boulanger and Bolt's Major *Randolph* Dorian). There are also good-natured and self-indulgent fathers (Emma's is a farmer) as well as red-faced priests (Emma's watcher is the athletic Father Bournisien, while Rosy has the whiskey-soaked Father Collins); and, in both *Madame Bovary* and *Ryan's Daughter*, consummation of the illicit affair between heroine and lover takes place in a misty forest among flowers and ferns. Finally, as was the case with Emma Bovary, it is somewhat difficult for the observer to sympathize with Rosy Ryan.

"I deliberately wrote the part of Rosy so that she had no confidante, nobody to whom she could talk—which meant that she couldn't talk to the audience," says Bolt. "You simply have to watch her sweating it out herself, and this is where an actress has to be able to convey a kaleidoscope of emotions."

He counts as these emotions, "First, the unreal adolescent idealization of the man she married. Then, the half-mature realization that he was not the man she had insisted upon his being, and, with that, the determination to see it through as a decent wife. Then, the cataclysmic impact of primitive sexuality, and finally the full mature realization that decency, simple decency, and her legitimate desires simply would not square, and that somehow she had got to come to some arrangement with herself."

"Poor old *Ryan's Daughter*," laments Lean. "The critics never caught on that it was really *Madame Bovary*."

Lean built his fictitious village of Kerry in Dingle, the farthest western point in Ireland—and, in 1927, the first land spotted by Lindbergh after he had crossed the Atlantic. Lean and his production designer, Stephen Grimes (John Box had temporarily abandoned his sketchbook in favor of a film producer's budget sheets), constructed the entire village from scratch.

"It was cheaper that way," says Lean. "To find a village of the period in the first place is next door to impossible. And then add to that a village in a desolate spot. Also, in a

Top: Stephen Grimes's sketch for Kerry's main street.

Above: Set under construction.

Opposite: The gathering storm.

171

"David's got a bit of a mean streak in him," says Sarah Miles. "I'm glad I never saw any of it."

real village, the shopkeepers want payments." That was true in Venice on *Summertime.*

Another cause for apprehension by Lean was "tourists." "If you own your own village, you see, you keep people out and run it like a studio. You arrange your own time, and time is money. Also you can pull it all about. The schoolhouse in *Ryan's Daughter* was built on a huge concrete raft, with walls as floaters so that you could pull them in and out to get the cameras and lights in. Same thing with the pub."

"When I first heard about *Ryan's Daughter,*" says John Mills, who won an Oscar for his portrayal of Michael, "I was told that the shooting would last for sixteen weeks, and

in my mind I made it a year. I was pretty right in my estimate, too. Mary and I took a little house in Dingle, had a boat, and I fished and had a ball. With the Irish weather—with those soft days and pouring rain—I knew it would take time. David wouldn't be hurried, and he wanted to put that country up there as it was on the screen. Some of the rest of the cast got, well, a little bit impatient."

Lean cast Robert Mitchum as Rosy's husband, and Mitchum got more than a little bit impatient. "Those two, Robert and David, got very silly," remembers Miles. "We shot for more than a year, and that whole time Mohammed would never go to the mountain, or vice versa."

"I had trouble with Mitchum," is Lean's statement on the matter. A member of the crew says, "David could not get Mitchum to shoot any scene after twelve noon." Mitchum had a reputation as a tippler.

Asked why he would cast the tough guy against type to play Rosy's limp husband, Lean replies, "Because I wanted a man with potential strength in him. A 'quiet, smooth, sweet' character actor would have been deadly boring. And I don't think Mitchum is. I knew nothing about him except what I'd seen in movies, and I remember him from years and years ago in a film nobody talks about called *Build My Gallows High,* at least that's what it was called in England. Some awful thing in a small town . . . I don't remember, but I remembered Mitchum."

Robert Bolt contacted Mitchum after the actor had been sent the *Ryan's Daughter* script. Mitchum had given it a careful read, reportedly declared it the best script ever written, and refused to do it—on the grounds of the enormity of his role and the demands that would place upon him.

"Is it the tenure of the schedule you find off-putting?" Bolt asked over the phone. If that were the case, the writer assured Mitchum, it could be arranged during production to give him "a fortnight or three weeks at a time on your own."

"It's not that at all," said Mitchum, declining as gracefully as possible. "Actually, I had planned to commit suicide."

Never at a loss for words, Bolt replied, "Well, if you would just do this wretched little film of ours and *then* do yourself in, I'd be happy to stand the expenses of your burial."

For the role of the priest, Lean wanted Alec Guinness. "I thought it was a terrible part," remembers Guinness. "Then David wrote me to say that the film would have this very exciting storm sequence with the priest out in the water bringing in his catch." Guinness's eyes focus skyward. "I answered him

back saying that the priest would have to be absolutely mad to go out like that. He should wait until the storm had passed."

Trevor Howard played the priest.

For the role of the British soldier who becomes Rosy's lover, for which Marlon Brando prepared, Lean viewed the film *The Looking Glass War,* which John Box had produced. "I wanted him to see Anthony Hopkins, who I thought was someone up-and-coming," says Box.

"That's right," says Lean, "but I couldn't keep my eyes off this other actor in the film, Christopher Jones."

"David thought Christopher looked perfect in *The Looking Glass War,*" says Miles of the young actor who at the time of *Ryan's*

"Christopher was very short," says Miles, "like a midget." She adds that the car accident he suffered while filming was a result of his not being able to reach the vehicle's pedals.

"David spent months on the storm scene," remembers Freddie Young, who shot *Ryan's Daughter* in seventy millimeter (it is believed to have been the last film photographed by the process). "It was a two-hours' journey to that particular bit of the coast," says Young. As the land rested closest to the ocean, he explains, "you got the whole force of the storm coming across the Atlantic. We'd get a storm warning and off we would go, and we would arrive and there would be this storm happening. We'd start shooting, work perhaps for an hour or two, and then the storm would die away. So we'd go back, get on to the other work, and wait for another storm warning."

Capturing the storm for the camera, Young says, involved "chaining the camera down to the rocks. And we all wore wet suits. To keep the lens dry, I devised a thing we called 'clear screen.' They have it on ships, and it's glass whirling around—I also put a plastic bag all around the camera—and this revolving glass went around at a thousand revs per minute. It could rain, or the sea could hit the camera, and the lens would just flatten out like a sheet of clear water."

One particularly damaging story about Lean sprang from the sumptuous look of *Ryan's Daughter*. He does not even need to have the anecdote identified before he addresses it. "It is rubbish," he says, "that I spent four months waiting to photograph the right cloud. Absolute rubbish." Lean blames the rumor on "some journalist who came to the set and asked if it wasn't true."

Young verifies Lean's account. "Completely wrong," he says of the cloudwatch. "An awful exaggeration." Both concede that there was a problem with getting shots to match, given the ever-changing nature of the Irish weather, but that would involve days, at most.

When time came to shoot the twilight suicide of Major Dorian, the terrain—and the seasons—of Ireland had been ex-

Trevor Howard as Father Collins. He was cool to Lean. "By the time David gets 'round to filming his *Gandhi*," Howard said, "Mahatma will have to be played by Katie Hepburn, because she'll be the only actor still talking to him."

Daughter bore a strong resemblance to James Dean, "and then he found out he was dubbed in that picture. David freaked out."

"We ended up having to dub Christopher in *Ryan's Daughter*," says Lean benevolently. "We used Stanley Holloway's son."

"He was a washout," says Miles, who also uses words like "midget" to describe her co-star. "And David helped drive him 'round the bend. Christopher wouldn't let anyone help him on the set. He was guarded by these two very bizarre [managers] who owned the house Sharon Tate was killed in, which, of course, happened while we were in Ireland. No one could get near Christopher to embrace his fears."

hausted. Eddie Fowlie found another location to set the explosion, on the coast of South Africa.

"We had to paint the rocks black, because they were white," Young says of the new location. "Otherwise it was a very good match. We did have two or three nights when the sunset was disappointing. Just as he was about to blow himself up, a big black cloud would come over the horizon and block the sun."

"I think M-G-M management changed hands about four times during the picture," remembers John Mills. Actually, it was three times, but in any event Lean's supporter Robert O'Brien was long departed. "Still, the picture was never canceled," says Mills. Lean's record on *Doctor Zhivago* ensured against that fate.

"David was also able to get his way with my makeup," says Mills. "But, there again, David also got his way with the casting. M-G-M didn't think I was right at all. They wanted a big, ugly, ungainly man, but David said, 'I think you should test Johnny.' They said, 'Oh, no. He couldn't possibly look right.' So David said to me, 'Look, Johnny, get hold of that makeup man, Charlie Parker,' who is a genius, 'and get it all on.' So I had a head almost twice the size, an enormous nose, and one eye—Lon Chaney, absolutely—and David said, 'Now let's show M-G-M.' And he showed them and they said, 'That's fine. We'll take him.'

"Then David said to Charlie Parker and me, 'Now let's get the makeup right.' So we went to town and took all that off and started from scratch. In two months we got this fantastic makeup which was hardly a makeup. I mean, it took sixteen minutes to put on in the morning. I just stuck a little nose on, stuck one ear out, and Charlie had those marvelous teeth made, which I clipped on and it twisted my face. I didn't feel made-up at all."

How was it working with Lean in the fifteen years since *Hobson's Choice*? "I no-

ticed a change in David, I suppose," says Mills. "When we were doing the domestic pictures in England, he was always learning, but already commanding a tremendous authority. He was able to handle anybody no matter who they were. Then, by *Ryan's Daughter,* he had 'arrived.' He had done *Lawrence* and *Zhivago,* and he was in the Great Director class. I'm not putting him down, but after that it was a very different kettle of fish."

While this may not have posed a problem with the technical crew, Mills suggests, it could perhaps have an effect on the talent.

"David's not really madly keen on actors," says Mills, "and he's very happy as

John Mills as the village idiot, Michael. Originally the film was to have been called *Michael's Day,* before the emphasis was shifted to Rosy Ryan.

Moving actors through the storm sequence: Lean, Arthur O'Sullivan (as Rosy's executioner, McCardle), and Leo McKern (Thomas Ryan, her doting father).

it with me. I got as far as leaning down on my knees, a most vulnerable position you can be sure, and he refused to do the love scene with me. This made it difficult, you see, because Rosy's first real climax was meant to be the most important moment of her life."

"Difficult situation," remembers Lean.

As Miles tells it, the crew moved to the appropriate spot in the woods, the butterflies were let loose, and Lean ran through the scene with his actors. " 'Okay,' he said," says Miles, " 'Sarah and Christopher come down from your horses, walk over here, Sarah, you kneel and wait for Christopher. Christopher, old boy, you go on your knees.' Christopher, meanwhile, is looking the other way. He told David that today was Sunday and he doesn't work on Sundays."

Monday, Lean repeated the run through with his actors. Miles says that this second time Christopher Jones blamed the rain for his lack of motivation, so Lean had the entire wooded area rebuilt inside a barn. Eddie Fowlie halfheartedly confirms this story. "David was furious," Miles remembers. "His knees were shaking through his trousers and he was puffing like mad on his cigarette holder." (Shortly after completing *Ryan's Daughter,* Lean gave up his sixty-to-eighty-cigarette-a-day habit.)

"Christopher told David, 'No way, *no way!* I'm not getting on my knees for you or anybody,' " says Miles. " 'Oh?' said David. 'Now, come on. You've signed for it. Don't embarrass me or Sarah any longer.' But Christopher wouldn't budge. Three days of this and finally the crew was saying, 'Hey, we'll do it with her.' "

"Words to that effect," remembers Lean.

"I was smelling my armpits," says Miles, "wondering what was wrong with me. I never felt so unwanted in my life."

Miles claims that she and Mitchum doctored Jones's breakfast cereal the next morning. "Christopher came out of his caravan weaving. David said, 'We'd better go down

soon as he gets the film done. In the preparation and in the cutting, I think, because he hasn't told me this, but that's where I think he finds the most pleasure—especially in the cutting room, because he likes to get the film in his fingers.

"So, as an actor, to be happy on a David Lean film, you've got to surrender your time, because it doesn't exist, period. And if you accept that, which you should, then you will be presented in the best possible way you can be presented.

"There won't be one bad shot."

"Do you want to know why David had to keep cutting away to shots of the bluebells and butterflies during the love scene?" asks Miles. "Because Christopher would not do

there and just shoot it, because at least this time he's here.' But Christopher was so ga-ga that he couldn't undo my buttons." She says that the crew undressed Jones and placed him in position.

"It was like having a wet fish on top of me," says Miles. "I'm doing everything, pretending I'm experiencing heaven, and he can't move a muscle. Obviously whatever Mitchum prescribed had too much of an effect. So David comes over to me and says, 'Can't you get any movement out of him at all?'"

Miles divulges that her trick to make Jones jump involved a quick but deft maneuver with her index finger. "He moved, and we got the shot."

Ryan's Daughter started shooting in March of 1969. Trevor Howard had broken an arm while horseback riding on the beach a week before the cameras rolled—his plaster cast was hidden under his priest's robe—and while doing their first scene in the film, Howard and John Mills capsized with their fishing boat. Mills blacked out, and the undertow swept him out to sea.

Frogmen carried both actors to shore.

"It was later said that during this near loss of life," wrote Trevor Howard's biographer Vivienne Knight, "David Lean's main concern was that no footprints should mar the sweep of virgin sand that formed the foreground to this visual of the scene."

"Rubbish!" says Lean.

Knight continues, "This canard is unacceptable if only because, with such a tricky location on his hands, David Lean could have had no desire to recast two leading roles and start again."

Ryan's Daughter opened at New York's Ziegfeld Theatre on November 9, 1970. "There wasn't a single good notice," says Lean. "The English notices were worse. I was afraid to show my face in restaurants."

"IT'S AN ALL-STAR SIX MILLION

QUID BORE" ranted a headline in *The Sun*. "Instead of looking like the money it took to make," Alexander Walker noted in *The Evening Standard*, "the film feels like the time it took to shoot." "*Ryan's Daughter*," pontificated John Russell Taylor in his lead for *The Times*, "is too bad even to be funny."

"The critics absolutely wee-weed all over

John Mills won the Oscar for playing Michael. "They should have given it to Trevor Howard," is Sarah Miles's sentiment.

us," says Sarah Miles. "It was horribly sad, because I think the film stands the test of time. I know it seems timeless now. But when it came out, nobody wanted a love story. I felt responsible, because not only was I in it, but I was the writer's wife. But then, the critics always hated me, and they've hated Robert, and they've hated David. This was their chance to get the three of us together.

"*Lawrence,*" she says, "got the most revolting reviews. One critic called it 'Four Pillars of Boredom.' Then out comes *Doctor Zhivago,* and the same critics said, 'What a shame this new piece of shit is compared to *Lawrence of Arabia.*'

"I think it's quite fashionable to hate David, because he did the big ones, didn't he? And he did them with quality, which is unforgivable."

"You know," says Lean philosophically, "I think I've become, well, it's coming back a bit now, but I became very unfashionable at one time, because I like to tell a story, and telling a story came to be completely unimportant in movies. I think there's a great danger making a movie without a story. I think the general public loves a story. It's deep in our blood. It started in caves, way back, and I don't believe that suddenly in the middle of the 1960s, it stopped to interest the human race.

"I don't believe it at all."

"After *Ryan's Daughter,* David was almost killed," says Maurice Jarre. "Not by the reviews themselves, but by the vindictiveness of some of the critics. The one that really got him was the one who said, 'When a director dies, he becomes a photographer.'"

The line actually opened Alexander Walker's review of *Doctor Zhivago,* but it was picked up by several reviewers when they went to work on *Ryan's Daughter.*

"That almost killed David," Jarre emphasizes. "I don't know why he took it as badly as he did. We all get bad reviews, and David

is a strong kind of Celtic.

"But that almost killed him."

The week of the film's premiere in New York, Lean was the invited guest of the National Society of Film Critics at a luncheon at the Algonquin Hotel. He was greeted by Richard Schickel of *Life* magazine, who, according to Lean, said, "How could the man who made *Brief Encounter* come up with a piece of shit like *Ryan's Daughter?*"

Fellow reviewers criticized the new film to the director's face for the better part of an hour, until Lean decided he had endured enough. Rising to leave, he told the critics, "You people obviously won't be happy until I make a film in sixteen millimeter and black-and-white." Pauline Kael of *The New Yorker* replied, "No. We'll let you use color."

David Lean was not to make another movie for fourteen years.

"It wasn't just the reviews on *Ryan's Daughter,*" speculates Freddie Young, "not that he wasn't upset by them. But David has a job finding a script that interests him. It's got to be something special, not just something ordinary. That's the problem with being a successful director. You have to find something which you feel is going to be a worthy successor to your last one."

"I know now what I did wrong with *Ryan's Daughter,*" says Lean. "The critics all said, 'Oh, Lean's gone over the top. He's in love. He's seeing the world through rose-colored glasses.' Well, so what?

"As a matter of fact, I *was* in love, and I was seeing the world that way. My mistake was in not stating that clearly in the picture. We shot the entire beginning to look absolutely flat—then, once Rosy falls in love, I should have had the priest say, 'Ah Rose, you're seeing the world through rose-colored glasses.'

"Because then we showed the rest of the picture as if it was seen through rose-colored glasses."

Opposite: Staging the film's opening, with Rosy's parasol. Bolt saw her as "a dream-ridden girl, expecting much of life. A humanist would say aspiring, a moralist would say greedy."

OCEANIA

The global traveler in Kenya, circa 1975.

"The main problem is finding a story you can really fall in love with," Lean has said time and again, publicly and privately.

Following *Ryan's Daughter,* which, despite its lambasting, eventually made a profit (as has every Lean film), Lean turned his full attention to indulging his love of travel. He started his lifelong journeys as a boy, going on holiday with his father and brother. Then, since finishing *Summertime,* he undertook a completely peripatetic life, settling down only those times he arrived on location to make a movie. Came his unofficial retirement in the 1970s, Lean qualified as the world's most stylish vagabond; his custom-built burgundy Rolls-Royce traveled everywhere with him, including on-

board the *Queen Elizabeth II.*

"I've driven across America twice," he says, claiming a particular liking for Charleston, South Carolina. When *Time* magazine peeked into Lean's wanderlust, the director told its reporter: "I've been through the Panama Canal twice, been to New Zealand, the Cook Islands, Tahiti, the Tuamotu Archipelago. I've sat on top of Mount Cook in a helicopter, had two Boston whalers docked out in French Polynesia, one in Bora-Bora, and one in Rangiroa, which is my favorite place in the world." Lean explains that Rangiroa is an island on the atolls, "an hour's flight from Tahiti. There's a lagoon there, fifty miles long and twenty-five miles wide. Just wonderful."

In addition to his treks across Europe (East and West), South America, India, North Africa, as well as the Middle East and the Orient, Lean calculates that, combined, his repeated trips to Kenya—where he shoots photographs, never animals—would total an entire year. The logos on the leather chairs in his London dining room bear the crest of the Mount Kenya Safari Club.

Lean prefers traveling by ship, and watching the sea go by, although he derives great pleasure from studying the light through the windows of planes. During an air trip, he seldom if ever takes in the movie.

Lean cannot claim that during the 1970s he entirely lost interest in making another film. What appears to have been lacking was the strong ambition to search for material. The truth is, if all had gone as planned, Lean probably would have unveiled a film around 1979, or 1980 at the latest.

In 1978, while in Polynesia, he and Robert Bolt investigated the life and times of explorer Captain James Cook, for the purposes of a film. "He was a wonderful, decent chap, a superb navigator who did his job extremely well, and who happened to get himself killed," says Lean. Cook's saga ran aground, according to Lean, beacause "it just wasn't very dramatic."

180

Writer and director, holed up at the Beachcomber Hotel in Papeete, next turned their sights to a revisionist look at Captain Bligh and the H.M.S. *Bounty,* with Lean convinced that Charles Nordhoff and James Norman Hall's *Bounty* trilogy from the 1930s (*Mutiny on the Bounty, Men at Sea,* and *Pitcairn's Island*) slandered the seaman with its fictitious account of what happened. "I think Nordhoff and Hall took the easy way out," Lean says of portraying Bligh as the villain. "I think the true story is more difficult but better. I think Captain Bligh was a wonderful man—a wonderful, dull man, and a superb navigator. [First mate Fletcher] Christian was knocked out by the exotica of the South Seas, and Bligh couldn't help but disapprove. I was raised a Quaker. I know about these things."

Warner Bros. announced Lean's project on June 22, 1977, and prepared a budget of seventeen million dollars. Fascinated by the material and the complexities of the characters and issues, Lean and Bolt expanded their idea into two separate but continuous epics. The first, to be called *The Law Breakers,* was to open with the ship's departure from Portsmouth—the mutiny en route began on April 28, 1789—and end with its arrival in Tahiti. The sequel, *The Long Arm,* would cover the events on Pitcairn Island, Bligh's ignominious return to England, the search for the mutineers, and the trial.

"They were fascinating," says Katharine Hepburn, who read both parts of the finished script. "It was a wonderful idea to tell the story of what happened before and after the mutiny."

Warners, facing a new budget of fifty million dollars, did not agree with Hepburn's assessment and bailed out. This brought producer Dino De Laurentiis to the project. "Spiegel was bad," Lean says with hindsight, "but I now have to say that Dino was worse."

John Box, who was to design the produc-

tion, and Lean disagreed about the proportions of the story and parted bitterly. Robert Bolt suffered a near-fatal heart attack and stroke in April of 1979, while still writing the script. Death blow number three was delivered by De Laurentiis himself, with Lean suddenly given six weeks "to get it out of a turnaround from Dino. I signed a paper saying if I couldn't find a buyer, Dino wouldn't owe me anything." Besides his investment of time and work, Lean had also purchased at his own expense two Boston whalers for use in location scouting.

Lean, desperate, approached his old partner Sam Spiegel. "I decided that the film had to be made in just one picture," Spiegel told columnist Roderick Mann. "I couldn't

Lost and Found, The Story of an Anchor was Lean's 1979 television documentary about a remnant of Captain Cook's explorations. Lean in New Zealand with cameraman Ken Roman and Wayne Turrell, the program's original director. He ended up as Lean's assistant.

181

see people going back again for Part II. David agreed and set about writing the script himself."

(Lean calls this Spiegel playing true to form. "Sam taking credit for making it *one* picture?" asks Lean. "I had already decided that by the time I went to him.")

With Spiegel's promise to find backing, Lean set about collaborating with the novelist Melvyn Bragg, writing at London's Berkeley Hotel, but by summer 1979 Lean embarked—solo—to Switzerland to continue the work. Spiegel, thinking the film and Lean were on a suicide course, withdrew.

"I tried to persuade David to abandon the project and work on something else," Spiegel told Mann, "but it was an *idee fixe* with him." Undaunted, Lean in 1980 interviewed actors, and saw Oliver Reed as Bligh and Christopher Reeve, who had played the lead in *Superman,* as Christian. "I thought Reeve was interesting," Lean recalls. "He flew his own private plane." Recalling his meeting with both Lean and Spiegel nearly a decade later, Reeve credited Katharine Hepburn with suggesting him for the role. "I thought I was going to have to jump through hoops to get the job," says the actor. "But, one phone call from Kate to David Lean and I already had it."

Lean to this day considers the condensation of the first two screenplays by Bolt and himself, "the best script I ever had," and the whole *Bounty* episode as "the worst experience of my entire career." He simply had to give away the two Boston whalers and walk away from the project, letting De Laurentiis forge ahead with it. In 1984, Roger Donaldson directed Anthony Hopkins as Bligh and Mel Gibson as Christian in the lackluster *The Bounty.*

"I lost everything I had in it," says Lean, who, with Bolt, is convinced that the very best scene they ever imagined in their nearly three decades working together is contained in their *Bounty* script.

Asking Bolt in 1988—ten years after their abortive collaboration—if he remembers what that scene is, Lean is instantly told by his screenwriter, "Ice."

CLOSE SHOT BLIGH. The wind whines louder and is suddenly filled with a rattling, metallic uproar. BLIGH looks up as:

MEDIUM LONG. The sails and rigging are partially obscured by a fusillade of hailstones . . .

CLOSE SHOT. The MEN in the rigging, heads down, barely visible through the sweeping clouds of ice and sleet . . .

LONG SHOT. The ship barely visible, the force of the squall driving the snow almost parallel to the sea. But it goes almost immediately, leaving the BOUNTY a white, ghost ship.

In the midst of preparing the never-to-be *Bounty* movie, Lean made a little-seen, forty-minute, sixteen-millimeter documentary about the underwater discovery and retrieval of a two-hundred-year-old anchor found off the coast of Tahiti and believed to have belonged to Captain Cook.

George Andrews, a New Zealand producer who had initiated the project, recounted for the March 1979 issue of *American Cinematographer* the adventures of working with Lean on what had originally been intended to be a simple television documentary. Lean, according to Andrews, agreed to finance the special provided the camera crews would properly record the first time the anchor had been moved in two centuries, and that a suitable narrator be found. Andrews suggested Lean himself, who accepted; he had, after all, narrated the British Movietone News.

Once Lean arrived to inspect the anchor site, he announced his ideas on how to open the program, and, furthermore, that Robert

Egypt, 1981.

Bolt had already scripted them. This surprised Andrews, who realized that in one swift, autocratic manuever Lean had overthrown the original documentary approach in favor of feature-filmmaking.

Not unexpectedly, nothing inhibited Lean's drive for perfection. Unable to control his underwater cameraman from his sea-level vantage point, Lean ordered the anchor hoisted from its long resting place and reburied in more shallow water. With the help of Eddie Fowlie, he also built a full-scale replica of the anchor, so he could rehearse on *terra firma* its movements with the cameraman.

"David made great demands," said a member of the crew, "and, to be frank, at times we cursed him for it."

Of the finished program, *Lost and Found,* which aired on Auckland's TV-2 in May of 1979, *Variety*'s reviewer said that it "lacks magic and shows no signs that it is the work of a major cinematic talent."

David Lean returned to the road.

183

"I'd given some thought to doing *Out of Africa,* based on the book by Isak Dinesen," says Lean, referring to a period around the summer of 1982, "only I never could figure out quite how to do it. Then the telephone rang and it was John Brabourne, asking about *A Passage to India.*"

Sydney Pollack ultimately directed his version of *Out of Africa* in 1985. Critics categorized it as "a David Lean–style picture." Lean later saw the film on television and did not particularly care for it.

A Passage to India is E. M. Forster's great 1924 novel about the delicate balance between the English and the Indians. The author—who died at ninety-one in 1970—initially collected his information while visiting India in 1911 (he was drawn there by a Muslim he had tutored while both were students at Cambridge). During a second trip in 1921, he revised his original notes and then wrote his story about the young British woman, Adela Quested, who is perhaps touched by the Indian, Dr. Aziz, while on a sightseeing tour of the dark, whispering Marabar Caves. The British community is outraged, and the question is raised: Was she raped?

That is why, when Brabourne rang Lean for the first time, the director knowingly picked up the phone by answering, "What do you think happened in those caves?"

Lean had read the novel years before and had seen a 1958 London stage adaptation by Santha Rama Rau. Lean had, in fact, attempted to purchase the rights at that time, but was rebuffed by Forster. "He was frightened," says Lean, "that whoever made it would come down on the side of the English or the Indians, and he wanted it balanced. Mind you, I don't think the book is balanced."

As for Santha Rama Rau's version, "It was a small play," Lean recalls. "It started in Fielding's house with Aziz doing the collar scene and ended up at the trial, which was obviously a clever way of doing it." Fielding

INDIA
A Passage to India (1985)

is the sympathetic English schoolmaster whose friendship with Aziz begins with this first visit to his house, during which Aziz rips off his own collar stud so Fielding will not have to go without.

Forster assigned the rights to his work upon his death to King's College, Cambridge, and Brabourne, who had produced a series of films based on Agatha Christie mysteries (including the 1974 *Murder on the Orient Express*), purchased *A Passage to India.*

185

In Kashmir. Directly behind Lean is Maggie Unsworth, his script supervisor since *In Which We Serve*. Noël Coward hired her directly out of school; referring to her then-hairstyle, he called her "the mad Degas."

Lean remembers meeting with the committee at King's College to assure them of his good intentions with the material "and," he says, "reminding them in any event that even if the film turned out a complete disaster, it would be gone in six months while the novel will go on living forever."

"I sat down and wrote the script and did six months in Delhi," says Lean, "because I wanted to be in the middle of things, in case I needed advice. I finished it off in Switzerland."

Lean believes he set right the balance on Forster's alleged bias against his own countrymen. "I evened it up a bit more because I wanted to be fair to both sides. I think

Forster was pretty tough on the English. He was in India and he was obviously not liked by the English he met—in those days they probably considered him a 'blasted little queer.'"

Lean also made Miss Quested less dreary. "I kind of 'upped' her a bit," he says. "I had to change her, otherwise audiences would have responded with an 'ugh.'" Lean similarly went to work on Forster's men. "In the book all the men are idiots, but in fact the British in India did a damned good job. I rather swung the balance against the women. It's a well-known saying that the women lost us the Empire. It's true."

Most noticeable is that Lean changed the story's famous ending. Instead of Forster's version, with Fielding and Aziz meeting after several years and, while on horseback, taking separate paths because of the forces of nature, Lean brings together East and West. Aziz and Fielding shake hands, and Aziz writes to Miss Quested in England, forgiving her for her wrong accusations of long ago. She reads his words by a window, where outside it is raining. This brings the film, which opens with her standing in the rain, looking inside the Thomas Cook office where she will book passage to India, full circle.

"I see now how I should have done it," says Lean in 1988. "After the trial I should have just quickly tied up the loose ends and ended it."

In October of 1982, producers Goodwin and Brabourne went to California to seek financing for David Lean's first picture since *Ryan's Daughter.* They were not greeted with open arms.

"We were surviving on good old American Express and a lot of unpaid bills," says Goodwin, adding that young turks in Hollywood were skeptical that a man of Lean's age—and reputation for time- and money-consuming perfection—could make a film in a practical, modern manner.

"Nobody believed we could make it for fourteen million," says Lean. "I think that people believed secretly that it was an art-house movie gone mad." One executive said he would give the green light if Lean would insert a brutal rape between Aziz and Miss Quested. Another wanted him to combine two characters, Miss Quested and the compassionate, elderly Mrs. Moore.

"They certainly talked a lot of cock about me," Lean says. "They talked about my waiting three days for a cloud, five days for a wave. I said, 'If I did that, how do you think I ever finished a picture?'

"Finally," he says, "Columbia put up some money, and Home Box Office put up the rest." The film was also partly financed

by EMI, private investors, and tax shelters. "We didn't have the money until two weeks before shooting," says Lean.

"It caused a great deal of anxiety."

Alec Guinness and his wife, the former Merula Salaman, were having dinner in London with Lean in 1983, and, the actor says, he could somehow sense that his first director was about to broach an important topic. Perhaps, Guinness went so far as to imagine, Lean was about to end his self-imposed retirement.

"David and I had seen a lot of each other at my house in the country," Guinness explains, "and then we had this dinner. He told me that the *Bounty* thing had been shelved, and that he might do this or that.

Peggy Ashcroft as Mrs. Moore; the actress had wanted to stay home and tend her garden.

Then he said, 'I'm interested in doing *A Passage to India.*' 'Oh, really?' I said, and asked him who would be playing what.

"He didn't know Peggy Ashcroft, who is a great friend of mine. He wanted her as Mrs. Moore, but she had just finished *Jewel in the Crown* [the 1982 television adaptation of the Paul Scott novel] and didn't want to go back to India again. She said, 'No, thank you. I'm tired. Please, oh please, just let me stay home'." Guinness takes credit for engineering Lean's introduction to the actress.

"I never met David Lean until he asked me to do the film," Ashcroft told an interviewer, Michael Buckley, "but we were both born in the same place and we both had brothers named Edward. David and I are almost the same age. I'm just a few months older."

David Lean was seventy-five when he began filming *A Passage to India* on November 14, 1983. Peggy Ashcroft at first tried begging off playing Mrs. Moore with the excuse of her advanced years. "But Peggy," countered Lean, "I'm as old as you are."

Peggy Ashcroft, who made her first film in 1933, won an Oscar for her portrayal of Mrs. Moore, whose compassion toward Aziz sums up eloquently her utter contempt for the British Raj.

"I asked who would play Fielding," says Guinness. Lean, who was to choose James Fox, later says, "That was difficult. Fieldings are not becoming roles for actors. Rather like casting test pilots."

"And," Guinness continues, "I asked who would play Dr. Aziz, which is a much bigger part." Lean found Victor Banerjee, whose attraction, Lean says, "is that you look at him, count to ten, and it's the young Charlie Chaplin. You laugh at him and laugh *with* him and you cry at him and cry with him. What I liked was, he grows very well."

"Then," says Guinness, "after a long breath, I asked who would play Godbole. I was met with a silence, and then an embarrassed pushing around of the fork."

Guinness imitates Lean's embarrassed pushing around of a fork. "David looked up and said, 'Well, I was rather hoping . . . you.'"

Guinness did not take kindly to stepping into the sandals of the cryptic Hindu sage. "I immediately complained, 'Oh, no. It must be played by a Hindu.'"

Part of Guinness's fear was having to look right. "I won't wear contact lenses," says the blue-eyed actor. "As it is, I'm practically blind in one eye already. And then I thought, 'Well, I did play Feisal in *Lawrence.* Perhaps with dark makeup my eyes would come out looking all right.'"

"We paid for that one," says Lean in retrospect of his casting an Englishman in an Indian role, a notion he still defends as being valid, "but I wanted a great character actor in a great character-actor part. It could have worked."

It looks not to. Critics complained. Guinness complained. Even Lean complains, somewhat.

"I tried to absorb something of an Indian nuance," says Guinness, "although all of Godbole's lines are forced. He's too heavily comic."

"Alec came to me," says Lean, "and said, 'You're asking me to play an Indian like Peter Sellers.'" The fire returns to Lean's eyes. "The bloody hell I was."

The real *contretemps* developed over a Hindu dance Guinness devised for the final scene in the picture. He had studied genuine gestures and rehearsed for two weeks. "David never came 'round to see it," he says, though Lean had noted at one point that Guinness should be playing Hindu cymbals, not the Tibetan brass pieces he was clasping in his hands.

Cymbals or no, Lean did not include the dance or any part of it in the finished film. Guinness carped bitterly of this to the press in much the same tone as his story about Lean's desiring Charles Laughton for *The Bridge on the River Kwai.*

"The dance," says Lean about the affair, "was ridiculous."

Through it all for the past forty years, the men obviously maintain an admiration for the other's talents. (Soon after completing *A Passage to India,* Guinness had dinner in Los Angeles with Geoffrey Horne. "I asked him how David was," says Horne, who was told by Guinness, "Oh, he's just lovely now. Not at all like he was on *Kwai.*") The only thing that occasionally, albeit dramatically, comes between them is their artistic temperaments, often based, perhaps, on the director's refusal to compromise.

Guinness does not refute this theory. "Ah yes," he says mock-serenely, as if one were listening to a cryptic Hindu sage. "David Lean is a perfectionist. I am not. I used to be, in my younger days as an actor, until I once ran across a line by G. K. Chesterton. It said, 'If a thing is worth doing, it is worth doing badly.'

"And I thought, 'Oh, thank God.'"

Asked whether, when it came to a working relationship, he preferred an elephant or a camel, Lean immediately replies, "No contest. Give me an elephant." Judy Davis, the Australian actress who played Adela Quested, was just as quick to decide the question of how she would perch herself atop such a beast when the time came for her ride to the Marabar Caves.

"I thought, 'All right now, Adela's had a long journey and she's feeling tired and wants to get comfortable, right?' So as we were about to do the scene, I took a deep breath and let my legs just sort of dangle apart. I couldn't imagine Lean would even notice."

He noticed. "Do sit with your legs together," he shouted. "You don't want to look unbecoming."

The words still make the actress cringe. She makes no bones about not getting along with David Lean, who, she says, "has an ego the size of America."

"We did not get along," says Lean, "until we came to the trial scene. Then, finally, she listened to me, and we stopped arguing."

Davis complains that Lean found the costumes she had chosen with designer Judy Moorcraft "dowdy" and he once commanded her to change her makeup, nearly wiping the paint off her face himself. Despite the passage of a few years since seeing one another, Davis still sounds petulant about working with Lean. "It's a bit difficult starting a very big project with someone you don't know," says Davis. She suggests, too,

Top: With Guinness as the Hindu sage Godbole; "We paid for that one," says Lean of the casting.

Above: Sandra Hotz played Fielding's wife at the end of the picture. In truth, she was Mrs. David Lean.

189

that Lean did not care for her first major film, *My Brilliant Career,* because it dealt with an independent woman.

"I wasn't as enamored of it as some of the critics," concedes Lean. He had first met Davis for two hours in London and found her "very bright, very intelligent," although a longer-lasting memory of that meeting was of their having been "chucked out of the EMI office, because they could no longer afford giving us the space."

"David Lean being David Lean is not an easy man to get along with," says Davis. "He tried to be approachable, I suppose, but I don't think he ever imagined anyone like me. He's not used to independent actresses."

Maggie Unsworth, Lean's script supervisor since 1942, disputes Davis's claim. "David got along fine with Kate Hepburn and Julie Christie," she says, "and they are two very independent actresses." Another crew member on *A Passage to India* suggests that Davis's lack of humor played an unquestionable role in exacerbating the differences between director and star.

John Box designed and built Lean's idealized India (or Forster's imaginary Chandrapore) on the grounds of a maharajah's palace in Bangalore, and, in Ramanagaram and Savandurga, Eddie Fowlie found Lean the right landscape to serve as the Marabar Caves. Three water tanks had to be built nearby, just to bathe and refresh the elephant.

"Whenever we drive around to find a location," says Fowlie, "you can practically read David's mind. He slumps in the seat if he is not interested, then sits well up when something excites him." When Lean first laid eyes upon the rock cliffs, "he jumped out of the car and scaled them faster than a kid. Or a mountain goat. Hell, he was like a bloody hare."

For Lean, *A Passage to India,* despite some personal criticisms he maintains about the

film, marked another turning point. He was back in the movie business. "David Lean's first film in fourteen years is a daring triumph for the old master," said *Time* magazine in an eight-page valentine that landed Lean on the news journal's front cover. A generation of new critics who were not part of the mainstream during Lean's earlier career were able to tip their hats as well.

"*A Passage to India* is large-scale and spectacular," wrote *New York* magazine's David Denby, "yet David Lean's movie is also debonair, intimate, light on its feet . . . a rather startling revival of the large-scale Anglo-American 'prestige' epic that many of us had taken for dead." (Because of the HBO connection, Lean did not shoot the film in widescreen, rather on a scale that would reduce easily to the television picture.)

On Lean's side of the Atlantic it was noted, "*A Passage to India* was the first offer he had from a British company in thirty-five years and is the first of his films to be British financed." So wrote Sue Summers of Lean's "triumphant return" in the February 17, 1985, *Sunday Times.*

"I originally left Britain because of income tax," Lean told Summers. "I was paying something terrible, keeping fourpence in the pound, and I was going bankrupt. I thought I was just going out for a year to get myself straight. But then I started making films for which no English company would have put up the money."

His efforts on behalf of the crown apparently did not go unnoticed; on June 18, 1984, David Lean was knighted. Also, after living in hotels for the past three decades (he had kept a house in Rome until it seemed that terrorists were taking over that city), David Lean set up a permanent residence, converting two empty warehouses in London's Wapping section into a luxurious riverside abode.

"I suppose," says Lean of the domestic turn his life was taking, "I just thought it was time to come home."

David Lean with Victor Banerjee. "Count to ten," the director says of the actor, "and he's Chaplin."

JOSEPH CONRAD
Nostromo (1990)

John Box's sketch for the opening of the film, "the first place you see cut off by mountains," says Lean. Conrad called the setting, Golfo Placido: "an enormous semi-circle and unroofed temple open to the ocean, with its walls of lofty mountains hung with the mourning draperies of cloud."

David Lean fell in love with the 1984 J. G. Ballard novel *Empire of the Sun,* the World War II story of an English boy lost in China at the outbreak of the Japanese invasion of Shanghai. In particular there was a dream-like image of a *Life* magazine cover falling from the sky that fueled Lean's imagination, "but," he says, "the book is like a kind of diary, and I could never get a handle on it to turn it into a film."

When Steven Spielberg made the movie version of *Empire of the Sun,* the majority of the critics said that the director was trying to enter "David Lean territory." Lean never saw the picture.

"Then," says Lean, double-checking his memory of a 1985 visit paid to a university, "I'm not sure it wasn't the Cambridge Film

Society . . . apparently they have a kind of questionnaire, as an examination for students. One of the questions was: 'What film would you suggest for David Lean as his next picture?'

"And an enormous percentage of them said, '*Nostromo.*'"

The response, says Lean, "sort of put the lid on the whole thing, because Maggie [Unsworth] and Robert Bolt had always said that *Nostromo* could make a wonderful picture. It was something I always remembered, because I have enormous respect for Robert's taste. Then, funnily enough, several other people were saying, 'Why don't you do *Nostromo?*'"

Lean took the first step by buying a copy of the five-hundred-page Joseph Conrad novel. "I found it terribly difficult to read," he says. "I made one attempt, got to fifty pages, and gave up. Then somebody else said something about it, so I went to a hundred pages—and gave up. That time, Maggie said, 'You've really, really got to read it,' which I did. I must say, around page one hundred eighty it takes off."

"Widely regarded as Conrad's own best novel, though not his least flawed," is how poet-critic Martin-Seymour Smith introduced one edition of the 1904 tale set in the imaginary Latin American Republic of Costaguana on the verge of brutal political revolution. Nostromo—"a fellow in a thousand" as Conrad ironically describes him—provides Lean with another hero who is both charismatic and enigmatic. Not only does he serve as an object of intense desire, but he absconds with the country's most valuable treasure, the ingots from the San Tomé silver mine.

"Number one," Lean says of the story's attraction, "it's got wonderful characters. Two, I like very much the great mixture of nationalities: English, French, German, South American, and Italian. It's a wonderful sort of bouillabaisse, and the characters are just beautifully written. [The Englishwoman] Mrs. Gould is the only 'good' character—not 'boring' character, 'good' character. But I like the brigands, too. They're outrageous, sort of double life-sized characters."

Although there have been perhaps twenty screen adaptations of different Conrad stories, the author is considered a tough nut to crack cinematically for his preponderance of internalized action and thought; moviemakers as a whole have also steered a clear circle around ironic pessimism, another Conradian trademark. Nevertheless, the Polish-born son of a writer and translator, who spent the first half of his life as an English sailor, has inspired those filmmakers willing to rise to his challenge. These include Alfred Hitchcock (*Sabotage,* from Conrad's *The Secret Agent*), Francis Ford Coppola (*Apocalypse Now,* from *Heart of Darkness*), and Carol Reed (*Outcast of the Islands,* which starred Trevor Howard and Ralph Richardson).

Lean wrote his initial script with the dramatist Christopher Hampton, after seeing Hampton's stage adaptation of *Les Liaisons Dangereuses.* The director then went back over the material with Robert Bolt, who describes Lean as "extraordinarily demanding, and it becomes a great challenge to match up to his expectations of concentration and intensity and to try and top them. In fact, sometimes when we're working, I think it gets a bit silly, and one or the other of us will look across at the other, both being cross-eyed with fatigue, and say, 'Look, we better just take a day off because we're so beat.' But we get so involved when we're working on a script that it requires discipline to break off, even for a day, rather than discipline to make ourselves work."

Despite the passage of time, little has changed in the working routine of the two collaborators. To shape *Nostromo,* they met several times a week in Lean's London home, where, says Lean, "we throw ideas for scenes at one another—Robert can get quite

bold sometimes and I love that—then he goes home and writes what we have outlined, and I go through his pages afterward, inserting the shots and camera angles, creating the blueprint for the film."

Working with Bolt at breakneck speed is possible, the director says, "because after all these years we've developed a kind of shorthand." Nor are their efforts hindered by Bolt's having suffered a debilitating stroke in 1978, at the time of the aborted *Bounty.*

In Lean's eyes, Bolt is "strong as ever. He's like some lovely rock on the coast of Cornwall. A great big wave may come and crash against it, but it still stands there, unconquered.

"Just great."

"*Nostromo,*" says Lean, "has a touch of *Lawrence* in it, except that instead of Arabia, this is South America. In one of the pieces of dialogue, Conrad says, 'Any one of these bandits who gets a few men collected together calls himself The General.'" The reference reminds Lean of Auda Abu Tayi in *Lawrence of Arabia.* "These bandits are outrageous characters. Baboons, really, without any brain or intellect, they're just barbarians, smashing and killing their way to the top," he says.

"The other thing about *Nostromo* that I like very much indeed is that it's so modern. It's about greed and making money. I'm always appalled by that."

Lean in his explanation draws an exacting parallel between the theme of *Nostromo* and the spirit of today's movie business—and not solely because of the struggle he faced in raising the thirty-two million dollars to mount *Nostromo* (one Hollywood studio executive professed the hope before reading Lean's script that it would be "just like *Rambo*")—but because of the shoddy quality of contemporary motion pictures and the emphasis the industry places on executive ego over excellence.

"The people who make movies today

hardly like movies," says Lean. "They like them because with a little bit of luck they can make a lot of money out of them, and the value of their company will go up by the end of the year.

"They don't think like the old villains, those great, big chaps like Harry Cohn, L. B. Mayer, Goldwyn, the rest of them. They were uneducated men who had a great love as it were for making films, supplying entertainment to huge audiences. They really did like movies. They may have been crude, but I think they were terrific in their way.

"I mean, my God, what we could do with an Irving Thalberg right now, yes?"

In 1988, David Lean turned eighty. "I always remember what Alex Korda used to say," he quotes, " 'The wonderful thing about getting old is, I don't mind admitting "I don't know." ' " Lean, it appeared, was allowed scant time for such a perspective. During the course of the year, tribute was paid him in Cannes by the British Film Industry, where he stood up in the packed Palais des Festivals and declared before a crowd that included some of the most notorious dealmakers in the world: "I think it's time that all us moviemakers band together to get rid of these crooks, every producer who has his hands in our pockets."

The reaction could be heard almost as far away as the jungles of Ceylon and the deserts of Jordan.

That same year, Lean's 1962 masterpiece *Lawrence of Arabia* was restored to its definitive glory as preparations were made to unveil it before a worldwide audience, including an entire generation that has never seen a "roadshow picture." When Lean first learned of the studio decision to reissue the picture, he was on holiday in Kenya. The next day he confessed to feeling "so excited that I couldn't sleep all night."

After several false hopes, *Nostromo* received its financing from the French producer Serge Silberman. Shooting was slated

to begin in late 1989 in Madrid and Almeria, where "There are very good clouds." Lean does not intend this as his swan song. Well before finishing the "blueprint" to *Nostromo,* he mentions his unrealized dream to create an original movie musical— he is a staunch fan of Stanley Donen's *Singin' in the Rain* and Bob Fosse's *Cabaret*—and he has long been at work refining in his mind a dramatic idea about Hollywood in the early days of movies.

First, however, will come *Nostromo.* As he did in the case of *Lawrence,* Lean has cast as his leading man an unknown stage actor. He is Georges Correface, who appeared in Peter Brooks's eleven-hour stage adaptation of *The Mahabharata.* In preparation for playing Nostromo, he spent a year changing his physical look and building up his muscles.

"I think," says Lean, "he'll be jolly good."

On the night of March 25, 1988, a birthday party in his honor was thrown in Lean's home, organized on short notice by his friend Sandra Cooke. Lean had opposed celebrating the landmark because, he said, "These are things I ordinarily ignore." The well-wishers prevailed.

The guests began arriving promptly at eight and included Bernard Miles—now Lord Bernard—who asked his host how many of the old gang he could expect to see. He would not be disappointed. Celebrants filled the entire second floor, from the entry hall to the living room, kitchen, and terrace. Robert Bolt sat on the sofa overlooking the river, his wife, Sarah Miles, beside him. Most were first-time visitors to the riverside residence.

"I haven't seen so many of my old mates in so long," said Sarah Miles, "it's as if we'd never had any arguments." Freddie Young told of the success of his recent cataract operation, which explained his wearing dark glasses. "I can take them off, really," Young volunteered.

"No, no, Freddie," said Lean warmly,

putting a hand on Young's arm. "Leave them on. They're very becoming."

Among the others to be found were Maggie Unsworth, John Box, Richard Lester, Melvyn Bragg, Nigel Havers, James Fox, and Christopher Hampton. Julie Christie was forced to send regrets from Australia, where she was shooting a movie for American television; Katharine Hepburn was booked into a previous family engagement in Florida; no luck in tracking down Omar Sharif, who was believed to be before the cameras in Ireland (he was, however, available that May to introduce Lean at the tribute in Cannes); and Maurice Jarre was facing a deadline in a sound studio in Los Angeles.

At 9:30, Sandra Cooke invited everyone to the terrace. From the garden, fireworks were launched, exploding in a brilliant aerial display over the Thames. Lean, who had no idea such entertainment was on the agenda, pronounced in a hushed tone after one particularly bright and loud explosion, "Jolly good." Then came the cake. Lean did not cut it alone. "Johnny," Lean said across the terrace to John Mills, who was standing with his wife, Mary. Mills, as it happened, had turned eighty the very week before, and Lean asked that he "come over here."

Holding hands, together they blew out the candles. The frosting on the cake bore the slogan, "GREAT EXPECTATIONS."

At half past eight on the night of the birthday revelry, once the majority of the guests had already arrived, the elevator doors opened and Eddie Fowlie accompanied into the entry hall a tall, gaunt figure puffing on a long, thin cigarette holder. Lean, deeply engaged in conversation with another couple in the room, did not see the pair. Separating from Fowlie, the new arrival silently stalked to a corner, stood in the shadow of a potted plant, and clasped his arms serenely against his chest.

In a moment's time, Lean looked up, ex-

David Lean in his eightieth year, Kenya.

cused himself to his guests, and crossed the room to greet the man with the imposing silhouette. His name was Peter O'Toole.

Lean first whispered something into O'Toole's ear, and then, after they both nodded in solid agreement, they embraced—and talked together the better part of the evening.

Later, Lean said, "I haven't seen Peter since *Lawrence*. People tried, I don't know, to sort of stir things up between us. They said he said things about me, and told him I'd said things about him. Very difficult." Obviously, bygones were bygones. "I remember," Lean says, "Sam coming to Jordan, we'd been shooting for weeks, and it had been a tremendous strain. Sam wouldn't send back the rushes, so we didn't know how any of the footage was turning out. Not a bit of it. Then Sam arrives and I said, 'Sam, how could you? Not even a cable. How is the footage?' And Sam said, 'Baby, it is of such low quality that I didn't have the heart to tell you.' I was crushed. I walked away from him, didn't say a word, and went under some canvas and collapsed in the shade. And I began to cry. And, as I was laying there, I suddenly felt this arm around my shoulder, and a face press against mine. It was Peter, and he said sympathetically, 'I know. I know.'

"I'll never forget Peter's doing that," says Lean. "He's a very great man."

Post Script

Lean receives his Lifetime Achievement Award from the American Film Institute, March 8, 1990. At the gala evening, he politely scolded Hollywood's power elite for caring more about profits than the quality of modern movies.

In Los Angeles the night after the triumphant studio screening of the complete *Lawrence of Arabia,* David Lean went to dinner with the two men who had instigated the restoration and worked under his final supervision, Bob Harris and Jim Painten. A few friends came along as well.

The three principals are physically and emotionally drained from their efforts on *Lawrence.* Still, it is a night to celebrate, express gratitude—and say goodbye. As often is the case, particularly in the company of more than one other, Lean spends several stretches of the evening immersed in his own silent thought. After the last remaining ounces of coffee and small talk are exhausted, however, the grand master of epic picture-making—and the greatest director of narrative in the English language—recharges his batteries.

In a stern but paternal voice, Lean addresses Harris and Painten. "Now look, you two," he says and, without benefit of notes or another's opinion, proceeds to review the full four hours of restored print scene by scene, from the volume and pitch of Maurice Jarre's overture to the final crawl of the restoration's credits—which he thinks come up too slowly. "Half your audience will be out of the cinema by then." Comments such as "Too yellow" or "We shot that scene at night so for God's sake print it darker" resound from him with a startling vitality as though he were shaking the sand from his shoes only yesterday.

"Now, what about the foreign versions?" Lean demands. "Dubbed or subtitled? Because I remember the dub Sam made for Germany. It was *awful.*" Harris ventures that this decision will have to be discussed with the studio.

"And the video?" asks Lean. He has a suggestion, tendered more in the form of an order. "The scene of Peter and the guide at the well when Omar makes his entrance. Take that, frame Peter on one side and the guide on the other, and make the whole picture as wide as that."

Harris assures Lean that the image will be "letter-boxed," a guarantee that a proper picture will be visible over television—via cable, cassette, and, Harris says, laser disc.

"Yes," says Lean. "That's good." Slowly he begins slipping back into his own thoughts. "Laser disc," he says before signing off momentarily.

He returns to life after a bit and says quietly but excitedly to this listener, "Can you imagine what entertainment will be like one hundred years from now? With telecommunications we'll be transmitting full lifelike images by satellite from one corner of the earth to the other in a matter of split seconds. Think of how that will be. Just marvelous."

He emits a small laugh. "I remember when sound came in," he says fondly, "and what everyone thought of that. It wasn't entirely positive, I can tell you. And color. That didn't go down well at all. The outcry was something terrible."

An amused look flashes across the whole of what Katharine Hepburn calls, simply, "that face." Lean folds his arms across the chest of his navy blue pullover as his blue eyes narrow into a penetrating stare.

"Moving pictures," he says. "You know, I've sort of been around to take part in their development."

Lean adds, without so much as a hint of sentimentality, "I feel rather fortunate."

Exit Music

David Lean could never quite believe his own accomplishments or his notable reputation, a result of his not quite measuring up in the eyes of his father, Francis Lean. For all of his monetary success, the homes around the world, the trophies (including an American Film Institute Life Achievement Award in March 1990, making him the first foreigner to be so honored), David Lean—even as an active octogenarian—failed to outgrow his sense of being "a complete dud" when he was young.

Taking this and Lean's ineluctable British reserve into account, one has the explanation of why sharp words from the critics stung him so; critics, he reasoned, represented the intellectual voice of the cinema audience and, therefore, something of a threat. Lean may have been a technical genius—what he really was was an artist—but he was no intellectual. His boyhood rival, his *younger* brother, held that singular distinction in the family. Lean never shook that.

Not that he spoke unkindly about his family, in those few instances when he sounded off about them at all. Then again, the warmest anecdote he managed to muster about his father had to do with the time the elder Lean had been to see his son's *Doctor Zhivago.*

"Now, David," his father advised him ingenuously, "why can't you go out and meet a nice girl, like that Julie Christie?"

That brings up what was another sore point with Lean, though he was aware that the fact raised eyebrows and some of them in admiration: his several marriages.

"I can't *believe* I've been married so many times," he would say, clasping his forehead. He conceded that most of his wives had been "very nice, indeed, although I think my big mistake was in marrying them and not the girlfriends, instead of the other way 'round."

There were exceptions. In 1986, Lean attended the London premiere of John Boorman's *Hope and Glory.* "This woman came up to me afterward and started talking," Lean recounted. "She mentioned several people we supposedly knew, and finally, after I felt I'd been polite long enough, I said, 'Well, dear, so nice to see you again.' I kissed her once on each cheek, and that was that. Then I walked over to Dick Lester and asked, 'Look, Dick, by any chance was that Ann Todd?'" It was indeed his third wife.

Then there was the time, two decades earlier, when Lean was married to his fourth wife, the former Leila Devi, who was a great friend of the Woolworth heiress, Barbara Hutton. The Leans frequently visited Hutton in Venice, where she maintained a villa directly across from the Gritti Palace Hotel. One night, during a large dinner party, several of the guests started good-naturedly chiding both Lean and Hutton for their many marriages. Finally, Hutton could take no more; turning to Lean, she said, "Listen, David, tell them to shut up. We're the moral ones. We marry them."

On December 14, 1990, David Lean wed again, this time to his companion since 1985, Sandra Cooke. Katharine Hepburn sent a present to the ceremony, which was held in the South of France.

"Which one is this," the star inquired before the package left her home in New York, "number four or five?" When informed that this would in fact be Lean's sixth wedding, Hepburn said with a hearty chuckle, "Oh, goody. Then there's still a chance for me."

When the line was repeated to both the new Lady Lean and Sir David, they roared with laughter.

The wedding festivities lasted an entire weekend. Indeed, there was much worth celebrating. The planned honeymoon in India would need to be postponed, but for a good reason: at long last, *Nostromo* was in preproduction at the Victorine Studios in Nice. Ironically, this is where Rex Ingram had gone to work after leaving Hollywood, which meant Lean was coming full circle: shooting what would conceivably be his last epic in the very same place where the man who had inspired him to become a movie maker had worked.

(*Nostromo* had already reached the screen once before, in 1926, as a silent six-reeler from the Hollywood pioneer William Fox. Its title was *The Silver Treasure.* The director was Rowland V. Lee, who later made Fu Manchu movies for Paramount. George O'Brien played Nostromo; and appearing as the gentle Mrs. Gould was an actress who later made her name as the gossip columnist Hedda Hopper.)

True to form, the undomesticated Lean abandoned his villa in the hills above Cannes and checked into Nice's Negresco Hotel, to oversee the building of sets before returning to London, where casting would be finalized. Tri-Star Pictures, an arm of Columbia Pictures, was in for seven million of the film's forty-million-dollar budget, in exchange for the American rights to the picture. (Producer Serge Silberman had obtained the bulk of his financing from French and British banks). It was Tri-Star that nixed the idea of an unknown to play the lead and was pushing for Kevin Kline, an Oscar winner for his comedic turn in *A Fish Called Wanda.* Eventually Dennis Quaid was hired as Nostromo, with Isabella Rossellini and Julian Sands set to play the Goulds. For the rest of his international cast, Lean gathered Klaus Maria Brandauer, Paul Scofield, Christopher Lambert, and Irene Papas, among others. A lot was at stake.

At Lean's wedding he looked fit for the first time in nearly two years. His health had taken a decided downturn after he returned to London following the 1989 American premieres of the restored *Lawrence of Arabia.* Termed only a "mystery lung ailment,"

Sir David and Sandra Cooke, the soon-to-be Lady Lean, on October 1, 1990, the day they became engaged. The wedding—his sixth—took place December 14, 1990, near their villa in the South of France.

that is precisely what the setback remained. Lean missed the London and Cannes premieres of his 1962 epic, for he was secretly in the hospital, being treated with cortisone—which immediately took effect upon his system. Lean's face and ankles swelled, and he was literally knocked off his feet.

"The doctor said, 'Well, now you'll start to look your age,'" Lean recalled with great irritation, reporting on when he'd been administered the first dosage of "the wonder drug." And age he did, quickly and irreversibly. Fit as Lean looked at his wedding, there was no mistaking it; the man also looked tired, and there was something horribly wrong with his voice, as if he had a bubble stuck in his throat.

On the Saturday night of the wedding weekend, fireworks greeted guests to his French villa. Lean himself did not last through the entire display; he claimed it was too chilly outside. Still, he cordially greeted each visitor, even gave a little speech the night before at the restaurant Moulins de Mougins, telling the forty special dinner guests from all over the map how "truly touched" he was by their presence, adding the curt admission that "I must be getting softer as I get older."

Nostromo had a start date of the first week of March, 1991.

"You know," said David Lean, once again utilizing his favorite preface before making an observation, "I've noticed something funny about myself." At the time he was seventy-nine years old and remarkably hale and hearty. The date was July 5, 1987. "I never thought I'd ever die. No, not me. But now, every morning, I read the obituaries in *The Times,* and I think, 'Well, it's possible.'"

One final insurance exam prior to the shooting of *Nostromo* took place the third week of January 1991. These medical ordeals had been going on for some years. This one, though, sent up a new red flag. A

headscan was immediately ordered in Paris. Lean was sent to London to receive six weeks of radiation therapy. David Lean had throat cancer.

To friends, who were the only ones made privy to this news, the frustrating delays on *Nostromo,* dating back to 1985, became more infuriating than ever. For his part, Lean was ready to do battle with the insult to his system. At the same time as he was receiving the treatments, he also continued to fine-tune the script for his epic. It was his way to take his mind off the pain.

David Lean beat the cancer. The radiation did knock it out of him. It also left him the worse for wear.

Sunday afternoon, April 14, David Lean visited the garden of his East End home, smelling the spring flowers. *Nostromo* had a new start date of July, and its director seemed to be well on his way to recovery. He was not. The effects of the radiation had left him highly susceptible to infection.

Double-pneumonia set in on Monday and he died, peacefully in bed, early the next day, April 16, 1991, after he had just been handed a bouquet of flowers from his garden.

Still adjusting to the news, Katharine Hepburn said, "It's going to be awfully difficult imagining life without David, isn't it?"

Nostromo was canceled. Tri-Star Pictures announced that it intended to collect the insurance money that would cover the preproduction expenses. Serge Silberman, of whom Lean had grown rather fond, issued a statement from Paris declaring that he had lost "a great friend." *Time* reprinted its 1984 cover with Lean for its Milestones column and noted, "Sir David cut as dashing a figure as any of his racked heroes." The magazine referred to him as "the raja of imperial cinema."

David Lean was cremated on April 22, 1991, and his ashes were scattered in India, the South of France, and Tahiti. Plans then got underway for his memorial service, held October 3 of that same year in London. The proceedings, labeled "A Service of Celebration and Thanksgiving for the Life and Work of David Lean," was, perhaps unsurprisingly, of epic proportions.

"One of the most extraordinary men of our age and our generation," was how the filmmaker was described by the Reverend Eric Evans, speaking to the eight hundred members of the congregation, which included Alec Guinness; Anthony Havelock-Allan; Ronald Neame; Fred Zinnemann; Valerie Hobson and John Profumo; Mrs. Jack Hawkins; James Fox; Nigel Havers; Victor Banerjee; Rita Tushingham; Christopher Hampton; the Second Master of the Leighton Park School, John Allinson; and four women who at various times had been married to David Lean.

Ann Todd, who attended, had told the press earlier in the week that when Lean walked out on her in 1954 after eight years of a stormy marriage, "it left me with a feeling of utter failure in life." Kay Walsh departed the ninety-minute ceremony ten minutes before it officially ended.

During that hour and a half, John Mills read an opening passage from *Great Expectations;* John Box cited Omar Sharif's entrance in *Lawrence of Arabia* as the prime example of Lean's mastery of his craft and read the lesson from Matthew; Robert Bolt assured his friend David Lean, "I am here"; Sarah Miles recited Celia Johnson's toast to the ship from *In Which We Serve;* and Peter O'Toole delivered John Donne's Holy Sonnet X, "Death, be not proud." Later Tom Courtenay read from *Doctor Zhivago,* Omar Sharif from *Seven Pillars of Wisdom,* and Georges Correface from *Nostromo.*

Melvyn Bragg delivered the eulogy and called Lean "meticulous and inflexible." David Lean, said the author and television commentator, "made films as if there was nothing else in the world he could do, and he made them with an intensity as if he feared each film would be his last." Lean's favorite word, said Bragg, was "Cut," and he suggested that those three letters could well serve as Lean's epitaph.

Maurice Jarre conducted members of the Royal Philharmonic Orchestra in the "Sunrise" portion of *Also Sprach Zarathustra* as Lean's Oscars and Directors Guild awards were placed before the podium. Other musical selections included Rachmaninoff's "Second Piano Concerto in C minor," "Fagin's Romp" from *Oliver Twist,* "The Willie Mossop Theme" from *Hobson's Choice,* "The Spitfire Ballet" from *The Sound Barrier,* and Jarre's own themes from the later epics.

One bit of music was not allowed inside the house of worship where the ceremony took place, due to the bawdy connotation of its tune. That was the "Colonel Bogey March" from *The Bridge on the River Kwai.* So the band of Blues and Royals played the infectious march as guests filtered out, which brings us back to the setting for this memorable morning: St. Paul's Cathedral.

Nearly six decades earlier, a similar tribute had been held there. That one was for T. E. Lawrence.

Academy Awards

David Lean and his films have been the recipients of countless international film prizes. From the Academy of Motion Picture Arts and Sciences, Lean's sixteen films to date have garnered fifty-six Academy Award nominations. These have resulted in twenty-seven Oscars, a record unequaled for someone who has never worked within the (now-defunct) Hollywood studio system.

Lean, while also recognized in other categories, has been nominated for Outstanding Achievement in Direction seven times, and has won twice, for *The Bridge on the River Kwai* and *Lawrence of Arabia,* making him the first British director ever to win, and the only British director, so far, to have won more than once. His was also the first-ever British director nomination, for *Brief Encounter.*

The following is a complete list of Academy Award nominations for Lean's films, with actual winning categories denoted by an asterisk (*).

IN WHICH WE SERVE

*Special Award (certificate) to Noël Coward for his outstanding production achievement.

BLITHE SPIRIT

*Special Effects (Visual): Thomas Allen. [Note: Says Lean, "All we did was throw a green light on Constance Cummings."]

BRIEF ENCOUNTER

Director: David Lean.
Actress: Celia Johnson.
Original Screenplay: Anthony Havelock-Allan, David Lean, Ronald Neame.

GREAT EXPECTATIONS

Picture: Ronald Neame, producer.
Director: David Lean.

Screenplay: David Lean, Ronald Neame, Anthony Havelock-Allan.
*Cinematography (black-and-white): Guy Green.
*Art Direction (black-and-white): John Bryan, Wilfred Shingleton.

THE SOUND BARRIER

Story and Screenplay: Terence Rattigan.
*Sound Recording: London Film Sound Department.

SUMMERTIME

Director: David Lean.
Actress: Katharine Hepburn.

THE BRIDGE ON THE RIVER KWAI

*Picture: Sam Spiegel, producer.
*Director: David Lean.
*Actor: Alec Guinness.
Supporting Actor: Sessue Hayakawa.
*Screenplay (Based on Material from Another Medium): Pierre Boulle [Note: Posthumous awards in 1985 to Carl Foreman and Michael Wilson; Lean, who wrote majority of script, says, "Mike Wilson deserved it."]
*Cinematography: Jack Hilyard.
*Musical Score: Malcolm Arnold.
*Filming Editing: Peter Taylor.

LAWRENCE OF ARABIA

*Picture: Sam Spiegel, producer.
*Director: David Lean.
Actor: Peter O'Toole.
Supporting Actor: Omar Sharif.
Screenplay (Based on Material from Another Medium): Robert Bolt.
*Cinematography: Fred A. Young.
*Art Direction/Set Decoration (Color): John Box, John Stoll; Dario Simoni.
*Sound: Shepperton Studio Sound Department; John Cox, sound director.

*Musical Score (Substantially Original): Maurice Jarre.
*Film Editing: Anne Coates.

DOCTOR ZHIVAGO

Picture: Carlo Ponti, producer.
Director: David Lean.
Supporting Actor: Tom Courtenay.
*Screenplay (Based on Material from Another Medium): Robert Bolt.
*Cinematography: Freddie Young.
*Art Direction/Set Direction: John Box, Terry Marsh; Dario Simoni.
Sound: M-G-M British Studio Sound Department; A.W. Watkins, sound director; and M-G-M Sound Department; Franklin E. Milton, sound director.
*Musical Score (Substantially Original): Maurice Jarre.
Film Editing: Norman Savage.
*Costume Design (Color): Phyllis Dalton.

RYAN'S DAUGHTER

Actress: Sarah Miles.
*Supporting Actor: John Mills.
*Cinematography: Freddie Young.
Sound: Gordon K. McCallum, John Bramall.

A PASSAGE TO INDIA

Picture: John Brabourne, Richard Goodwin, producers.
Director: David Lean.
Actress: Judy Davis.
*Supporting Actress: Peggy Ashcroft.
Screenplay (Based on Material from Another Medium): David Lean.
Cinematography: Ernest Day.
Art Direction/Set Direction: John Box; Hugh Scaife.
Sound: Graham Hartstone, Nicolas Le Messurier, Michael A. Carter, John Mitchell.
*Original Score: Maurice Jarre.
Film Editing: David Lean.
Costume Design: Phyllis Dalton.

Filmography

IN WHICH WE SERVE

A Two Cities Film. Directors: Noël Coward and David Lean. Producer: Noël Coward. Associate Producer: Anthony Havelock-Allan. Screenplay: Noël Coward. Photography: Ronald Neame. Camera Operator: Guy Green. Art Director: David Rawnsley. Art Supervisor (to Noël Coward): G. E. Calthrop. Editor: Thelma Myers. Sound: C. C. Stevens. Rerecording: Desmond Dew. Unit Manager: Michael Anderson. Production Manager: Sidney Streeter. Music: Noël Coward.

Cast: Noël Coward (Captain "D" Kinross), Bernard Miles (Chief Petty Officer Walter Hardy), John Mills (Ordinary Seaman "Shorty" Blake), Celia Johnson (Alix, Mrs. Kinross), Kay Walsh (Freda Lewis), Derek Elphinstone (Number One), Michael Wilding ("Flags"), Robert Sansom ("Guns"), Philip Friend ("Torps"), James Donald (Doctor), Ballard Berkeley (Engineer Commander), Chimmo Branson ("Snotty"), Kenneth Carten (Sub-Lieutenant Royal Naval Volunteer Reserve), George Carney (Mr. Blake), Kathleen Harrison (Mrs. Blake), Wally Patch (Uncle Fred), Richard Attenborough (Young Stoker), Penelope Dudley Ward (Maureen Fenwick), Hubert Gregg (Pilot), Frederick Pipe (Edgecombe), Caven Watson (Brodie), Johnnie Schofield (Coxswain), Geoffrey Hibbert (Ablebodied Joey Mackridge), John Boxer (Ablebodied Hollert), Leslie Dwyer (Parkinson), Walter Fitzgerald (Colonel Lumsden), Gerald Case (Captain Jasper Fry), Dora Gregory (Mrs. Lemmon), Lionel Grosse (Reynolds), Norma Pierce (Mrs. Scatterthwaite), Ann Stephens (Lavinia), Daniel Massey (Bobby), Jill Stephens (May Blake), Eileen Peele (Mrs. Farrell), Barbara Waring (Mrs. Macadoo), Kay Young (Barmaid), Juliet Mills (Freda's Baby).

Running time: 113 minutes.

Released September, 1942, by British Lion (Great Britain), and October, 1942, by United Artists (United States).

THIS HAPPY BREED

A Two Cities Film. Director: David Lean. Producer: Noël Coward. In Charge of Production: Anthony Havelock-Allan. Screenplay: Noël Coward, from his own play. Adaptation: David Lean, Ronald Neame, and Anthony Havelock-Allan. Photography: Ronald Neame. Camera Operator: Guy Green. Color Directors: Natalie Kalmus, Joan Bridge, and Harold Hayson. Sound: C.C. Stevens, John Cooke, and Desmond Dew. Conductor: Muir Matheson (London Symphony Orchestra). Art Direction: C.P. Norman. Art Supervisor (to Noël Coward): G.E. Calthrop. Editor: Jack Harris. Production Managers: Ken Horne and Jack Martin. Assistant Director: George Pollack. Dress Supervisor: Hilda Collins. Makeup: Tony Sforzini. Hairdresser: Vivienne Walker. Special Effects: Percy Day.

Cast: Robert Newton (Frank Gibbons), Celia Johnson (Ethel Gibbons), John Mills (Billy Mitchell), Kay Walsh (Queenie Gibbons), Stanley Holloway (Bob Mitchell), Amy Veness (Mrs. Flint), Alison Leggatt (Aunt Sylvia), Eileen Erskine (Vi Gibbons), John Blythe (Reg Gibbons), Guy Verney (Sam Leadbitter), Merle Tottenham (Edie), Betty Fleetwood (Phyllis Blake).

Running time: 111 minutes, in Technicolor.

Released June, 1944, by Eagle-Lion (Great Britain), and April, 1947, by Universal-International (United States).

BLITHE SPIRIT

A Cineguild-Two Cities Film. Director: David Lean. Producer: Noël Coward. Screenplay: Noël Coward, from his own play. Adaptation: David Lean, Ronald Neame, and Anthony Havelock-Allan. Photography: Ronald Neame. Special Effects: Tom Howard. Color Directors: Natalie Kalmus and John Bridge (Associate). Sound: John Cooke and Desmond Dew. Music: Richard Addinsell. Conductor: Muir Matheson (London Symphony Orchestra). Art Direction: C.P. Norman. Art Supervisor to Noël Coward: G.E. Calthrop. Editor: Jack Harris. Unit Managers: Norman Spencer and S.S. Streeter. Assistant Director: George Pollack. Costumes: Rahvia. Dress Supervisor: Hilda Collins. Makeup: Tony Sforzini. Hairdresser: Vivienne Walker.

Cast: Rex Harrison (Charles Condomine), Constance Cummings (Ruth), Kay Hammond (Elvira), Margaret Rutherford (Madame Arcati), Joyce Carey (Mrs. Bradman), Hugh Wakefield (Doctor Bradman), Jacqueline Clark (Edith).

Running time: 96 minutes, in Technicolor.

Released April, 1945, by General Film Distributors (Great Britain), and September, 1945, by United Artists (United States).

BRIEF ENCOUNTER

A Cineguild Production. Director: David Lean. Producer: Noël Coward. Executives in charge of production: Anthony Havelock-Allan and Ronald Neame. Screenplay: David Lean, Ronald Neame, and Anthony Havelock-Allan, based on the play *Still Life,* by Noël Coward. Adaptation: Noël Coward. Photography: Robert Krasker. Camera Operator: B. Francke. Sound: Stanley Lambourne and Desmond Dew. Music: Rachmaninoff's "Second Piano Concerto," played by Eileen Joyce. Conductor: Muir Matheson (National Symphony Orchestra). Art Direction: L.P. Williams. Art Supervisor to Noël Coward: G.E. Calthrop. Editor: Jack Harris. Associate Editor: Harry Miller. Production Manager: E. Holding. Assistant Director: George Pollack. Continuity: Margaret Sibley.

Cast: Celia Johnson (Laura Jesson), Trevor Howard (Dr. Alec Harvey), Cyril Raymond (Fred Jesson), Joyce Carey (Barmaid), Stanley Holloway (Station Guard), Valentine Dyall (Stephen Lynn), Everly Gregg (Dolly Messiter), Margaret Barton (Beryl), Dennis Harkin (Stanley).

Running time: 86 minutes.

Released November, 1945, by Eagle-Lion (Great Britain), and August, 1946, by Universal (United States).

GREAT EXPECTATIONS

A Cineguild Production for the J. Arthur Rank Organization. Director: David Lean. Producer: Ronald Neame. Executive Producer: Anthony Havelock-Allan. Screenplay: David Lean, Ronald Neame, and Anthony Havelock-Allan, with Kay Walsh and Cecil McGivern, from the novel by Charles Dickens. Photography: Guy Green. Camera Operator: Nigel Huke. Sound: Stanley Lambourne, Desmond Dew, and Gordon K. McCallum. Music: Walter Goehr, Kenneth Pakeman, and G. Linley. Art Direction: Wilfred Shingleton. Production Designer: John Bryan. Conductor: Walter Goehr (National Symphony Orchestra). Editor: Jack Harris. Production Manager: Norman Spencer. Costumes: Sophie Harris (of Motley) and Margaret Furse (Assistant). Continuity: Margaret Sibley. Choreography: Suria Magito.

Cast: John Mills ("Pip"), Valerie Hobson (Estella), Bernard Miles (Joe Gargery), Francis L. Sullivan (Jaggers), Finlay Currie (Magwitch), Martita Hunt (Miss Havisham), Anthony Wager ("Pip" as a boy), Jean Simmons (Estella as a young girl), Alec Guinness (Herbert Pocket), Ivor Barnard (Wemmick), Freda Jackson (Mrs. Joe Gargery), Torin Thatcher (Bentley Drummle), Eileen Erskine (Biddy), Hay Petrie (Uncle Pumblychook), George Hayes (Compeyson), Richard George (The Sergeant), Everly Gregg (Sarah Pocket), John Burch (Mr. Wopsle), Grace Denbigh-Russell (Mrs. Wopsle), O. B. Clarence (The Aged Parent), John Forrest (The Pale Young Gentleman), Anne Holland (A Relation), Frank Atkinson (Mike), Gordon Begg (Night Porter), Edie Martin (Mrs. Whimple), Walford Hyden (The Dancing Master), Roy Arthur (Galley Steersman).

Running time: 118 minutes.

Released December, 1946, by General Film Distributors (Great Britain), and May, 1947, by Universal-International (United States).

OLIVER TWIST

A Cineguild Production for the J. Arthur Rank Organization. Director: David Lean. Producer: Ronald Neame. Screenplay: David Lean and Stanley Haynes, from the novel by Charles Dickens. Photography: Guy Green. Camera Operator: Oswald Morris. Sound: Stanley Lambourne and G.K. McCallum. Music: Sir Arnold Bax. Conductor: Muir Matheson (Philharmonic Orchestra of London, Harriet Cohen solo pianoforte). Art Direction: John Bryan. Editor: Jack Harris. Production Manager: Norman Spencer. Assistant Director: George Pollack. Costumes: Margaret Furse. Makeup: Stuart Freebourne. Continuity: Margaret Sibley.

Cast: Robert Newton (Bill Sikes), Alec Guinness (Fagin), Kay Walsh (Nancy), Francis L. Sullivan (Mr. Bumble), Henry Stephenson (Mr. Brownlow), Mary Clare (Mrs. Corney), John Howard Davies (Oliver Twist), Josephine Stuart (Oliver's Mother), Henry Edwards (Police Official), Robert Truman (Monks), Anthony Newley (The Artful Dodger), Hattie Jacques and Betty Paul (Singers at the "Three Cripples"), Kenneth Downy (Workhouse Master), Gibb McLaughlin (Mr. Sowerberry), Kathleen Karrison (Mrs.

Sowerberry), Amy Veness (Mrs. Bedwin), W. G. Fay (Bookseller), Maurice Denham (Chief of Police), Frederick Lloyd (Mr. Grimwig), Ivor Barnard (Chairman of the Board), Deirdre Doyle (Mrs. Thingummy), Edie Martin (Annie), Fay Middleton (Martha), Diana Dors (Charlotte), Michael Dear (Noah Claypole), Graveley Edwards (Mr. Fang), Peter Bull (Landlord of the "Three Cripples"), John Potter (Charlie Bates), Maurice Jones (Workhouse Doctor), Michael Ripper (Barney).

Running time: 116 minutes (censored to 104 minutes for release in the United States).

Released June, 1948, by Eagle-Lion (Great Britain), and July, 1951, by United Artists (United States).

THE PASSIONATE FRIENDS
(AMERICAN TITLE: ONE
WOMAN'S STORY)

A Cineguild Production for the J. Arthur Rank Organization. Director: David Lean. Producer: Ronald Neame. Assistant Director: George Pollack. Screenplay: Eric Ambler, based on the novel by H.G. Wells. Adaptation: David Lean and Stanley Haynes. Photography: Guy Green. Camera Operator: Oswald Morris. Production Designer: John Bryan. Assistant Art Director: T. Hopwell-Ashe. Set Decorator: Claude Manusey. Editors: Jack Harris (Supervisor) and Geoffrey Foot. Sound Recording: Stanley Lambourne and Gordon K. McCallum. Sound Editor: Winston Ryder. Costumes: Margaret Furse. Music: Richard Addinsell.

Cast: Ann Todd (Mary Justin), Trevor Howard (Steven Stratton), Claude Rains (Howard Justin), Isabel Dean (Pat), Betty Ann Davies (Miss Layton), Arthur Howard (Man-servant), Guido Lorraine (Hotel Manager), Marcel Poncin (Hall Porter), Natasha Sokolova (Chambermaid), Helen Buris (Flowerwoman), Jean Serrett (Emigration Official), Frances Waring (Charwoman), Wanda Rogerson (Second Bridge Guest), Wilfred Hyde-White (Solicitor).

Running time: 91 minutes.

Released January, 1949, by General Film Distributors (Great Britain), and June, 1949, by Universal-International (United States).

MADELEINE

A Cineguild Production. Director: David Lean. Producer: Stanley Haynes and David Lean. Screenplay: Nicholas Phipps and Stanley Haynes, based on the actual case of Madeleine Hamilton Smith. Photography: Guy Green. Music: William Alwyn. Conductor: Muir Matheson (Royal Philharmonic Orchestra). Editor: Geoffrey Foot. Costumes: Margaret Furse. Assistant Director: George Pollack. Art Direction: John Bryan.

Cast: Ann Todd (Madeleine Smith), Ivan Desny (Emile L'Angelier), Norman Woland (William

Minnoch), Leslie Banks (Mr. Smith), Barbara Everest (Mrs. Smith), Susan Stranks (Janet Smith), Patricia Raine (Bessie Smith), Elizabeth Sellars (Christina), Edward Chapman (Doctor Thompson), Jean Cadell (Mrs. Jenkins), Eugene Deckers (Monsieur Thuau), Ivor Barnard (Mr. Murdoch), David Horne (Lord Justice); Harry Jones (Lord Advocate); Andre Morell (Dean of Faculty), Henry Edwards (Clerk of the Court), Amy Veness (Miss Aiken), John Laurie (Scots Divine), Kynaston Reeves (Dr. Penny), Cameron Hall (Dr. Yeoman), Douglas Barr (William), Irene Brown (Mrs. Grant), Alfred Rodriguez and Moira Fraser (Highland Dancers), James McKechnie (Narrator).

Running time: 114 minutes.

Released February, 1950, by General Film Distributors (Great Britain), and September, 1950, by Walter Reade and Universal-International (United States).

THE SOUND BARRIER
(AMERICAN TITLE: BREAKING
THE SOUND BARRIER)

A London Films Production. Director: David Lean. Producer: David Lean. Screenplay: Terence Rattigan. Photography: Jack Hildyard, John Wilcox, Peter Newbrook, and Jo Jago (Aerial Sequences). Music: Malcolm Arnold. Conductor: Muir Matheson (London Philharmonic Orchestra). Art Direction: Vincent Korda, Joseph Bato, and John Hawkesworth. Production Manager: John Palmer. Associate Producer: Norman Spencer. Editor: Geoffrey Foot. Aerial Unit Director: Anthony Squire.

Cast: Ralph Richardson (Sir John Ridgefield), Ann Todd (Susan Ridgefield Garthwaite), Nigel Patrick (Tony Garthwaite), John Justin (Philip Peel), Dinah Sheridan (Jess Peel), Joseph Tomelty (Will Sparks), Denholm Elliot (Chris Ridgefield), Jack Allen (Windy Williams), Ralph Michael (Fletcher), Douglas Muir and Leslie Philips (Controllers), Robert Brooks Turner (Test Bed Operator), Anthony Snell (Peter Makepeace), Jolyon Jackley (John), Vincent Holman (A.T.A., Officer).

Running time: 118 minutes.

Released July, 1952, by British Lion (Great Britain), and November, 1952, by Lopert Films/United Artists (United States).

HOBSON'S CHOICE

A London Films Production. Director: David Lean. Producer: David Lean. Associate Producer: Norman Spencer. Screenplay: David Lean, Norman Spencer, and Wynard Browne, based on the play by Harold Brighouse. Photography: Jack Hildyard. Camera Operator: Peter Newbrook. Sound: John Cox (Supervisor), Buster Ambler, and Red Law. Music: Malcolm Arnold. Conductor: Muir Matheson (Royal Philharmonic Orchestra). Editor: Peter Taylor.

Production Manager: John Palmer. Assistant Director: Adrian Pryce-Jones. Costumes: John Armstrong and Julia Squire. Makeup: Tony Sforzini and George Parleton. Hairdresser: Gladys Atkinson. Continuity: Margaret Shipway.

Cast: Charles Laughton (Henry Hobson), Brenda de Banzie (Maggie Hobson), John Mills (Will Mossop), Daphne Anderson (Alice Hobson), Prunella Scales (Vicky Hobson), Richard Wattis (Albert Prosser), Derek Blomfield (Freddy Beenstock), Helen Haye (Mrs. Hepworth), Joseph Tomelty (Jim Heeler), Julien Mitchell (Sam Minns), Gibb McLaughlin (Tudsbury), Philip Stainton (Denton), Dorothy Gordon (Ada Figgins), Madge Brindley (Mrs. Figgins), John Laurie (Dr. McFarlane), Raymond Huntley (Mr. Beenstock), Jack Howart (Tubby Wadlow), Herbert C. Walton (Printer).

Running time: 107 minutes.

Released February, 1954, by British Lion (Great Britain), and June, 1954, by United Artists (United States).

SUMMERTIME
(BRITISH TITLE: SUMMER MADNESS)

A London Film Production in Association with Lopert Films. Director: David Lean. Producer: Ilya Lopert. Assistant producer: Norman Spencer. Screenplay: David Lean and H. E. Bates, based on the play *Time of the Cuckoo,* by Arthur Laurents. Photography: Jack Hildyard. Camera Operator: Peter Newbrook. Sound: Peter Handford and John Cox. Music: Alessandro Cicognini (Rossini's *La Gazza Ladra*). Art Direction: Vincent Korda. Assistant Art Directors: Bill Hutchinson and Ferdinand Bellan. Editor: Peter Taylor. Production Managers: Raymond Anzarut and Franco Magli. Production Assistant: Robert J. Kingsley. Assistant Directors: Adrian Pryce-Jones and Alberto Cardone. Makeup: Cesare Gamberelli. Hairdresser: Gracia de Rossi. Continuity: Margaret Shipway.

Cast: Katharine Hepburn (Jane Hudson), Rossano Brazzi (Renato Di Rossi), Isa Miranda (Signora Fiorina), Darren McGavin (Eddie Jaeger), Mari Aldon (Phyl Jaeger), Jane Rose (Edith McIlhenny), MacDonald Parke (Lloyd McIlhenny), Gaetano Audiero (Mauro), Andre Morell (Englishman on train), Jeremy Spencer (Vito), Virginia Simeon (Giovanna).

Running time: 100 minutes, in Technicolor. Filmed on location in Venice.

Released May, 1955, by British-Lion (Great Britain), and June, 1955, by Lopert Films/United Artists (United States).

THE BRIDGE ON THE RIVER KWAI

A Sam Spiegel/David Lean Presentation. Director: David Lean. Producer: Sam Spiegel for Horizon Pictures. Screenplay: Pierre Boulle, based on his novel. Photography: Jack Hildyard. Camera Operator: Peter Newbrook. Sound: John Cox and John Mitchell. Music: Malcolm Arnold (Royal Philharmonic Orchestra), *Colonel Bogey March* by Kenneth J. Alford. Art Direction: Donald M. Aston and Geoffrey Drake (Assistant). Editor: Peter Taylor. Production Manager: Cecil F. Ford. Production Executive: William N. Graf. Assistant Directors: Gus Agnosti and Ted Sturgis. Construction Manager: Peter Dukelow. Technical Advisor: Major-General L. E. M. Perowne. Consulting Engineers: Husband and Company, Sheffield (Bridge constructed by Equipment and Construction Company, Ceylon). Wardrobe: John Apperson. Continuity: Angela Martelli.

Cast: William Holden (Shears), Alec Guinness (Colonel Nicholson), Jack Hawkins (Major Warden), Sessue Hayakawa (Colonel Saito), James Donald (Dr. Clipton), Geoffrey Horne (Lieutenant Joyce), Andre Morell (Colonel Green), Peter Williams (Captain Reeves), John Boxer (Major Hughes), Percy Herbert (Grogan), Harold Goodwin (Baker), Ann Sears (Nurse), Henry Okawa (Captain Kanematsu), K. Katsumoto (Lieutenant Miura), M. R. B. Chakrabanhu (Yai), Viliaiwan Seeboonreaung, Ngamta Suphaphongs, Javanart Punchychoti, Kannikar Dowklee (Siamese Girls).

Running time: 161 minutes, in Technicolor and CinemaScope. Filmed on location in Ceylon.

Released December, 1957, by Columbia Pictures.

LAWRENCE OF ARABIA

A Sam Spiegel/David Lean Presentation. Director: David Lean. Producer: Sam Spiegel for Horizon Pictures. Screenplay: Robert Bolt, based on *Seven Pillars of Wisdom,* by T. E. Lawrence, and other sources. Photography: F. A. Young. Camera Operator: Ernest Day. Second Unit Cinematography: Skeets Kelly, Nicolas Roeg, and Peter Newbrook. Second Unit Directors: Andre Smagghe and Noel Howard. Sound: Paddy Cunningham. Sound Editor: Winston Ryder. Music: Maurice Jarre, *Voice of Guns* by Kenneth J. Alford. Music Arranger: Gerard Schurmann. Music Co-ordinator: Morris Stoloff. Conductor: Sir Adrian Boult (London Philharmonic Orchestra). Art Director: John Stoll. Assistant Art Directors: Roy Rossotti, George Richardson, Terry Marsh, and Anthony Rimmington. Set Dresser: Dario Simoni. Editor: Anne V. Coates. Production Manager: John Palmer. Assistant Director: Roy Stevens. Casting Director: Maude Spector. Construction Managers: Peter Dukelow and Fred Bennett (Assistant). Location Manager: Douglas Twiddy. Property Master: Eddie Fowlie. Chief Electrician: Archie Dansie. Costumes: Phyllis Dalton. Wardrobe: John Apperson. Makeup: Charles Parker. Hairdresser: A. G. Scott. Continuity: Barbara Cole.

Reconstruction and Restoration: Robert A. Harris. Restoration Producers: Robert A. Harris and Jim Painten. Editorial Consultant: Anne V. Coates. Sound Consultant: Richard L. Anderson. Re-recorded in Six-track Dolby Spectral Recording at the Goldwyn Sound Facility. Re-recording Mixer: Gregg Landakar. 65mm Negative Restoration: Metrocolor Laboratories. 70mm Prints: Metrocolor. 35mm Prints: Deluxe. Production Assistants: Jude Schneider, Maggie Field, Joanne Lawson. With Special Thanks to Martin Scorsese, Steven Spielberg, Jon Davison, and Sir David Lean.

Cast: Peter O'Toole (Thomas Edward Lawrence), Alec Guinness (Prince Feisal), Anthony Quinn (Auda Abu Tayi), Jack Hawkins (General Allenby), Jose Ferrer (Turkish Bey), Anthony Quayle (Colonel Brighton), Claude Rains (Mr. Dryden), Arthur Kennedy (Jackson Bentley), Donald Wolfit (General Murray), Omar Sharif (Sherif Ali Ibn el Karish), I. S. Johar (Gasim), Gamil Ratib (Majid), Michel Ray (Farraj), Zia Mohyeddin (Tafas), John Dimech (Daud), Howard Marion Crawford (Medical Officer), Jack Gwillim (Club Secretary), Hugh Miller (R.A.M.C. Colonel).

Running time: 222 minutes—with interval—at London premiere (cut to 200 minutes before New York premiere, then cut to 184 minutes by Sam Spiegel for 1971 re-release; restored to full 222 minutes, 1989), in Technicolor and Super Panavision-70. Filmed on location in Jordan, Spain, Morocco, and England.

Released December, 1962, by Columbia Pictures. Re-issue of restored version, February, 1989.

DOCTOR ZHIVAGO

A Carlo Ponti/David Lean Production for Metro-Goldwyn-Mayer. Director: David Lean. Producer: Carlo Ponti. Executive Producer: Arvid L. Griffen. Screenplay: Robert Bolt, based on the novel by Boris Pasternak. Photography: Fred A. Young. Camera Operator: Ernest Day. Second Unit Cameraman: Manuel Berenguer. Sound: Paddy Cunningham. Re-recording: Franklin Milton and William Steinkamp. Sound Editor: Winston Ryder. Music: Maurice Jarre (Composer and Conductor). Production Designer: John Box. Art Direction: Terence Marsh and Gil Parrondo (Associate). Assistant Art Directors: Ernest Archer, Bill Hutchinson, and Roy Walker. Set Decoration: Dario Simoni. Editor: Norman Savage. Production Supervisor: John Palmer. Production Managers: Agustin Pastor and Douglas Twiddy. Assistant Directors: Roy Stevens and Pedro Vidal. Second Unit Director: Roy Rossotti. Dialogue Coach: Hugh Miller. Costumes: Phyllis Dalton. Makeup: Mario van Riel. Hairdressers: Gracia de Rossi and Anna Christofani. Continuity: Barbara Cole. Special Effects: Eddie Fowlie. Chief Electrician: Miguel Sancho. Construction: Gus Walker and Fred Bennett. M-G-M Representative: Stanley H. Goldsmith.

Cast: Geraldine Chaplin (Tonya Gromeko), Julie Christie (Lara), Tom Courtenay (Pasha/

Strelnikov), Alec Guinness (Yevgraf Zhivago), Siobhan McKenna (Anna Gromeko), Ralph Richardson (Alexander Gromeko), Omar Sharif (Yuri Zhivago), Rod Steiger (Komarovsky), Rita Tushingham (Tonya), Adrienne Corri (Amelia), Geoffrey Keen (Professor Kurt), Jeffrey Rockland (Sasha), Lucy Westmore (Katya), Noel Willman (Razin), Gerard Tichy (Liberius), Klaus Kinski (Kostoyed), Jack Mac Gowran (Petya), Maria Martin (Gentlewoman), Tarek Sharif (Yuri age 8), Mercedes Ruiz (Tonya age 7), Roger Maxwell (Colonel), Inigo Jackson (Major), Virgilio Texeira (Captain), Bernard Kay (Bolshevik), Erik Chitty (Old Soldier), Jose Nieto (The Priest), Mark Eden (Young Engineer), Emilio Carrer (Mr. Sventytski), Gerhard Jersch (David), Wolf Frees (Comrade Yelkin), Gwen Nelson (Comrade Kaprugina), Jose Caffarel (Militiaman), Brigette Trace (Streetwalker), Luana Alcaniz (Mrs. Sventytski), Lili Murati (Raddled Woman), Catherine Ellison (Raped Woman), Mario Vico (Demented Woman), Dodo Assad Bahador (Dragoon Colonel), Peter Madden (Political Officer).

Running time: 197 minutes—with interval—at New York premiere (cut by David Lean to 180 minutes), in Metrocolor and Panavision. Filmed in Spain, Finland, and Canada.

Released December, 1965 (United States), and April, 1966 (Great Britain), by Metro-Goldwyn-Mayer.

RYAN'S DAUGHTER

A Faraway Production for Metro-Goldwyn-Mayer. Director: David Lean. Producer: Anthony Havelock-Allan. Associate Producer: Roy Stevens. Screenplay: Robert Bolt. Photography: Fred A. Young. Camera Operator: Ernest Day. Second Unit Cameramen: Denys Coop and Robert Huke. Sound: John Bramall. Rerecording: Gordon K. McCallum and Eric Tomlinson (Music). Music: Maurice Jarre (Composer and Conductor). Production Designer: Stephen Grimes. Art Direction: Roy Walker and Derek Irvine (Assistant). Set Decoration: Josie MacAvin. Editor: Norman Savage. Production Manager: Douglas Twiddy. Assistant Directors: Pedro Vidal and Michael Stevenson. Second Unit Directors: Charles Frend and Roy Stevens (Storm Sequence). Production Liaison: William O'Kelly. Construction Manager: Peter Dukelow. Location and Property Master: Eddie Fowlie. Costumes: Jocelyn Rickards. Makeup:

Charles Parker. Hairdresser: A.G. Scott. Continuity: Phyllis Crocker. Special Effects: Robert Macdonald.

Cast: Sarah Miles (Rosy Ryan), Robert Mitchum (Charles Shaughnessy), Trevor Howard (Father Hugh Collins), Christopher Jones (Major Andrew Doryan), John Mills (Michael), Leo McKern (Tom Ryan), Barry Foster (Tim O'Leary), Marie Kean (Mrs. McCardle), Arthur O'Sullivan (Mr. McCardle), Evin Crowley (Moureen Cassiday), Douglas Sheldon (Driver), Gerald Sim (Captain), Barry Jackson (Corporal), Des Keogh (Private), Niall Toibin (O'Keefe), Philip O' Flynn (Paddy), Donal Neligan (Moureen's Boyfriend), Brian O'Higgins (Constable O'Connor), Niall O'Brien (Bernard), Owen Sullivan (Joseph).

Running time: 196 minutes—with interval—for roadshow engagements (165 minutes for United States general release), in Metrocolor and 70mm Super Panavision. Filmed on the West Coast of Ireland.

Released December, 1970, by Metro-Goldwyn-Mayer.

A PASSAGE TO INDIA

A David Lean Film. Director: David Lean. Producers: John Brabourne and Richard Goodwin, in association with John Heyman and Edward Sands and Home Box Office, Inc. Screenplay: David Lean, based on the novel by E. M. Forster and the play by Santha Rama Rau. Photography: Ernest Day. Editor: David Lean. Music: Maurice Jarre (Composer and Conductor, with the Royal Philharmonic Orchestra; *Freeley Maisie* tune composed by John Dalby). Production Designer: John Box. Couturier: Germinal Rangel. Assistant Directors: Patrick Cadell, Christopher Figg, Nick Laws, Arundhati Rao, and Ajit Kumar. Camera Operator: Roy Ford. Focus: Frank Elliot. Clapper: Martin Kenzie. Second Camera Focus: John Fletcher. Second Unit Photography and Effects: Robin Browne. Sound Editor: Winston Ryder. Music Editor: Robin Clarke. Assistant to Maurice Jarre: Christopher Palmer. Dialogue Editor: Archie Ludski. Effects Editor: Jack T. Knight. Sound Recorders: Graham V. Hartstone, Nicolas Le Messurier, Michael A. Carter, Richard Lewzey, and Lionel Strut. Boom Operator: Kenneth Pamplin. Sound Engineer: Ron Butcher. Assistant Editors: Anne Sopel and Kees 'T Hooft.

Assistant Sound Editor: Peter Dansie. Assistant Dialogue Editor: Jeremy Baylis. Production Assistant: Pat Pennelegion. London Contact: Pamela Allen. Production Secretary (India): Eleanor Chaudhuri. Delhi Liaison: Monini Banerji. Unit Manager (India): Rashid Abbassi. Government Liaison (India): P.N. Parthasarathy. Location Secretary: Brioni Pereira. Customs Liaison: Marcus Wilford. Art Directors: Leslie Tomkins, Clifford Robinson, Ram Yedekar, and Herbert Westbrook. Set Decorator: Hugh Scaife. Wardrobe Mistress: Rosemary Burrows. Wardrobe Master: Keith Morton. Makeup: Jill Carpenter and Eric Allwright. Hairdressers: Elaine Bowerbank and Vera Mitchell. Production Accountant: Charles Cannon. Location Accountant: Rex Saluz. Publicity: Diana Hawkins. Stills: Frank Connor. Property Master (United Kingdom): Bert Hearn. Props: Mickey Pugh and Steve Short. Grip: Chunky Huse. Electricians: Alan Martin and Bill Pochety. Transport: Pamela Wells. Color Timing: Ron Lambert. Production Supervisor: Barrie Melrose. Location and Props: Eddie Fowlie. Production Managers: Jim Brennan and Shama Habibullah. Sound Recording: John Mitchell. Casting: Priscilla John. Costumes: Judy Moorcroft. Associate Editor: Eunice Mountjoy. Continuity: Maggie Unsworth.

Cast: Judy Davis (Adela Quested), Victor Banerjee (Dr. Aziz), Peggy Ashcroft (Mrs. Moore), James Fox (Fielding), Alec Guinness (Professor Godbole), Nigel Havers (Ronny), Richard Wilson (Turton), Antonia Pemberton (Mrs. Turton), Michael Culver (McBryde), Art Malik (Ali), Saeed Jaffrey (Hamidullah), Clive Swift (Major Callendar), Ann Firbank (Mrs. Callendar), Roshan Seth (Amritrao), Sandra Hotz (Stella), Rashid Karapiet (Das), H.S. Krishnamurthy (Hassan), Ishaq Bux (Selim), Moti Makam (Guide), Mohammed Ashiq (Haq), Phyllis Bose (Mrs. Leslie), Sally Kinghorne (Ingenue), Paul Anin (Clerk of the Court), Z.H. Khan (Dr. Panna Lai), Ashok Mandanna (Anthony), Dina Pathak (Begum Hamidullah), Adam Blackwood (Mr. Hadley), Mellan Mitchell (Indian Businessman), Peter Hughes (P&O Manager).

Running time: 160 minutes, in Technicolor and Panavision. Filmed on location in India and at Shepperton Studios, Middlesex, England.

Released December, 1984 (United States), and February, 1985 (Great Britain), by Columbia Pictures.

Selected Bibliography

Aldgate, Anthony, and Richards, Jeffrey. *Britain Can Take It: The British Cinema in the Second World War*. New York and London: Basil Blackwell, 1986.

Anderegg, Michael A. *David Lean*. Boston: Twayne Publishers, 1984.

Andersen, Christopher. *Young Kate*. New York: Henry Holt, 1988.

Armes, Roy. *A Critical History of the British Cinema*. New York: Oxford University Press, 1978.

Bach, Steven. *Final Cut*. New York: William Morrow and Company, 1985.

Barr, Charles (editor). *All Our Yesterdays: Ninety Years of British Cinema*. London: British Film Institute Books, 1986.

Barsacq, Leon (revised and edited by Elliot Stein). *Caligari's Cabinet and Other Grand Illusions: A History of Film Design*. Boston: New York Graphic Society, 1976.

Boulle, Pierre (Fielding, Xan, translator). *The Bridge Over the River Kwai*. New York: Vanguard Press, 1954.

Castelli, Louis P. (with Cleeland, Caryn Lynn). *David Lean: A Guide to Resources and References*. Boston: G. K. Hall and Company, 1980.

Castle, Charles. *Noël*. Garden City, New York: Doubleday and Company, 1973.

Conrad, Joseph. *Nostromo*. Harmondsworth, Middlesex: Penguin Books, Ltd., 1983.

Coward, Noël. *Future Indefinite*. New York: Doubleday and Company, 1954.

Coward, Noël (Payn, Graham, and Morley, Sheridan, editors). *The Noël Coward Diaries*. Boston and Toronto: Little, Brown, 1982.

Coward, Noël. *Three Plays*. New York: Grove Press, 1979.

Darlow, Michael, and Hodson, Gillian. *Terence Rattigan: The Man and His Work*. London: Quartet Books, 1979.

Dickens, Charles. *Great Expectations*. London: Oxford University Press, 1953.

Dickens, Charles. *Oliver Twist*. Oxford: Oxford University Press, 1966.

Eells, George. *Robert Mitchum: A Biography*. London: Robson Books, 1984.

Flaubert, Gustav (Russell, Alan, translator). *Madame Bovary*. Harmondsworth: Penguin Books, Ltd., 1950.

Forster, E. M. *A Passage to India*. New York: Harcourt, Brace, and World, 1924.

Freedman, Richard. *The Novel*. New York: Newsweek Books, 1975.

Guinness, Alec. *Blessings in Disguise*. London: Hamish Hamilton, Ltd., 1985.

Halliwell, Leslie. *Halliwell's Filmgoer's Companion (Seventh Edition)*. London: Granada Publishing Ltd., 1983.

Harrison, Rex. *Rex: An Autobiography*. London: Macmillan Ltd., 1974.

Hawkins, Jack. *Anything for a Quiet Life*. New York: Stein and Day, 1974.

Higham, Charles. *Charles Laughton: An Intimate Biography*. Garden City, New York: Doubleday and Company, 1976.

Hingley, Ronald. *Pasternak: A Biography*. New York: Alfred A. Knopf, 1983.

Kanin, Garson. *Hollywood*. New York: The Viking Press, 1974.

Katz, Ephraim. *The Film Encyclopedia*. New York: Perigee Books, 1979.

Kemp, Peter (editor). *The Oxford Companion to Ships and the Sea*. Oxford: Oxford University Press, 1976.

Korda, Michael. *Charmed Lives*. New York: Random House, 1979.

Knight, Vivienne. *Trevor Howard: A Gentleman and a Player*. New York: Beaufort Books, 1987.

Lanchester, Elsa. *Elsa Lanchester Herself*. New York: St. Martin's Press, 1983.

Lawrence, T. E. *Seven Pillars of Wisdom*. Garden City, New York: Doubleday Doran, 1937.

Lawrenson, Helen. "Letter Home," *Esquire*. December, 1965, pages 132–40.

Lean, David. "Brief Encounter," *The Penguin Film Review 4*. Middlesex: Penguin Books, Ltd., October 1947.

Leyda, Jay. *Voices of Film Experience*. New York: Macmillan Publishing Company, 1977.

Maugham, W. Somerset. *The Summing Up*. London: William Heinemann, Ltd., 1938.

Mills, John. *Up in the Clouds, Gentlemen, Please*. London: Ticknor and Fields, 1980.

Minney, R. J. *"Puffin" Asquith*. London: Leslie Frewin, 1973.

More, Kenneth. *More or Less*. London: Hodder and Stoughton, 1978.

Moseley, Roy (with Masheter, Philip, and Masheter, Martin). *Rex Harrison: A Biography*. New York: St. Martin's Press, 1987.

Moss, Robert F. *The Films of Carol Reed*. London: Macmillan Press, Ltd., 1987.

O'Connor, Gary. *Ralph Richardson: An Actor's Life*. London: Hodder and Stoughton, 1986.

Orwell, George. *A Collection of Essays*. New York: Harcourt Brace Jovanovich, 1946.

Parrish, Robert. *Hollywood Doesn't Live Here Anymore*. Boston and Toronto: Little, Brown, 1988.

Pasternak, Boris (Hayward, Max, and Harari, Manya, translators). *Doctor Zhivago*. New York: Pantheon Books, 1958.

Perry, George. *The Great British Picture Show*. Boston and Toronto: Little, Brown, 1985.

Phillips, Gene D. *The Moviemakers: Artists in an Industry*. Chicago: Nelson-Hall Company, 1973.

Pratley, Gerald. *The Cinema of David Lean*. London: The Tantivy Press, 1974.

Powell, Michael. *A Life in Movies*. London: William Heinemann, Ltd., 1986.

Quinlan, David. *British Sound Films: The Studio Years 1928–1959*. London: B. T. Batsford, 1984.

Silver, Alain, and Ursini, James. *David Lean and His Films*. London: Leslie Frewin Publishers, Ltd., 1974.

Sinclair, Andrew. *Spiegel: The Man Behind the Pictures*. Boston and Toronto: Little, Brown, 1988.

Slide, Anthony. *Fifty Classic British Films, 1932–1982*. New York: Dover Publications, 1985.

Taylor, John Russell. *Alec Guinness: A Celebration*. Boston and Toronto: Little, Brown, 1984.

Thomas, Bob. *Golden Boy: The Untold Story of William Holden*. New York: St. Martin's Press, 1983.

Todd, Ann. *The Eighth Veil*. New York: G. P. Putnam's Sons, 1981.

Vermilye, Jerry. *The Great British Films*. Secaucus, New Jersey: Citadel Press, 1978.

Von Gunden, Kenneth. *Alec Guinness: The Films*. Jefferson, North Carolina and London: McFarland and Company, 1987.

West, Anthony. *H.G. Wells: Aspects of a Life*. New York: Random House, 1984.

Index

210

Photograph Credits

The author and publishers would like to thank the following studios, photographers, and individuals who have generously contributed photographs and/or granted permission for their publication. All references are to page numbers.

Film copyrights: *Blithe Spirit* (54, 55, 56, 57) Courtesy of Janus Films. *The Bridge on the River Kwai* (114, 115, 116, 117, 118, 119, 120, 121, 124) © 1957, renewed 1985 Columbia Pictures Industries, Inc. *Brief Encounter* (58, 59, 60, 61, 62, 63, 64) by Courtesy of the Rank Organisation Plc. *Doctor Zhivago* (150, 151, 152, 154, 155, 156–57, 158, 159, 160, 161, 162, 163, 164, 165) © 1965 Metro-Goldwyn-Mayer Inc. Courtesy Turner Entertainment Co. *Great Expectations* (66–67, 68, 69, 70, 71, 73) by Courtesy of the Rank Organisation Plc. *Hobson's Choice* (94, 95, 96, 98, 99) Courtesy of Janus Films. *In Which We Serve* (37, 41, 42, 43, 45, 46, 47, 48) by Courtesy of the Rank Organisation Plc. *Lawrence of Arabia* (2–3, 4, 6–7, 126, 127, 128, 129, 130, 131, 132, 134–35, 136, 137, 138, 139, 140, 141, 142, 143, 144–45, 149) © 1962 Horizon Pictures (GB). All rights reserved. Courtesy Columbia Pictures Industries, Inc. *Madeleine* (86, 87, 88, 89) by Courtesy of the Rank Organisation Plc. *Oliver Twist* (74, 75, 76, 77, 79, 80, 81) by Courtesy of the Rank Organisation Plc. *A Passage to India* (184, 185, 186, 187, 189, 191) © 1984 Thorn E.M.I. Films Finance Plc. *The Passionate Friends* (82, 83, 85) by Courtesy of the Rank Organisation Plc. *Ryan's Daughter* (1, 168, 169, 170, 171, 172, 173, 174, 175, 176, 177, 179) © 1970 Metro-Goldwyn-Mayer Inc. Courtesy Turner Entertainment Co. *The Sound Barrier* (90, 91, 92, 93) Courtesy of Janus Films. *Summertime* (12, 13, 14, 15, 100, 101, 103, 104, 105, 106–7, 108, 109, 110, 111, 112) Courtesy of Janus Films. *This Happy Breed* (50, 51, 53) Courtesy of Janus Films.

Photos: Photograph by and collection of George Andrews. 181. Associated Press: 146. Collection John Box: 143, 151. British Film Institute: 12, 34–35, 90, 91, 92, 93, 94, 100, 105, 119, 120, 121, 141, 142, 154, 185, 186, 187, 189. Courtesy Columbia Pictures Industries, Inc.: 2–3, 6–7, 126, 127, 128, 129, 132, 134–35, 136, 137, 138, 139. Collection Robert A. Harris: 150, 152, 156–57, 158, 161, 162, 163, 164, 165. Collection Katharine Hepburn, photograph by Per Olow: 9, 13, 14, 15, 101, 103, 104, 106–7, 108, 109, 110, 111, 112. Collection David Lean: 16, 18, 19, 20, 21, 22, 23, 27, 31, 32, 39, 113, 117, 124, 130, 131, 159, 160, 167, 171, 180, 183, 191; photograph by Sandra Cooke: 195; photograph by Ken Danvers: 1, 4, 140, 144–45, 147, 149, 168, 169, 170, 172, 173, 174, 175, 176, 177, 179. Collection Lady Lean: 198. Photofest: 114, 115, 116, 118, 155, 184. Photograph by Robin Platzer: 148. Collection David Robinson: 36. Photograph by Lee Salem: 197. Photograph by Tim Unsworth: 192.

Acknowledgments

The author wishes to express grateful appreciation to
Lady Lean
as well as to the following:
Lindsay Anderson, George Andrews, Carol Atkinson, Sue Barton, John Box, Melvyn Bragg, Michael Caine, Judith Crist, Hollace Davids, Margaret Denk, Donna Edge, Phyllis Flood, Sarah Foster, Eddie Fowlie, Richard Freedman, Patricia Funt, Renée Furst, Paul Gottlieb, Lee Gross, Bob Harris, Mary Jacobson, Garson Kanin, William Kenly, Christine LaMonte, Alfred Lowman, Ron Mandelbaum, Barbara and David Morowitz, Nancy Morowitz, Catherine Olim, Ronald Paquet, David Robinson, Luis Sanjurjo, Paul Stolper, Helga Stephenson, Judy Strang, Jerry Tallmer, Margaret Unsworth, Tim Unsworth, Archer Winsten.

Supplementary research was conducted in the Performing Arts Library of Lincoln Center in New York City, the Margaret Herrick Library of the Academy of Motion Picture Arts and Sciences in Beverly Hills, and the British Film Institute, London. The manuscript was written in New York, London, and Tuscany.

This book is dedicated to Shirley.

About the Author

Stephen M. Silverman, for years the chief entertainment correspondent for the New York Post, has written about film for nearly every major American publication, including *American Film, Esquire,* the *Los Angeles Times, New York, The New York Times, Playboy, The Village Voice,* and *Vogue.* He is the author of three previous books, *Public Spectacles* (1981), *The Fox that Got Away: The Last Days of the Zanuck Dynasty at Twentieth Century-Fox* (1988), and *Where There's a Will: Who Inherited What and Why* (1991). Born in Los Angeles, Silverman lives in New York City, where he is currently at work on a Broadway musical.